JULIA KRISTEVA

A leading literary critic and psychoanalyst, Julia Kristeva is one of the most significant French thinkers writing today. In this up-to-date survey of her work, John Lechte outlines fully and systematically her intellectual development. He traces it from her work on Bakhtin and the logic of poetic language in the 1960s, through her influential theories of the 'symbolic' and the 'semiotic' in the 1970s, to her analyses of horror, love, melancholy, and cosmopolitanism in the 1980s. He provides an insight into the intellectual and historical context which gave rise to Kristeva's thought, showing how thinkers such as Roland Barthes, Emile Benveniste, and Georges Bataille have been important in stimulating her own reflections. He concludes with an overall assessment of Kristeva's work, looking in particular at her importance for feminism and postmodernist thought in general.

Essential reading for all those who wish to extend their understanding of this important thinker, this first full-length study of Kristeva's work will be of interest to students of literature, sociology, critical theory, feminist theory, French studies, and psychoanalysis.

A former student of Julia Kristeva, John Lechte is Tutor in Sociology at Macquarie University, Australia.

CRITICS OF THE TWENTIETH CENTURY
General Editor: Christopher Norris, University of Wales, College of Cardiff

Julia Kristeva

JOHN LECHTE

London and New York

First published 1990
by Routledge
11 New Fetter Lane, London EC4P 4EE

Simultaneously published in the USA and Canada
by Routledge
a division of Routledge, Chapman and Hall, Inc.
29 West 35th Street, New York, NY 10001

Reprinted 1991

© 1990 John Lechte
Data converted to 10/12pt Baskerville
by Columns Ltd
Printed in England by
Clays Ltd, St Ives plc

British Library Cataloguing in Publication Data
Lechte, John
  Julia Kristeva. (Critics of the twentieth century)
  1. Literature. Criticism. Kristeva, Julia, 1941–
  I. Title II. Series
  801′.95′0924
  0 415 00809 3 hbk
  0 415 00834 4 pbk

Library of Congress Cataloging in Publication Data
also available

Contents

Contents

Editor's foreword

The twentieth century has produced a remarkable number of gifted and innovative literary critics. Indeed it could be argued that some of the finest literary minds of the age have turned to crticism as the medium best adapted to their complex and speculative range of interests. This has sometimes given rise to regret among those who insist on a clear demarcation between 'creative' (primary) writing on the one hand, and 'critical' (secondary) texts on the other. Yet this distinction is far from self-evident. It is coming under strain at the moment as novelists and poets grow increasingly aware of the conventions that govern their writing and the challenge of consciously exploiting and subverting those conventions. And the critics for their part – some of them at least – are beginning to question their traditional role as humble servants of the literary text with no further claim upon the reader's interest or attention. Quite simply, there are texts of literary criticism and theory that, for various reasons – stylistic complexity, historical influence, range of intellectual command – cannot be counted a mere appendage to those other 'primary' texts.

Of course, there is a logical puzzle here, since (it will be argued) 'literary criticism' would never have come into being, and could hardly exist as such, were it not for the body of creative writings that provide its *raison d'être*. But this is not quite the kind of knock-down argument that it might appear at first glance. For one thing, it conflates some very different orders of priority, assuming that literature always comes first (in the sense that Greek tragedy had to exist before Aristotle could formulate its rules), so that literary texts are for that very reason possessed of superior value. And this argument would seem to find commonsense support in the difficulty of thinking what 'literary criticism' could *be* if it seriously renounced all sense of the distinction between literary and critical texts. Would it not then find itself in the unfortunate position of a discipline that had willed its own demise by declaring its subject non-existent?

But these objections would only hit their mark if there were indeed a special kind of writing called 'literature' whose difference from other kinds of writing was enough to put criticism firmly in its place. Otherwise there is nothing in the least self-defeating or paradoxical about a discourse, nominally that of literary criticism, that accrues such interest on its own account as to force some fairly drastic rethinking of its proper powers and limits. The act of crossing over from commentary to literature – or of simply denying the difference between them – becomes quite explicit in the writing of a critic like Geoffrey Hartman. But the signs are already there in such classics as William Empson's *Seven Types of Ambiguity* (1928), a text whose transformative influence on our habits of reading must surely be ranked with the great creative moments of literary modernism. Only on the most dogmatic view of the difference between 'literature' and 'criticism' could a work like *Seven Types* be counted generically an inferior, sub-literary species of production. And the same can be said for many of the critics whose writings and influence this series sets out to explore.

Some, like Empson, are conspicuous individuals who belong to no particular school or larger movement. Others, like the Russian Formalists, were part of a communal enterprise and are therefore best understood as representative figures in a complex and evolving dialogue. Then again there are cases of collective identity (like the so-called 'Yale deconstructors') where a mythical group image is invented for largely polemical purposes. (The volumes in this series on Hartman and Bloom should help to dispel the idea that 'Yale deconstruction' is anything more than a handy device for collapsing differences and avoiding serious debate.) So there is no question of a series format or house-style that would seek to reduce these differences to a blandly homogeneous treatment. One consequence of recent critical theory is the realization that literary texts have no self-sufficient or autonomous meaning, no existence apart from their after-life of changing interpretations and values. And the same applies to those *critical* texts whose meaning and significance are subject to constant shifts and realignments of interest. This is not to say that trends in criticism are just a matter of intellectual fashion or the merry-go-round of rising and falling reputations. But it is important to grasp how complex are the forces – the conjunctions of historical and cultural motive – that affect the first reception and the subsequent fortunes of a critical text. This point has been raised into a systematic programme by critics like Hans-Robert Jauss, practioners of so-called 'reception theory' as a form of historical hermeneutics. The volumes in this series will therefore be concerned not only to expound what is of lasting significance but also to set these critics in the context of present-day argument and debate. In some cases (as with Walter Benjamin) this debate takes the form of a struggle for interpretative power among disciplines with sharply opposed ideological view-points. Such controversies cannot simply be ignored in the interests of achieving a clear and balanced account. They point to unresolved tensions and problems which are there in the critic's work as well as in the rival appropriative readings. In the end there is no way of drawing a neat methodological line between 'intrinsic' questions (what the critic really thought) and those other, supposedly 'extrinsic' concerns that have to do with influence and reception history.

The volumes will vary accordingly in their focus and range of coverage. They will also reflect the ways in which a speculative approach to questions of literary theory has proved to have striking consequences for the human sciences at large. This breaking-down of disciplinary bounds is among the most significant developments in recent critical thinking. As philosophers and historians, among others, come to recognize the rhetorical complexity of the texts they deal with, so literary theory takes on a new dimension of interest and relevance. It is scarcely appropriate to think of a writer like Derrida as practising 'literary criticism' in any conventional sense of the term. For one thing, he is as much concerned with 'philosophical' as with 'literary' texts, and has indeed actively sought to subvert (or deconstruct) such tidy distinctions. A principal object in planning this series was to take full stock of these shifts in the wider intellectual terrain (including the frequent boundary disputes) brought about by critical theory. And, of course, such changes are by no means confined to literary studies, philosophy and the so-called 'sciences of man'. It is equally the case in (say) nuclear physics and molecular biology that advances in the one field have decisive implications for the other, so that specialized research often tends (paradoxically) to break down existing divisions of intellectual labour. Such work is typically many years ahead of the academic disciplines and teaching institutions that have obvious reasons of their own for adopting a business-as-usual attitude. One important aspect of modern critical theory is the challenge it presents to these traditional ideas. And lest it be thought that this is merely a one-sided takeover bid by literary critics, the series will include a number of volumes by authors in those other disciplines, including, for instance, a study of Roland Barthes by an American analytical philosopher.

We shall not, however, cleave to theory as a matter of polemical or principled stance. The series will extend to figures like F. R. Leavis, whose widespread influence went along with an express aversion to literary theory; scholars like Erich Auerbach in the mainstream European tradition; and others who resist assimilation to any clear-cut line of descent. There will also be authoritative volumes on critics such as Northrop Frye and Lionel Trilling, figures who, for various reasons, occupy an ambivalent or essentially contested place in modern critical tradition. Above all the series will strive to resist that current polarization of attitudes that sees no common ground of interest between 'literary criticism' and 'critical theory'.

CHRISTOPHER NORRIS

Preface

The discipline of semiotics – or semiology – is now well established in Europe, or at least in the French and Italian university and intellectual systems. It has become much better known in the last decade in Anglo-Saxon countries – especially in film studies – although it is not always treated with the respect it has achieved on the Continent. Julia Kristeva's work, the subject of this book, derives much from the development of modern semiotics, even if it is also distanced from it to a certain extent.

Although enough of an introductory nature has now been written on semiotics,[1] a brief remark about its nature and scope are appropriate in order that we may better take our bearings in relation to Kristeva's work.

Seminal texts explaining the nature of the discipline of semiotics, such as those of Barthes[2] and Eco,[3] apart from showing how it is dependent on a theory of the sign and signification, also point towards the breadth of its researches. Barthes speaks for example of 'extra-linguistic' sign systems: the food, car, furniture, clothing, and architecture systems.[4] Eco goes much further than Barthes, and shows that there is hardly any field of human endeavour which does not potentially fall within the province of semiotic studies. Eco's list of studies includes, *inter alia*: zoosemiotics; olfactory signs; tactile communication; paralinguistics (including one study of 'vocal characterizers' such as laughing, crying, whimpering, sobbing . . . etc.); medical semiotics; kinesics and proxemics ('the idea that gesturing depends on cultural codes'); musical codes; visual communication; systems of objects (objects cultures); formalized languages (algebra, chemistry); aesthetic texts; mass communication; and rhetoric.[5] Clearly, hardly an aspect of social and cultural life fails to have a signifying/communicative aspect. And this means that, despite the claims sometimes made to the effect that semiotics 'occludes material relationships',[6] hardly an aspect of cultural and social life is uniquely instrumental (geared to the satisfaction of needs), or narrowly material (a concrete object). Broadly speaking, semiotics has challenged the notion that the material, instrumental dimension of human life does not also have symbolic implications.

Especially in its early phase, Julia Kristeva's work constitutes a particular version of semiotic studies increasingly influenced by psychoanalysis. No doubt due to the specific character of French (or Parisian) intellectual life, certain aspects of semiotic theory may seem highly elaborated, if not obscure, to an Anglo-Saxon audience. My position is that the difficulties of reading Kristeva outside France are as much due to a particular Anglo-Saxon intellectual disposition as they are due to the intrinsic nature of her work. Kristeva herself speaks – admittedly in 1980 – of 'the *difference* in mental and intellectual habits that persist in spite of recently increased cultural exchanges between the United States and Europe'.[7] One aim of this book is to transcend these 'mental and intellectual' habits, and to throw light on Kristeva's *oeuvre* for people outside the Hexagon.

To the extent that Kristeva's name is known outside France, it is usually in connection with so-called French feminism. But while Kristeva has indeed commented publicly, and written about issues relevant to the position of women in western society, there is a sizeable other dimension to her writing which has been somewhat neglected in the literature on her work. This book is principally a consideration of this 'other dimension'. It includes Kristeva's theory of society and culture as inspired by Freud and avant-garde art; her consideration of writing as a practice, and elaborations of psychoanalytic theory with respect to 'horror', 'love' and 'melancholy'. It is especially these latter three topics which contribute to raising fundamental questions about social life in advanced capitalist – postmodern – societies. Not to be neglected, in this regard, is Kristeva's postition as exile and foreigner. Her book, *Etrangers à nous-mêmes* published late in 1988, provides an important insight here.[8]

The assumption made throughout this study is that some readers of Kristeva not only have difficulty in following each step in her thinking, but try to read her work on the wrong level. I have attempted, therefore, to bring into focus the appropriate dimension involved, or the general region where one's gaze should be directed. The aim, nevertheless, is not to read Kristeva *for* someone else; it is rather to help people read Kristeva for themselves. And this means to help them truly to confront the difficulties involved. The point, then, is not to have these difficulties (supposedly) resolved in a secondary text which 'simplifies' them. A profound thinker is just not open to simplification in this way. To be cast in the role of 'teacher' is often to be cast in the role of simplifier in this sense. As Heidegger said, however, teaching is much more difficult than learning because 'the real teacher, in fact, lets nothing else be learned than – learning'.[9] Here, we see that teaching has nothing to do with the transmission of knowledge in a simplified form, but with learning to let people themselves learn. I have just such an aim in the following pages.

Finally, all quotations from French texts are in my own translation unless otherwise indicated.

Notes

1 See Terence Hawkes, *Structuralism & Semiotics*, New Accents Series (London, Methuen, reprinted 1982).

2 Roland Barthes, *Elements of Semiology*, trans. Annette Lavers and Colin Smith (New York, Hill & Wang, 1977).

3 Umberto Eco, *A Theory of Semiotics*, Advances in Semiotics Series (Bloomington, Indiana University Press, first Midland Book edition, 1979).

4 See Roland Barthes, *Elements of Semiology*, pp. 25–7, and pp. 62–3.

5 Eco, *A Theory of Semiotics*, pp. 9–14.

6 See Raymond Williams, *Marxism and Literature* (Oxford, Oxford University Press, 1977), p. 169:

> To occlude these [material and social relationships], by reducing their expressed focus to a linguistic system, is a kind of error closely related, in effect, to that made by the theorist of 'pure' expression for whom, also, there was no materially and socially differential world of lived and living practice; a human world of which language in, and through its own forms, is itself always a form.

7 Julia Kristeva, *Desire in Language: A Semiotic Approach to Literature and Art*, trans. Thomas Gora, Alice Jardine and Leon S. Roudiez (New York, Columbia University Press, reprinted 1984), p. vii. Kristeva's emphasis.

8 Julia Kristeva, *Etrangers à nous-mêmes* (Paris, Fayard, 1988).

9 Martin Heidegger, 'What calls for thinking' in David Farrell Krell (ed.), *Martin Heidegger: Basic Writings* (London, Routledge & Kegan Paul, 1978), p. 356

Acknowledgements

Gill Bottomley most of all deserves my thanks for her support and for so willingly discussing many of the issues raised in this book. Thanks are also due to Andrew Benjamin for his encouragement, and to the students of the Philosophy Department at Warwick University for their invaluable response to a version of Chapter 1, in May 1988. Thanks, too, to Julia Kristeva for one particularly important interview at Jussieu in May 1988 when she answered questions on things I was still uncertain about. I, of course, take responsibility for the way I have interpreted these answers. Murray Domney kindly checked some of my French translations and saved me from making a number of errors. Responsibility for the final version of these passages is of course mine. Helen Easson unfailingly typed the manuscript with great accuracy – even after her retirement. And colleagues, Vivien Johnson and Sue Foskey willingly lightened my teaching load in the book's final stages.

Introduction

Since the end of the nineteenth century, 'poetry' has deliberately
maintained the balance between sociality and madness, and we
view this as the sign of a new era.

Julia Kristeva, *Revolution in Poetic Language*

Recent developments in the sciences, both physical and human, are
such an affront to our sense of self-certainty, to our attachment to
identity, to our belief in unity and reality – to our senses, in a
word, to our common sense(s) – that thinking is no longer the same
as it was even thirty years ago. A few early indications of this
upheaval in thought were Freud's theory of the unconscious, Georg
Cantor's concept of the infinite in mathematics, Einstein's shaking
of our Newtonian world with his theory of relativity, and, more
recently, Heisenberg's 'uncertainty principle'.[1] To these early
indications of an upheaval in thought may be added – for those
who have a penchant for thinking in neat categories – the
movements of structuralism, and its successors, poststructuralism[2]
and postmodernism.[3] It was in this second phase of the upheaval
in western thought that 'man' died: or rather the theoretical 'form-
man' – to use the philosopher Gilles Deleuze's term[4] – began to
pass away and something else, something as yet not entirely
discernible, began to take its place. It was in this context that the
famous final lines from Michel Foucault's *The Order of Things*,
published in the mid-1960s, were destined to create quite a storm:

As the archaeology of our thought easily shows, man is an
invention of recent date. And one perhaps nearing its end.

1

If those arrangements were to disappear as they appeared, if some event of which we can at the moment do no more than sense the possibility – without knowing either what its form will be or what it promises – were to cause them to crumble, as the ground of Classical thought did, at the end of the eighteenth century, then one can certainly wager that man would be erased, like a face drawn in the sand at the edge of the sea.[5]

Julia Kristeva's work is situated within this upheaval in thought to which Foucault's words refer, and has in fact contributed significantly to it. Indeed, Kristeva writes in light of the 'death of man', a death which seems to be echoed by the Italian writer, Italo Calvino, when he says that the sixties 'profoundly changed many of the concepts we are dealing with', and that 'we do already know that there has been a revolution of the mind, an intellectual turning point'.[6]

To make that part of this upheaval – of this 'revolution' – which Kristeva has brought about accessible, is the aim of this book. There are, however, very real barriers to achieving this aim. One of these – alluded to in the Preface – is that, for many people, these developments have been registered as something extremely difficult and complex, and certainly intimidating and inaccessible to the non-specialist – much as are higher mathematics, or *Finnegans Wake*. Thus, right from the moment when it came to be better known outside France, Kristeva's work has been characterized, almost above all else, by its difficulty.[7] And at least this suggests that a wider audience than might otherwise have been expected is looking for enlightenment about the 'revolution of the mind' which continued apace in the 1960s. In other words, to register the 'revolution' as difficulty is an advance on complete indifference.

There are those, however, who would propose that the very (as they see it) arcane character of this upheaval in thought holds out great dangers. For 'the people' (i.e., the harbingers of common sense) will be alienated from such developments in thought, almost by definition. The 'people', then, or those, as Pierre Bourdieu says, without the specific code necessary for coming to terms with what is difficult, come 'to feel lost in a chaos of sounds and rhythms, colours and lines, without rhyme or reason'.[8] We could simply add 'words' to the 'chaos of sounds', etc., to show that Bourdieu describes something he would see as being applicable to Kristeva: Kristeva's work would be difficult for common sense because people lack the appropriate code for making sense of it. For Bourdieu, western (especially European) society produces the codes for understanding just as it produced the alienation that an absence of the 'right' code is destined to bring. Thus in Bourdieu's view, alienation from 'high', avant-garde art and intellectual endeavour, is more or less structurally inescapable in the kind of society in question. From Bourdieu's perspective, it is difficult to see how 'popular', and 'high' culture cannot be locked in a battle for supremacy – a battle of classes in the end – for which the fruit of victory is to remain, or to become, the exclusive wielder of power.[9] In short, 'cultural capital' (i.e., 'legitimate' taste as refinement and the means of acquiring it) becomes an important instrument of domination.

Bourdieu's argument, and with it the idea of the 'popular' as broadly democratic – as broadly petty bourgeois and working class, perhaps – is incomprehensible without recognizing the role played by the market and consumerism. For the market is what allows taste as refinement to become the mark of the distance deemed to exist between necessity as a kind of 'brutish' and 'vulgar' drive for survival,[10] and luxury. The popular would thus not rank highly in the established hierarchy of taste because it is too close to unrefined nature (i.e. necessity), a state from which it would only be possible to escape if the monetary means existed for doing so. The popular in capitalist society, as Bourdieu analyses it is simply too close to nature to be 'refined'. Indirectly, then, it is wealth which makes refinement, and thus legitimate taste, possible. Without the market, there would be no 'consumers of cultural goods', and thus no hierarchy of modes of consumption – the material base, as it were, of the hierarchy of taste.

But is Bourdieu's argument, seen as a sophisticated version of the notion of the popular aesthetic as the mark of the dominated class,[11] really adequate? Or might it not rather be that there is enormous pressure, in a so-called 'mass society' – albeit one produced by *real* post-industrialism – to resist all those things which can be viewed as a potential challenge to the hegemony of unselfconscious 'reason', a 'reason' quite content and supposedly identical with itself? We could even go further and suggest that with unselfconscious 'reason', unreflective pleasure (particularly in consuming) becomes the condition of possibility of representation – and thus stereotypes; these, then, oil the machinery of a market-based consumer society – a society of the simulacrum, and a highly centralized mass communications network. This network produces identities where once there might have been differences. These are identities which the mass market accepts without a murmur in the race to divest itself of the last vestiges of God and the Enlightenment. From this perspective, too, there are strong indications of an increasing homogenization of society, or a 'putting into discourse', as Foucault might say, of what was once 'outside', and 'other' to representation.

From another perspective, however – that of the individual artist or intellectual who is not rich – the situation could have been described in its essentials by Marx when he said that no one is free to speak and write as they please if their livelihood depends on what they say and write. Seen in this light, the freedom of the artist or intellectual is also the freedom from an employer, and from the market and its attendant consumerism. If the market is the expression of what people want (i.e. the expression of unreflective desire), then the intellectual's freedom is in part based on not presenting the people with what they want (to hear). The intellectual/artist is increasingly confronted by the market which creates homogeneity (abolishes differences, and even individuality). This is why the so-called 'popular' of the people is also what makes for a *commercial* success. New thought is then difficult in this context because it 'calls for thinking',[12] is not inscribed in a stereotype, or convention, and challenges the *doxa*. It will only have a reduced chance of commercial success.

Julia Kristeva's work calls for thinking and thereby challenges the market mentality in doing so. It by-passes the stereotype, and opens the way – for those who allow themselves to be challenged by it – to an experience of analysis. Such is the context in which we may read her work with love: love defined as an 'open system'[13] – open to the other, the different, the foreign.

Julia Kristeva's intellectual trajectory

In the succeeding chapters, each of what I see as three periods of Kristeva's intellectual trajectory will be covered. Broadly considered these are, firstly, the writings of the 1960s and early 1970s which outline a theory of semiotics capable of describing poetic language both as the 'productivity' of the text, and as a specific form of negativity. Kristeva scrutinizes linguistics, various logics, and some aspects of mathematics in order to see whether they offer a rigorous way of developing a theory of the dynamic and unrepresentable poetic dimension of language: its rhymes, rhythms, intonations, alliterations – melody; the music of language, in short; music which is even discernible in everyday speech, but which is in no sense reducible to the language of communication. It is a question, for example, of creating a way of analysing the poetic aspect of Joyce's writing. This writing is illustrated in *Ulysses* by Molly's monologue. Consider for instance the repetition of 'yes' in the final lines of the latter:

> I was a Flower of the mountain yes when I put the rose in my hair like the Andalusian girls used or shall I wear a red yes and how he kissed me under the Moorish wall and I thought well as well him as another and then I asked him with my eyes to ask again yes and then he asked me would I yes to say yes my mountain flower and first I put my arms around him yes and drew him down to me so that he could feel my breasts all perfume yes and his heart was going like mad and yes I said yes I will Yes.[14]

Kristeva will enable us to become aware, in her writings of the late 1960s, that each 'yes' in this passage from *Ulysses* does not have the same meaning as it does in the language of communication. In effect, there is here a poetic 'yes' *and* the 'yes' of communication. Kristeva begins to provide a way of speaking about such a poetic 'yes'. Whereas before we relied on intuition, now it is possible to speak about what used to be unspeakable. Such then is one of the major strengths of Kristeva's work of this time.

The second discernible period of Kristeva's trajectory is the 1970s. Here, particularly with the publication of *La Révolution du langage poétique*,[15] Kristeva takes up the issue of the theory of the subject in relation to language – and especially poetic language. This is the period of the refinement of the concept of '*le sémiotique*' designed to help articulate the realm of the pre-symbolic, or that dimension of language which constitutes the basis of poetic language. At this time, too, Kristeva's debt to psychoanalysis begins to become more evident with the 'feminine' coming to disrupt the Name-of-the-Father as the embodiment of the paternal function (of father/mother/child triad – see Chapter 2), and thus the Symbolic as the order of language and signification. As we shall see, the feminine element as '*chora*' (a receptacle, as well as a distinctive mark) corresponds to the 'poetic' in language. For the feminine would be located in language's unrepresentable material-ity – its indeterminate and almost ephemeral aspect – the aspect which places in question all modes of formalization traditionally associated with 'nationality' (masculinity). Certain kinds of text highlight the materiality of language more than others (the poems of Mallarmé more than the novels of Balzac), and these can be analysed, as Kristeva illustrates, in relation to the socio-historical context in which they emerge. The possibility of poetic language becoming evident (visible) is thus linked to the nature of social relations at a particular moment in history. In the highly normalized, regularized, ordered society of *fin de siècle* France of the last century, poetic language assumes the role of the major ethical function of art. Kristeva thus begins to sketch out the political significance of the avant-garde, and at the same time offers insights into the way psychoanalytic theory can throw light on social relations. Poetry becomes, in Kristeva's analysis, a way of maintaining social bonds through what is destructive of the social, and conducive to madness. Poetry is capitalist society's carnival, a way of keeping death and madness at bay. Poetry is a refusal of a 'flight into madness'.[16]

Finally, Kristeva's work has focused even more closely on psychoanalytic theory during the 1980s. *Powers of Horror*[17] marks a turning point in this regard for at least two reasons. Firstly, while psychoanalysis and semiotics remain the principal instruments of explication, there is in this text a strong sense that the origin of psychoanalysis itself might be brought into the picture, via the notion of abjection. This is the effect of focusing on Freud's more 'anthropological' writings and thence on religious practices in general. Secondly, however, as several writers have noted,[18] *Powers of Horror* introduces a marked 'lightening' of style with a more liberal use of the first person and the more frequent inclusion of personal experience as illustrative of points being made. In this respect, we find Kristeva tacitly acknowledging her debt to Roland Barthes. Moreover, whereas prior to 1980, semiotics and psycho-analysis were brought to bear on works of art (cf. poetic language), now the tendency is to invoke works of art in order to illuminate, or even explain, concepts such as abjection. Céline's work is, for instance, used in this way.

A similar stylistic approach appears in two other works of the 1980s, namely, *Tales of Love (Histoires d'amour*[19]) and *Soleil noir*.[20] These examine, through a psychoanalytic prism, aspects of love in western culture, and depression and melancholia, respectively. Both books are personal and theoretical odysseys which at the same time illuminate the nature of personal experience in the west in the 1980s. Art (both painting and literature), both past and present, is put in service of studies of the ego (cf. narcissism) and its vicissitudes – one outstanding example being Kristeva's analysis of Hans Holbein the Younger's 'The Corpse of Christ in the Tomb' painted in 1521.[21] The orientation of Chapter 7 below will be, in part, directed towards a consideration of the extent to which Kristeva succeeds in explaining certain tendencies evident in western culture and society in the 1980s. Given their focus on individual experience, can these works really explain broader social and cultural developments? And if they do, to what extent do they help people to cope with the negative side of these?

An adequate understanding of Kristeva's intellectual trajectory requires some knowledge of the intellectual and historical context in which it emerged. The main purpose of Chapter 1 will be to provide a sketch of this context. In effect, an attempt will be made to explain and outline aspects of cultural and intellectual history from the 1960s to the 1980s, paying particular attention to the fact that it is things 'French' with which we are concerned. Does this make any real difference to our understanding? Such is the question which guides our reflection here.

The focus of reading

For the remainder of this introduction, I would like to speak about one of the issues raised in writing a book about Kristeva.

To begin, let us consider the possibility that all disciplines are similar when it is a question of whether or not they are themselves included in the discourses they produce. The problem here is no different for mathematics than it is for literary criticism. As soon as we speak of the 'set of all sets' in mathematics, or of the 'literary' quality of criticism, or of the sociology of sociology, etc., a division emerges – or, more rigorously, a threat to the integrity of the discipline emerges – which cannot be pasted over. Certain British mathematicians-cum-philosophers such as Bertrand Russell were very much concerned precisely with this problem throughout their lives. Unfortunately, those in other disciplines have tended to shun it. Ironically, perhaps, this very threat to the integrity of the disciplines potentially bridges the gap between the natural sciences and the other disciplines. A brief indication of what is at stake may be gained by pointing out that when we speak, a tension is introduced between the act of speaking and the completed statement. Recognition of this may amount to little more than a fleeting evocation in my mind, or in that of my addressee that, after all, these are only words being uttered. And if someone *says*, 'These are only words I am uttering' it becomes clear that what is being said may well refer to the act of speaking itself and create a dilemma; for it becomes unclear as to whether the speaking (or discourse) is, or is not to be included in what is being spoken about. In addition to the literary critic and sociologist already mentioned, we could point to the European anthropologist who writes about European culture; the university academic who writes about the university; the philosopher who writes about philosophy; the linguist who speaks about language, etc. To repeat: it does not matter which discipline is involved, the structure of the problem is the same. It is a problem which transcends disciplines. And it is the line of thought which Kristeva pursues in her essay, 'Pour une sémiologie des paragrammes'.[22] It is also present in J. L. Austin's distinction between 'performative' and 'constative' utterances,[23] as it is in Emile Benveniste's work.[24]

Do we have to conclude, then, that it really *is* the case that in France, and elsewhere on the Continent, there is greater awareness of the kind of problem we have been considering, and that, as a result, the gap between the natural sciences and the humanities tends to be greater in Anglophone countries than in Continental Europe? Maybe our exploration in Chapter 1 of some aspects of the French intellectual scene will provide the basis for an answer to this question.

Notes

1 See Shoshana Felman, 'Psychoanalysis and Education: Teaching terminable and interminable', *Yale French Studies*, no. 63 (1982), p. 29. Werner Heisenberg's Principle of Uncertainty states that we can never know the world, or reality, exactly. As Bronowski puts it: 'Heisenberg's principle says that no events, not even atomic events, can be described with certainty.' *The Ascent of Man* (London, BBC, reprinted 1976), p. 365.

2 The work of the French philosopher, Jacques Derrida, is often thought to have inaugurated poststructuralism. See Robert Young, 'Post-

structuralism: the end of theory', *The Oxford Literary Review*, vol. 5, nos 1 and 2 (1982), pp. 3–15.

3 Postmodernism is explained by Jean-François Lyotard in his *La Condition postmoderne: rapport sur le savoir* (Paris, Minuit, 1979); in English as *The Postmodern Condition*, trans. Geoff Bennington and Brian Massumi (Manchester, Manchester University Press, 1984). However, Lyotard has said that his book, *Le Différend* (Paris, Minuit, 1983), contains the philosophy of postmodernism.

4 Gilles Deleuze, *Foucault* (Paris, Minuit, 1986), pp. 131–41.

5 Michel Foucault, *The Order of Things* (New York, Vintage, 1973), p. 387.

6 Italo Calvino, 'Right and wrong political uses of literature', in *The Uses of Literature*, trans. Patrick Greagh (San Diego, Harcourt, Brace, and Jovanovich, 1986), p. 90.

7 To give but two examples. The first is from the late 1970s where it is said that:

> Any understanding of Kristeva's theory demands a willingness on the part of the reader to come to terms with her unfamiliar and, as such, difficult terminology.

Steve Burniston, Chris Weedon, 'Ideology, subjectivity and the artistic text' in *On Ideology*, Centre for Contemporary Cultural Studies (London, Hutchinson, 1978), p. 218. Secondly, in her 'Preface' to *The Kristeva Reader* (Oxford, Basil Blackwell, 1986), Toril Moi writes that,

> To think the unthinkable: from the outset this has been Julia Kristeva's project. (p. vi)

Also,

> Given the conceptual and theoretical difficulty of her texts, each essay [in *The Kristeva Reader*] has been provided with a short introduction. . . . (ibid.)

8 Pierre Bourdieu, *Distinction: A Social Critique of the Judgment of Taste*, trans. Richard Nice (London, Routledge & Kegan Paul, 1986), p. 2.

9 Not that Bourdieu himself is usually as 'unsubtle' as this in his presentation – far from it. Power relations are never obvious, visible, or even easily deduced. Rather, they are always 'concealed', 'camouflaged', 'masked', 'hidden', 'disguised', 'invisible', etc. See ibid., pp. 99–112. But see also ibid., p. 228 where Bourdieu explicitly links the acquisition of cultural capital to the struggle between social classes.

10 See ibid., pp. 372 ff.

11 ibid., pp. 32–3.

12 See Martin Heidegger, 'What calls for thinking' in David Farrell Krell (ed.), *Martin Heidegger: Basic Writings* (London, Routledge & Kegan Paul, 1978), pp. 341–67.

13 See Julia Kristeva, *Tales of Love*, trans. Leon S. Roudiez (New York,

Columbia University Press, 1987), pp. 13–16.

14 James Joyce, *Ulysses*, the corrected text (London, The Bodley Head, 1986), pp. 643–4.

15 *L'Avant-garde à la fin du XIXe siècle, Lautréamont et Mallarmé* (Paris, Seuil, 1974); first part in English as *Revolution in Poetic Language*, trans. Margaret Waller (New York, Columbia, 1984).

16 Kristeva, *Revolution in Poetic Language*, p. 82. See also pp. 81–4.

17 *Powers of Horror: An Essay on Abjection*, trans. Leon S. Roudiez (New York, Columbia University Press, 1982).

18 See Leon S. Roudiez 'Translator's Note' in ibid., p. vii, and Guy Scarpetta in *Le Nouvel Observateur*, (19 May 1980) cited by Roudiez in ibid.

19 Paris, Denoel, 1983.

20 Paris, Gallimard, 1987.

21 ibid., pp. 119–50.

22 *Tel Quel*, no. 29 (1967), pp. 53–75, reprinted in *Séméiotiké: Recherches pour une sèmanalyse* (Paris, Seuil, 1969), pp. 174–207.

23 See J. L. Austin, *How to Do Things with Words*, ed. J. O. Urmson and Marina Sbisa (Oxford, Clarendon Press, 2nd edn, reprinted 1980).

24 See Emile Benveniste, 'Subjectivity in language' in *Problems in General Linguistics*, trans. Mary Elizabeth Meek, Miami Linguistics Series, no.8 (Coral Gables, Florida, University of Miami Press, 1971), pp. 223–30; and 'Analytical philosophy and language', in ibid., pp. 231–8.

Part One

Context and influences

1
"'Too French . . .'"?
Setting the intellectual scene

'Too French' means: love affairs, libertinism, witticisms, fickle-
ness, lack of substance and seriousness, fashion, petite Parisian
women, economic incompetence, Pigalle, Folies-Bergère,
Moulin-Rouge, banks of the Marne, Impressionism, the tradition of the eighteenth century, too frivolous, too much froth and
bubble. . . .

Philippe Sollers, *Théorie des Exceptions*

Frenchness

There are probably few nations, if not few people, in the world –
and, certainly in the Western world – for whom 'French' does not
evoke a specific set of images relating to food, fashion, politics,
sexuality, language, rural and intellectual life, etc. – images
precisely like those enumerated above by Sollers.[1] How could it be
otherwise? For as the historian, Theodore Zeldin clearly recognizes, no 'nation has tried harder to find and express its identity'[2]
– especially outside France, we could add. Even though, as Zeldin
also recognizes, the task of describing a typical French person is
well-nigh an impossible one, 'Frenchness', because it is a perceived
set of images, styles, and behaviours divorced from any particular
individual, is much easier to define.

Here, we need only recall the image – even if it is a somewhat
faded one – of the intellectual *engagé*, or, more simply, the very idea
of 'intellectual'. Thus an intellectual is certainly a person who takes
a stand, goes against the tide, is provocative, opposes the
establishment, and generally has a sense of moral, or political
commitment; but in its non-Sartrean version, an intellectual can

13

also be someone who loves art and ideas for their own sake, who may enjoy putting on a show (cf. Lacan), and who does not necessarily need to be paid in order to think.

And so while a difference exists between the image of 'Frenchness' and the reality, we need above all to recognize that before being able to appreciate and understand intellectual and artistic endeavour in France, we must, firstly, discount images of 'Frenchness' deriving from self-promotion; and, secondly, look critically at the often negative stereotypes deriving from an overreaction to 'Frenchness' outside France. In this regard, Philippe Sollers might well have added 'Parisian intellectual' to his list of what 'too French' means. American or British books and articles on intellectual movements in France – especially since 1945 – rarely fail to refer to the effects on thought of Parisian intellectual life.[3] More specifically, in the early years of structuralism in America and elsewhere, being a French intellectual often meant being seen by Anglophones as monstrously difficult to understand;[4] or, if the figure was Jacques Lacan, simply a monstrosity.[5]

Julia Kristeva's work is written in this milieu which, for some, is 'too French'. That she is highly sensitive to this milieu, is illustrated by the following remarks:

> From the time of my arrival [in Paris], I found, in this milieu, a distrustful and cold hospitality, that was nevertheless effective and dependable. A hospitality which has, moreover, never failed. Whatever the xenophobia, the antifeminism or the antisemitism of some, I maintain that French cultural life as I have come to know it has always been marked by a reserved but generous curiosity, one that is reticent but, everything considered, receptive to the nomad, the outlandish, the implant, and the exogamous of all kinds. The greater tolerance of the English, and the greater American capacity for assimilation no doubt offer more existential opportunity. But they are, finally, because of their lower *resistance*, less propitious to the production of new thought.[6]

As a foreigner in France for whom being in exile has taken on both an intellectual and personal significance,[7] Kristeva becomes a perceptive witness of the intellectual environment that I discuss in the following pages of this chapter. Indeed, in what follows, I attempt to provide a pre-text for Kristeva's text, one to which Kristeva has responded from the moment of her arrival in Paris in the mid-1960s to the present day.

Thought and its concerns in France

Beginning in particular in the 1930s with the lectures of Alexander Kojève,[8] Hegel, and then Marx will permeate Parisian intellectual life for the next thirty or more years. Whatever version of their thought becomes current in France up until 1968, it is impossible to dissociate it from a political cutting edge. Interest in these thinkers shakes philosophy from its narrowly institutional – that is, academic – slumber perhaps characteristic of the Bergson era. Kristeva's work certainly bears the mark of this influence – especially in texts such as *La Révolution du langage poétique*.[9]

Sartrean Existentialism, too, is more or less unthinkable outside a framework set by the Hegel–Marx nexus. As Sartre wrote in 1960: 'the unsurpassable framework of Knowledge is Marxism; and in as much as this Marxism clarifies our individual and collective *praxis*, it therefore determines us in our existence.'[10]

The study of Hegel and Marx focused attention on the foundations of thought and society. Theories of politics, ideology, and subjectivity, which would give French intellectual life its unique stamp immediately before and after the Second World War, begin to come to the fore. At the same time begins the ascendancy of the French Communist Party as the main focus for progressive intellectual and cultural activity: it becomes the prime organizer of colloquia on social and cultural issues, the main harbinger – almost despite itself – of intellectuals and avant-garde writers and artists in the late sixties and early seventies.[11] Stalin had been denounced in 1956; the party's bureaucratic apparatus was deemed cumbersome and authoritarian, but the party as patron of intellectual activity, together with Marxist philosophy, would not receive its final *coup de grâce* until the mid to late seventies with the publication of *The Gulag Archipelago*, the rise of the so-called 'new philosophers' (who called, in part, for a return to the moral ideas of Kant and the Enlightenment), and the emergence of the Solidarity movement in Poland.

Somewhat less visible to a wider public than Hegelianism or Marxism, was phenomenology. Phenomenology comes to provide a more sophisticated backdrop for the development of a theory of subjectivity and language – a theory of which Marxism was bereft. Phenomenology, too, provided the impetus for Sartre's existentialist humanism, although Sartre's 'innovation' here was to try to rid his humanism of any trace of transcendence, or any entity prior to

15

consciousness in the world. In fact, in privileging consciousness, Sartre eliminated the difference between subject and object: the ego would become absolute master of itself and of the objective world for it would be continuous with it. The phenomenological strand found in Sartre is therefore somewhat aberrant; nevertheless, it doubtless inspired the move to see Marxism as a humanism, thus bringing the latter under fire from structuralism in the 1960s. According to Michel Foucault,[12] Marxism was, after 1945, always fundamental, but was variously 'married' to other parallel systems of thought, or intellectual movements. Of these, phenomenology was, in Foucault's eyes, by far the most important – to the extent that 'everything which took place in the sixties arose from a dissatisfaction with the phenomenological theory of the subject, and involved different escapades, subterfuges, break-throughs, according to whether we use a negative or a positive term, in the direction of linguistics, psychoanalysis or Nietzsche'.[13] As we shall see,[14] Julia Kristeva's work is also strongly marked by the influence of phenomenology and its theory of the subject. Rather than rid thought of the distinction between subject and object, Kristeva's Freudian approach leads to an investigation of the preconditions for the constitution of the subject–object division. This kind of focus, let us note, was quite inimical to the Analytic–Empiricist tradition. For it, too, like Marxism, failed to pay close attention to a theory of the subject.

Nietzsche constitutes another underlying reference point in French thought for the generation coming after Sartre. In particular, writers such as Georges Bataille and Maurice Blanchot – assiduous readers of Nietzsche – influenced those, who, like Foucault and Gilles Deleuze, wanted to ecape the restrictiveness of academic philosophy and Marxism alike. Nietzsche was not only challenging and refreshing as a thinker, and captivating as a prose stylist, but was also seen as a way of gaining a new insight into contemporary culture. If, then, Sartre had somewhat cavalierly dismissed God and the transcendental ego at almost a single stroke, Nietzsche had shown, firstly, that God cannot be abolished so readily, but that, secondly, were He to be, man would also be a casualty, with nihilism taking up the slack. If the writer was Georges Bataille, Nietzsche would even stimulate a renewed interest in the sacred. Thus, in the early 1970s, Kristeva writes that:

Bataille's work seems to me to bear on this precise moment: it is that following the ending of Christianity, with its affirmation posing the subject and knowledge, thus opening up society as well as modern philosophy, Bataille proclaims a new practice. Rather than being ignorant of it, or avoiding it, Bataille's approach takes the conclusion of Christian idealism as its point of departure.[15]

Part of Bataille's attraction for Kristeva and others is in showing that the death of God is not the end of the story – either philosophical or historical. In its continuation, this story – especially as it is taken up by the writer – refuses to bypass the horror and death (man's own death) which Christianity masked, and which humanity must now confront alone, if it can confront it at all. In short, Bataille would counter Sartre's humanist naïveté and point toward an understanding of the knife edge upon which the existence of society is poised in the battle between the sacred transgression (cf. sacrifice) and the Law as the basis of the social pact.

Structuralism

The movement publicly designated 'structuralism',[16] which emerged in France in the 1960s became, in many respects, the strongest force against philosophical humanism. Most fundamentally, the structuralist endeavour restored the difference between subject and object that Sartre's philosophy in particular had erased. Such is the significance of the emphasis on the study of language as both a relatively autonomous realm, and at the same time constitutive of the conscious subject. For Sartre, it was important to show how language could be transparent, and a perfect representation of the world. Although approached from different directions by a variety of thinkers, the structuralist concern was to show that representation as such was not innocent, but symptomatic of a particular kind of society. The journal *Tel Quel* (publisher of most of Kristeva's writing), pointed out in its editorials and articles in the late 1960s, and especially in 1968, that representation, knowledge, and consciousness could not be separated from one another in a bourgeois, capitalist society. The point was to avoid being naïve about representation and to see it, like language, as being one aspect of existence, not the equivalent of the thing itself. The structuralist move was in part, then, aimed at breaking the nexus between words and things which various forms of empiricism seemed determined to maintain at all costs through the workings of representation.

Furthermore, structuralist studies began to show that the kind of relation between elements of any system (be that system linguistic or cultural) and not the elements in themselves is the source of meaning (cf. Saussure's famous notion of the arbitrary relation between signifier and signified). These relations are, in particular, those of opposition and difference. Saussure's famous 't' can be written in a variety of ways, for the letters surrounding it in a word or phrase will constitute it as having the value of the letter 't': 'the value of the letters is purely negative and differential'.[17] From this Saussurian perspective – where language is a system of differences 'without positive terms' – all empirical manifestations of phenomena only attain their significance and value in the context of the often invisible (to consciouness) system of relations which constitutes them. Saussure designated this level as '*la langue*' (language), as opposed to '*la parole*', or the particular speech act – the empirical manifestation of language. '*La langue*', in short, would constitute the 'rules of the game' (cf. Saussure's chess game illustration) which produce meaning to take place in 'la parole'.

One of the most important consequences of the structuralist endeavour, together with its poststructuralist aftermath (see Derrida), was to undermine the privileging of consciousness. For consciousness, it was contended, tends to attribute meaning exclusively to things 'in themselves', rather than to the negative and differential relations between them. As far as consciousness is concerned, objects ('positive terms') can be represented, but relations are another matter. In effect, the level of 'la langue' is denied in favour of a privileging of both the referent and the transparence of language.

This insight, that language is a system of differences not only gave structuralism its impetus, but also made it the object of hostility for many Anglo-American Marxists and more empirically minded academics alike. No doubt the most notorious diatribe in this regard, was that mounted by E. P. Thompson against the structuralist Marxism of Louis Althusser.[18] More urbanely, Jeffrey Mehlman referred to the Anglo-American's 'fascination or exasperation at the remarkable speculative activity' associated with such figures as Claude Lévi-Strauss and Jacques Lacan.[19] The hostility – or fascination – accompanying the emergency of structuralism no doubt highlights a philosophical disagreement; however, more fundamentally, it highlights a difference in intellectual orientation – as though, for the Anglo-American, it is precisely out of Paris that such an incredibly complex and obscure theoretical movement like an 'anti-humanist' structuralism would come. This movement, in other words, is just a little 'too French'.

This notion of structuralism as 'too French' can be seen in the fact that although the structuralist tendency to dethrone consciousness took on vastly different forms according to the thinker involved, at a distance this tendency quickly assumed a homogeneity which, to many, had more to do with its being perceived as a peculiarly French phenomenon, than it had to do with any real homogeneity. Thus in the 'Conclusion' to her book on structuralism, Edith Kurzweil writes that 'Structuralism could not become popular in America in the way that it did in France... For the pursuit of knowledge, in France and America, proceeds from different traditions: we are empirical, the French are philosophical ....'[20] The question turns, however, on the extent to which the nature of the issues raised are indeed explicable simply in terms of two 'different traditions'.

A paradise for intellectuals?

Once, the intellectual in France would have evoked some of the ideals of the French Enlightenment: rather than remaining trapped within the naïveté of the limited, immediate, and closed world of one's own culture, society, or country, the intellectual *qua* intellectual could reflect, and meditate – invoke reason as a counter to prejudice and ignorance, and thereby transcend particularity. This transcendence of particularity would lead to the promotion of reason and thought as universal values not limited by time or place. Enlightenment philosophy would enjoin all people to arrive at the 'age of reason' and thus gain the means to their freedom. No people, once having attained the age of reason, could then unthinkingly accept tyranny. The idea of the social contract as the *rational* and universal origin of society thus becomes one of the clearest expressions of Enlightenment political thought.

Perhaps it was Julien Benda's *La Trahison des clercs* (translated as *The Betrayal of the Intellectuals*), bemoaning the passing of the

Enlightenment intellectual as the bearer and defender of the universal, which is crucial here.[21] Or perhaps Sartre was in fact the last truly Enlightenment intellectual, one who fought in the name of universal freedom; but whatever the case, a transformation of the role of the intellectual has occurred. Now, the reason of the Enlightenment has been found at best to be a particular historical form of reason. A self-image which made it possible for the intellectual to speak in the *name of others* has been brought into question,[22] and the language of contestation or commitment (*engagement*) has itself been contested.

Despite all this, philosophy in France continues to prosper – even if it is coming under increasing pressure in the education system from so-called reforming governments.[23] Belief in the universal and in the age of reason may be over, but philosophy – including the history of philosophy – is able to claim some rights in 'postmodern' France, and fulfil its historical role as a kind of icon of French culture.[24] This is particularly true if we remember that philosophy in France permeates all the arts, including literature.

This is how it has come about that intellectuals-cum-philosophers in France today are often concerned with the subversiveness of thinking for its own sake. In fact, May 1968 marked an important turning point for the fortunes of the intellectual *engagé*. *Tel Quel*, for example, stormed at the time that:

> We are not 'philosophers', 'savants', 'writers' according to the representative definition admitted by the society whose material operation and theory of language stemming from it, we attack . . .[25]

The theory of language in question is the one invoked by the '*discours engagé*'. This theory claims that politically committed language is a transparent language – a language which would reveal the world as it is so that no one could say that they were ignorant of, or not responsible for, its injustices. On this basis, the writer's political position about the Algerian war, for example, is what he, or she explicitly writes about that war. The events of May 1968, however, marked a fundamental reappraisal of this Sartrean position of the '*discours engagé*'.

According to Philippe Sollers, the divergence from Sartre's notion of the political role of literary activity had already begun for him at the time of the foundation of *Tel Quel*, precisely at the height of the Algerian war in 1960.[26] Despite the journal's opposition to the war, no explicit declaration against it appeared in the first number in March 1960. On the other hand, Sollers' 'Requiem' [27] describes (new novel style) a soldier's funeral (the funeral of Sollers' friend killed in Algeria, as it turned out). 'Requiem' proposes to be an oblique, quite indirect – and *therefore* literary – political statement. Through the opaque pathos of writing, the shadow of death and the oblique political gesture become one and the same. With this gesture, the writer is an intellectual – not by being the vehicle of a moral or political message, but by becoming a writer in the fullest sense possible: by becoming the opponent of all normalizations and stereotypes, and the *practitioner* of his/her art.

In this spirit of being a writer, Sollers would give – also in 1960 – a lecture at the august Sorbonne on the (at the time) marginal poet, Francis Ponge. Not at all 'academic' by the standard of the times, Sollers is, like Sartre in a sense, a breath of non-academic fresh air in an all-too-moribund academic establishment.[28] The intellectual of the early 1960s thus aims to break out of accepted *forms* governing thought and writing; literature – writing – does not *become* political, but has political effects *as* literature.

The intellectual in the spirit of *Tel Quel* becomes, in the late sixties, a materialist writer: the sounds and rhythms of language are highlighted, and together display a plurality of meanings. In brief: a mechanism of perpetual movement is sought out, and a transformation brought about – for example, by the coincidence of narrative and the act of writing as such.

The Enlightenment intellectual has, then, more or less passed from the French intellectual scene. If he or she is still there as an essayist committed to revealing the dangers of various tendencies in social and political life, it is as but one of many equally audible voices borne along by the plurality of discourses that is an inescapable part of postmodern reality.

Whatever the case, it is no doubt as much in her role of avant-gardist and materialist writer, as in that of Enlightenment *philosophe* that the French intellectual has been dubbed by the outsider as just a little 'too French'.

The other side of reality and the limits of writing

Roland Barthes writing on Fourier and Loyola,[29] Michel Foucault examining, 'archaeologically', the thought of the Renaissance and the modern era,[30] Jacques Derrida on the history of writing and philosophy,[31] or Julia Kristeva herself writing on Saint Bernard of Clairvaux and Jeanne Guyon in *Tales of Love*, are but some examples of how the history of thought and the text makes its way into the present in French cultural life. What is at stake is the analytic value of reading such thinkers, of working out *what* their texts are saying, and *how* they are saying it, even if there can be little consensus about the value of the content of the writing in question. As intimated by our earlier reference to Philippe Sollers, the 'how', or the practice of writing became, for Kristeva and *Tel Quel* in the late 1960s, just as important and significant as what was being written. Thus Sollers strove, when writing his novels *Drame* and *Nombres*, to make the 'act of writing' and the story coincide.[32] This act of writing as writing is another side of writing, another side of 'reality'. This act of writing, too, has formed the basis of Kristeva's analyses of Sollers' *Nombres*, and another novel, *H*.[33] For Kristeva, this approach to writing as such, was almost unique – as she pointed out in 1983:

> For the first time in modern history, with the exception of the very brief association of futurism and formalism crushed by the Stalinist régime in the USSR, a form of thought was emerging having as its basis – as the object of analysis but above all as its principal stimulus – the practice of writing in process.[34]

Seen in the above light, the French and Anglo-Saxon traditions embody two different tendencies: the former has well-nigh legitimated a flamboyance and an intensity which the latter tradition often finds – in its perceived excessiveness – difficult to fathom. This excessiveness often seems like Pascal's 'joy of the hunt' incarnate – or it would do if joy (jouissance) were not also the subject of serious reflection – as it is, for example, in the work of Lacan.[35]

Joy is but another form of the 'unnameable' – the other side of reality as such – which, together with Being and death, drives thought beyond itself, beyond its own limits, putting it in touch with infinity, particularly in the sense that the part becomes equal to the whole.[36] The limited truths of positivism do not sit easily in such circumstances. As Foucault once wrote in response to Gilles Deleuze's work – work carried out in the spirit of tapping the unthinkable beyond tradition and history: 'new thought is possible, [therefore] thought is again possible'.[37] To put it simply: not to have thought continually producing new thought – which means producing new problems – is to have it die. Such would be the basis of a French cultural tragedy alluded to by the words of Pierre Bourdieu when he says: 'I doubt . . . that real freedom exists other than as the knowledge of necessity.'[38] Freedom of thought is thus a knowledge of limits. In Bourdieu's case, these are the limits of necessity. Thought, too, is caught up in the dialectic of freedom and necessity, so that to embrace this necessity (the limit) becomes a way of transcending it, of creating new thought.

The limit also ushers in the notion of writing as an experience. Here, a distinction may be made – following Roland Barthes – between writing that in no way signals an awareness of its own style and productivity, and one that does. Writing treated purely as an instrument (as in scientific discourse), and writing which engenders jouissance – and even perversion to the extent that here, writing does not *produce* anything – correspond to Barthes' '*écrivance*' and '*écriture*', respectively. Only 'unreadable' writing, says Barthes, 'is a limit-literature, a literature of experience'.[39] This is a writing (*écriture*) which transcends the instrumental view (*écrivance*), and thereby disturbs existing perceptions of the possibilities of writing, and perhaps art in general.

Writing and limits undermine the idea of language as purely transparent. Transparence is implied within an empiricist framework when the latter presents language as the coincidence of words and things where there would be complete adequation between language and reality or, in Locke's terms, between ideas and reality. For Locke, reality is the cause of ideas, or representations:

> External objects furnish the mind with the ideas *of sensible qualities*, which are all those different perceptions they produce in us; and the *mind furnishes the understanding with* ideas of its own *operations*.[40]

The implicit acceptance of the notion of language as transparent corresponds to pure *écrivance*. Within this framework, the proper function of language is the communication of a message – originating in reality and filtered through the senses – to a receiver. If the words are *adequate* to the message, communication takes place. From the position of the receiver there must, however, be a double mediation brought about by the fact that the message is based on an *other's* experience and is, therefore, a representation of a representation. Looked at from this position, *écrivance* is brought into question and language is on the way to becoming opaque.

23

However, to analyse language from the position of the receiver of the message, and not simply from the perspective of the sender, or the hypothetically isolated individual speaker, is to begin to analyse it at the level of the community of speakers, and not simply in terms of the relationship between words and things. The more empiricist the framework, the more the consequences of the socio-linguistic basis of language tend to go unacknowledged. In the 1950s, the concern of Anglo-American philosophy to justify the notion of truth as adequation still presupposed the fundamental transparence of language.

Even before the heyday of Analytic philosophy in the 1950s, Bertrand Russell proposed that no sentence without 'object-words' to connect language to non-linguistic reality could have meaning, unless it was a product of pure logic or mathematics; 'all empirical statements contain object-words, or dictionary words defined in terms of them', says Russell. And he continues by saying:

> Thus the meaning of object-words is fundamental in the theory of empirical knowledge, since it is through them that language is connected with non-linguistic occurrences in the way that it makes it capable of expressing empirical truth or falsehood.[41]

Clearly, to the extent that language is founded on 'object-words' connected to reality (truth), it is also fundamentally transparent, and limited to being no more than *écrivance*. For thinkers and writers in France – such as Barthes, Derrida, Kristeva and Sollers – the point is to go beyond *écrivance* and towards the analysis or production of writing as opaque, as jouissance and an 'experience of limits'.[42]

The missed (Anglo-Franco) encounter

In the story of Don Juan, two different conceptions of language can be seen in operation. The first is what Shoshana Felman, in her book on J. L. Austin, calls the 'cognitive' or 'constative' conception of language, while the second is the conception of language as 'performative'.[43] The antagonists and victims of Don Juan subscribe to the first view of language, Felman points out, whereas Don Juan himself subscribes to the second view. As cognitive and constative (descriptive), Felman explains, language is conceived as

an instrument for the transmission of *truth*, that is an instrument of know-how (*savoir*), of *knowledge* (*connaissance*) of the real. The truth is a relation of perfect adequation between a statement (*énoncé*) and its referents and, more generally, between language and the reality it represents.[44]

By contrast, the *performative* as analysed by Austin and employed by Don Juan, is

> *to do: to act* on an interlocutor, to modify the situation and its relations of strength. Performative, and not informative, language for [Don Juan] is a field of enjoyment (*jouissance*) and not of knowledge (*connaissance*); as such, he is not susceptible to truth or falsity, but rather, very exactly, to felicity or infelicity, to success or failure.[45]

Not only does Shoshana Felman here set out an analytic framework of great clarity and succinctness, but, as will have been noted, she also offers two conceptions of language corresponding precisely to the empiricist view, and the view of writing as an experience of limits: as *écriture* and jouissance. Hence, just as Don Juan's victims do not grasp language in its performative dimension, and so fail to have a real encounter with him, so too would there be a 'missed encounter', according to Felman, between English and French styles of thinking.

Furthermore, according to Felman, the reality of this missed encounter is well-nigh unsymbolizable. Both sides, however, are attributed a certain genius: the 'ironically empirical and pragmatic genius of the English' contrasts with the 'sophisticated, allusive, speculative genius of the French'.[46] For Felman, therefore, these two different styles of thinking, especially in the early 1960s, engaged in what amounted to a non-confrontation between two different philosophical traditions. The question of whether or not the notion of 'non-confrontation' really goes to the heart of the matter, is less relevant to our discussion than the specific style of Felman's approach itself. This quite unique approach throws further light on the interaction between the styles of thought in question.

In essence, Felman seeks to focus on the difference, or differences between two philosophical traditions which are so much taken for granted, that they are 'missed', or not taken into account. With Felman's guidance, we would come to see that there is *always* another, unrecognized dimension in this encounter. Consequently,

Felman draws attention to J. L. Austin's 'anaphoric' style – a style of 'mis-fires' and 'recommencements'. In fact, she shows us Austin's Don Juanesque face in his commitment to the performative, his fascination with new beginnings and a joy in philosophizing which undermines the goal of bringing his theorizing to a final conclusion. Indeed, to be entirely true to Austin's philosophy, as much attention should be paid to Austin's own act of stating, as to his statements of truth or falsity – his descriptive, constative statements. And this, says Felman, is because the spirit of Austin's thought is always drawing us towards the performative dimension of language. If the performative is 'doing things with words' – thus I make a promise when I say 'I promise' – Felman wants to highlight what Austin himself is doing with words while he engages 'seriously' in the business of elaborating his theory of the performative.

In this regard, the humour of Austin's style is very much part of the performative aspect of his way with language. But here, it is precisely humour, argues Felman, that has not been given due consideration; its full significance has indeed been missed. Far from being incidental, or merely a quirk of style, humour centres Austin's theory in the '*force d'énonciation*' – the 'force of uttering': the dimension in which humour may be displayed so scandalously, and so subversively that nobody sees it as Austin's trump-card. 'If I had broken your dish or your romance', says Austin on excuses, 'perhaps the best defence I can find is clumsiness.'[47] Austin's humour is never thematized, never explicitly commented upon, never subjected to the criterion of truth or falsity by the philosopher himself. Humour rather insists in his discourse and, in this way, simultaneously seduces, and produces jouissance in, the listener/reader. Like Don Juan, suggests Felman, Austin always promises results: he promises, for example, to provide a rigorous distinction between 'performative' and 'constative', but in the end the initial firmness of the distinction begins to evaporate:

Were these distinctions [between 'performative' and 'constative'] really sound? Our subsequent discussion of doing and saying certainly seems to point to the conclusion that whenever I 'say' anything (except perhaps a mere exclamation like 'damn' or 'ouch') I shall be performing both locutionary [constative] and illocutionary [performative] acts, and these two kinds of acts seem to be the very things which we tried to use, under the

26

names of 'doing' and 'saying', as a means of distinguishing performatives from constatives.[48]

The purists, as Felman notes, are not at all happy with this state of affairs. For them, it is like giving up the whole basis of the theory of the distinction between 'constative' and 'performative' when it has hardly begun. These purists – who may come from either side of the Channel – miss the 'fun' of Austin's philosophizing; they miss the fact that Austin's *How to Do Things with Words* is also an instance of *doing* philosophy which is as much performative as it is constative – that is, as it is about finding answers to problems posed. In light of such a recognition, Austin can be ranged alongside, Don Juan; but he can also be ranged alongside Jacques Lacan and Nietzsche: two men of style.

We can agree that Felman's thesis is quite sustainable and that the performative is a destabilizing factor that some would prefer to ignore, or even suppress. However, Felman's mode of analysis itself is more in keeping with the aspect of recent French thought associated with a structural/poststructural framework. Felman makes liberal use, for example, of Lacan's work. It is illuminating, I think, to reflect briefly upon Felman's own performative, in order to see if there is not what some would see as just a little (too much) 'Frenchness' in this way with theory.

To begin with, it strikes us quite forcibly that Felman's mode of analysis is highly nuanced, endlessly reflexive, and analytically sophisticated. Furthermore, the focus of her study is as much, if not more on the unconscious level of Austin's text, as it is on the conscious level. Even more incontrovertibly, however, the use of Don Juan, Nietzsche, and Lacanian psychoanalysis turns Austin into a divided figure where, amongst other things, the philosopher's own act (style) is never entirely in harmony with his analytical philosophical bent. In short, in keeping with a structural/post-structural framework, Felman herself clearly illustrates an aspect of the French – as opposed to the Anglo-American – style of thinking. For she seeks to exploit the evidence of a division in the subject and the barely symbolizable terrain this opens up. A new Austin seems possible for Felman, because the joy of the game (philosophizing) is as important as the gravity of the capture (truth or falsity). Again, like important thinkers in the French philosophical tradition, Felman does not see her task as one of avoiding Don Juanesque scandals in thought, but rather of provoking them to the maximum extent possible. And above all, the scandal committed by the Don Juans of history is to infuse a joy of language into language as communication.

Quite significantly, then, Shoshana Felman (who lives and teaches (at Yale) in the United States) decides to publish her book on Austin in French, rather than in English – a tacit admission on her part that she knows very well where the bulk of her audience is to be found.

In fact, the tenor of Felman's approach points us precisely in the direction taken by Julia Kristeva's work. For it, too, takes account, not only of the communicative aspect of language, but also of its scandalous and, as we shall see, semiotic aspect.

Kristeva's work on writers from Baudelaire to Duras, passing by, amongst others, Joyce, Céline, and Sollers, will show us what is happening in modern writing and its French variant:

> And what if something were to happen? What if a novel written in French were revealed as being very important? No, it is not possible, it *must* not be possible.
>
> You quote such and such a name, a title or two, and, straight away, they burst out (certain, amused, offhand, feverish) '*Mais c'est trop français! Too French!*' How many times I have heard this exclamation, this cry at once superior, sorrowful and quietly fearful. Too French? What does it mean?[49]

Notes

1 See Philippe Sollers, '"Too French!"' in *Théorie des exceptions* (Paris, Gallimard, 1986), pp. 303–7 – whence comes the title of this chapter.

2 Theodor Zeldin, *The French* (London, Collins, 1983), p. 6.

3 Thus in her book, *The Age of Structuralism: Lévi-Strauss to Foucault* (New York, Columbia University Press, 1980), Edith Kurzweil writes that: 'I was struck by the diverse reactions to Lévi-Strauss' notions – reactions which could only partly be attributed to the fact that he is French, but which had to do with the appeal and respect accorded Parisian intellectuals' (p. ix). Or again, as Zeldin writes: 'Any exploration of the French must include a visit to a Parisian intellectual, because he belongs to a small group that have cast a magic spell on the way the French are perceived by themselves and by foreigners' (*The French*, p. 398).

4 See Richard Klein, 'Prolegomena to Derrida', *Diacritics* (Winter, 1972), p. 29.

5 See Stuart Schneiderman, 'Afloat with Jacques Lacan', *Diacritics* (Winter, 1971), p. 27.

6 Julia Kristeva, 'Mémoire', *L'Infini*, no. 1 (Winter, 1983), p. 42.

7 See below, Chapter 3.

8 According to a number of observers, Alexandre Kojève's lectures on Hegel at the Ecole Pratique des Hautes Etudes from 1933 to 1939 were quite fundamental here. See Vincent Descombes, *Modern French Philosophy*, trans. L. Scott-Fox and J. M. Harding (Cambridge, New York, Melbourne, Cambridge University Press, 1980), pp. 10–12.

9 See, for example, pp. 375–96. While the whole of Kristeva's text is indebted to Hegel, but see especially, *Revolution in Poetic Language*, pp. 109–64.

10 Jean-Paul Sartre, *Search for a Method*, trans. Hazel E. Barnes (New York, Vintage, 1968), p. 178.

11 See Julia Kristeva, 'Mémoire', pp. 48–9.

12 See Gérard Raulet, 'Structuralism and post-structuralism: an interview with Michel Foucault', trans. Jeremy Harding, *Telos*, no. 55 (Spring, 1983), pp. 195–211.

13 ibid., p. 199.

14 Especially Chapter 5, below.

15 Julia Kristeva, 'L'Expérience et la pratique' (first published in 1973), reprinted in *Polylogue* (Paris, Seuil, 1977), p. 109.

16 Note that figures such as Foucault rejected any such categorization of their work.

17 See Ferdinand de Saussure, *Course in General Linguistics*, trans. Wade Baskin (London, Fontana, 1973), p. 119.

18 E. P. Thompson, *The Poverty of Theory and Other Essays* (London, Merlin Press, 1979), pp. 193–397. See also, Raymond Williams, *Marxism and Literature* (Oxford, Oxford University Press, 1977), p. 27 where Saussure is seen to put forward a 'reified understanding of language', and p. 168 where the Saussurian principle of the arbitrary nature of the sign is seen to be a veil hiding an alienating bourgeois social reality.

19 Jeffrey Mehlman, 'The "floating signifier": from Lévi-Strauss to Lacan', *Yale French Studies*, no. 48 (1972), p. 10.

20 Kurzweil, *The Age of Structuralism*, p. 243.

21 This is the argument, for example, of Alain Finkielkraut in his *La Défaite de la pensée* (Paris, Gallimard, 1987), pp. 13 ff.

22 See Gilles Deleuze's and Michel Foucault's discussion, 'Intellectuals and power' in Michel Foucault, *Language and Counter-Memory Practice: Selected Essays and Interviews*, trans. Donald F. Bouchard and Sherry Simon, ed. Donald F. Bouchard (Ithaca, New York, Cornell University Press, 1977). Foucault says, for example:

> The intellectual's role is no longer to place himself 'somewhat ahead and to the side' in order to express the stifled truth of the collectivity. . . . (pp. 207–8)

23 Attempts – the most recent being in November 1986 by the Chirac government – to restructure French universities in light of technocratic goals have been vigorously contested – particularly by students – so that the government was forced to back down on its proposed 'reforms' affecting the place of philosophy in the education system.

24 In June 1979, '*Les Etats Généraux de la philosophie*' ('The Estates General of Philosophy') was convened by, amongst others, Jacques Derrida. Its goal: to defend the teaching of philosophy at all levels of the education system from the threat of abolition or reduction. See Jacques Derrida, 'Philosophie des Etats Généraux', *Libération*, 20 June 1979, pp. 14–15. Also to be noted in this regard is the establishment of the *Collège International de Philosophie* set up in Paris in October 1983. This institution provides the opportunity for an interchange between French and foreign philosophers – especially on themes not covered by teaching and research in philosophy in mainstream institutions.

25 'La Révolution ici, maintenant', *Tel Quel*, no. 34 (1986), p. 3.

26 Philippe Sollers, *Vision à New York* (interviews with David Hayman) (Paris, Grasset, 1981), p. 83.

27 Philippe Sollers, 'Requiem', *Tel Quel*, no. 1 (1960), pp. 33–8.

28 See, too, the comment by Gilles Deleuze that Sartre was – especially just after the War – 'our Outside'. Gilles Deleuze, Claire Parnet, *Dialogues* (Paris, Flammarion, 1977), p. 18.

29 Roland Barthes, *Sade/Fourier/Loyola*, trans. Richard Miller (New York, Hill & Wang, 1976).

30 See Michel Foucault, *The Order of Things* (New York, Vintage, 1973).

31 See Jacques Derrida, *De la grammatologie* (Paris, Minuit, 1967), in English as *Of Grammatology*, trans. Gayatri Chakravorty Spivak (Baltimore and London, The Johns Hopkins University Press, 1976).

32 See Philippe Sollers, *Drame* (Paris, Seuil, 1965); and *Nombres* (Paris, Seuil, 1968). For the reference to writing and story coinciding, see Sollers, *Vision à New York*, p. 100.

33 See Julia Kristeva, 'L'Engendrement de la formule' (on *Nombres*) in *Séméiotiké: Recherches pour une sèmanalyse*, pp. 278–371 and, 'The novel as polylogue' in *Desire in Language*, pp. 159–209.

34 Julia Kristeva, 'Mémoire', p. 45.

35 See Jacques Lacan, 'De la jouissance' in *Le Séminaire, livre XX: Encore* (Paris, Seuil, 1975), pp. 9–18. Hereafter cited as *Encore*.

36 See below, Chapter 4.

37 Michel Foucault, 'Theatrum Philosophicum' in *Language and Counter-Memory Practice*, p. 196.

38 Pierre Bourdieu, *Questions de sociologie* (Paris, Minuit, 1980), p. 77.

39 Roland Barthes, *Sur la littérature* (Grenoble, University of Grenoble Press, 1980), p. 42.

40 John Locke, *An Essay Concerning Human Understanding*, vol. I, ed. J. W. Holton (London, Dent; New York, Dutton, Everyman's Library,

revised edition, reprinted, 1967), pp. 78–9. Locke's emphasis.

41 Bertrand Russell, *An Inquiry into Meaning and Truth* (the William James lectures for 1940 delivered at Harvard University), (London, Unwin Paperbacks, reprinted 1985), p. 29.

42 See Philippe Sollers, 'Le Roman et l'expérience des limites' in *Logiques* (Paris, Seuil, 1968), pp. 226–49, and especially p. 242.

43 Shoshana Felman, *Le Scandale du corps parlant: Don Juan avec Austin ou la séduction en deux langues* (Paris, Seuil, 1980).

44 ibid., p. 33.

45 ibid., p. 34. Felman's emphasis.

46 ibid., p. 124.

47 J. L. Austin, *Philosophical Papers*, ed. J. O. Urmson and G. L. Warnock (London, Oxford, and New York, Oxford University Press, 1970), p. 177, cited by Felman at p. 165.

48 J. L. Austin, *How to Do Things with Words*, ed. J. O. Urmson and Marina Sbisa (Oxford, Clarendon Press, 2nd edn, reprinted 1980), p. 133.

49 Sollers, '"Too French!"', p. 303.

2

The effect of the unconscious

The unconscious is structured like a language.

Jacques Lacan

On 7 November 1955, Jacques Lacan – doctor of medicine, psychoanalyst, friend of surrealism – 'officially' announced his famous 'return to Freud' in a paper given at a neuro-psychiatric clinic in Vienna.[1] Unofficially, the 'return' had been under way at least since the end of the Second World War[2] and probably since Lacan's first presentation of the 'mirror stage' in 1936 – although the notion of 'return' is not explicitly mentioned there. The concept of the mirror stage would dislodge the ego from its position of ascendancy – a dislodgement fundamental to the Lacanian 'return to Freud'.

And so, in the Vienna of the 1950s, the clinicians, psychiatrists and all those who worked to ensure the dominance of the medical model of psychoanalysis are told that their way is unfaithful to Freud's thought, that the 'Freudian thing' is not the ego or the 'self' – much less a personality, or a diseased brain – but the subject of the unconscious: 'it' speaks.

With the success of ego-psychology under the hand of Heinze Hartmann, America was hardly willing to accept the news; and the British, always a little uneasy about things French, would continue to insist on the primacy of clinical experience over and above the realm, as they saw it through the eyes of Anna Freud, of 'theory'.[3] Already in 1954, the International Psychoanalytic Association had ceased to recognize the 'Société française de psychanalyse', ostensibly because of Lacan's 'short' analytic sessions. In fact, the

32

Lacanian 'return' undermined the hegemony of the psychologistic paradigm founded on a privileging of the unity of consciousness and the identification of the subject in psychoanalysis with this consciousness. The ego in psychology was not therefore to be confused with the subject in psychoanalysis. To do so, Lacan said, was to misunderstand the full import of Freud's concept of the unconscious; it was to resist the effects of the fact that 'it' speaks in psychoanalysis.

Despite clear differences – largely related to the person of Lacan, and the promotion of a doctrine – no part of the psychoanalytic community in France has remained unaffected by Lacan's influence in raising the concept of the unconscious to a position of pre-eminence in interpreting Freud's thought. And Julia Kristeva is no exception. The decentring of the ego and the dethronement of consciousness are also her points of departure. For Kristeva, this decentring does not only take place in, or through psychoanalysis, but also within the realms of literature, art, and to some extent theology. Kristeva's work can be seen, in fact, as a prolonged meditation on the effect of the unconscious in human life, an effect psychoanalytic discourse is charged with rendering thinkable, symbolizable, and perhaps explicable. Because of his influence on her work, it is worth spending some time discussing the nature of the unconscious according to Lacan. In particular, I shall be concerned both with what Lacan means by the term, the unconscious, as well as how he specifically uses this term in interpreting literary texts. Indeed, the status of literature in relation to psychoanalysis is what is at issue in the following pages of this chapter. With respect to literary and artistic work in general, Lacan's conception of the unconscious is limited in the end, because of its heavy emphasis on formalization. In highlighting this limitation, we can see what the parameters of Lacan's theory are, as well as outline the point at which Kristeva's theory of both signification and the unconscious tends to go beyond it.

The increasingly numerous books and articles explicating the work of Lacan[4] make it unnecessary to go into detail concerning Lacanian psychoanalytic theory in general. Moreover, our explication of Kristeva's work in subsequent chapters[5] will throw further light on fundamental aspects of psychoanalytic theory.

Language and the unconscious system

According to Lacan, the 'unconscious is structured like a language'. Or, as a later formulation would have it:

> If I have said that language (*langage*) is what the unconscious is structured like, this is because language, to begin with, does not exist. Language is what we try to know concerning the function of *lalangue*.[6]

What precisely is the significance of Lacan's formulations? To answer this question, we must approach the problem indirectly, and recall first of all that the unconscious is a separate system; it is not part of consciousness. In fact, the very mode of appearance of the unconscious has always been problematic, in that knowledge (as opposed to truth), together with natural languages and symbols, both belong to, and form, the consciousness system. Moreoover, the logic of the unconscious is fundamentally different from that of Cartesian reason and self identity. The unconscious is characterised precisely by what is not identical with itself, with what cannot be totalized. With this last term, we can return to Lacan's formulation, cited above. The overall structure of language as a system of differences is like the unconscious in that it cannot be represented. This is to say that language as such is not embodied within any number of speech acts; for it is not contained within the empirical realm of speech, but is equivalent to the condition of possibility of all speech-acts. Language as such is something akin to the implicit, coded structure of rules (e.g. syntactical and grammatical) which are – unconsciously – invoked by the speaking being. If the unconscious is, for Lacan, 'like' this realm of language, let us give full weight to this term. Let us not say, for instance, that the unconscious is – even in its structure – equivalent to the realm of language, that realm denoted by the French word '*langage*'. One fundamental difference is that language lends itself too readily to formalization, whereas the unconscious is precisely what poses a problem of formalization. Through slips of the tongue, jokes – especially puns – the poetic dimension of language (to the extent that it is *full* of ambiguity, and therefore full of meaning), the dream as a rebus, and forms of nonsense, we glimpse the unconscious. More succinctly: the unconscious both calls for interpretation and cannot be exhausted by interpretation.

34

By implication, then, the unconscious cannot be assimilated by the consciousness system, but rather poses a problem for consciousness because it cannot be represented: *it* speaks. Or in Lacan's words: 'there is no metalanguage'. There is no discourse over and above discourses of the consciousness system (such as the scientific) which can represent the unconscious. On the contrary: *it* appears. In short: 'The unconscious is the testimony of a knowledge in as far as for the most part it escapes the speaking being.'[7] Poetic meaning escapes the speaking subject by being a condensation of meaning – that is, a potential plurality of meanings. Poetic language, then, is *full* of meaning (Lacan's 'full' word) calling for interpretation. This fullness differentiates it from the communicative language of everyday life. Or, more precisely: in communicative language, the presence of a fullness of meaning passes unnoticed by consciousness. It passes over, or resists, the possible plurality of meanings evident in the language of communication in the form of ambiguity and nonsense. Sometimes, however, this plurality of meaning seems to 'insist' in a person's speech – even to the extent of becoming a symptom. Consciousness and its agent, the ego, thus have a tendency to resist poetry – to resist the notion that consciousness, too, is a product of language, and that the subject is thereby divided between two heterogeneous systems: the conscious and the unconscious.

The privileging of the ego in the psychoanalysis of the 1950s (in France as elsewhere) is hardly surprising given that the scientific paradigm of the time was positivist and thus predominantly empirical, if not empiricist. The empirical basis of knowledge clearly gives precedence to knowledge which may be verified (or falsified) experimentally to the satisfaction of egos in the *concordia discours*. This '*discours*' remains, in Lacan's terms, at the level of the 'empty' word, or at the level of signification and the message of communicative language. For Lacan, the symbol itself has made the human being human;[8] the ego, however, not without a hint of paranoia,[9] claims to be the only true origin of the subject.

As Lacan announced in 1955 in the introduction to the famous seminar on Edgar Allen Poe's, 'The Purloined Letter', 'the subject who speaks is beyond the *ego*'.[10] Granting that this be so, there is still a question of whether the unconscious is a language, or a discourse which can be understood by someone. Before we reply too hastily and say that it is the analyst who hears the unconscious beyond the ego – and 'receives his own message back in reverse form' – the question remains as to what, precisely, the analyst hears. Does the analyst receive a message from the analysand which may be transcribed into a discourse readily grasped by symbolic processes and by consciousness? If so, the unconscious would seem to become the site of distorted communication, or perhaps the site of a 'disorder' that needs to be dissipated in the interests of the ego and the proper functioning of language as communication. Such an understanding renders the unconscious a kind of pale, indeed faulty, reflection of consciousness; the relative autonomy of the unconscious is effaced in light of the dominance of consciousness. For Lacan, the notion of a relation between the two realms implies that the 'full' poetic word is an aberration to be eliminated in the interest of clarity and the complete transparence of the word. Clearly, Lacanian discourse does not accept such an understanding. On the other hand, the evolution of Lacan's doctrine itself shows an oscillation between the notion that 'the unconscious is structured like a language' – in which case we could presume that it is susceptible to being articulated and formalized – and the notion that the unconscious is always equivocal, between the lines, the irreducibly poetic where a plurality of meanings resonates – the subject's 'style' (the subject as style), impossible to translate into the language of communication.

The baroque

From another angle, the unconscious would 'speak' in the very baroque style of Lacan's seminar, one which made the possibility of the seminar's publication a doctrinal issue.[11] Roudinesco describes the Lacanian performance in the amphitheatre of Saint-Anne hospital in Paris where the seminar was held for ten years from 1954:

> He gave up his Prince of Wales suits for more extravagant clothes. Henceforth, he dresses in a style resembling his baroque syntax . . . he speaks in a wavering, syncopated or thundering voice, spiced with sighs and hesitations. He notes down in advance what he is going to say, then, before the public, he improvises like an actor from the Royal Shakespeare Company who has Greta Garbo as a teacher of diction and Arturo Toscanini as spiritual director. Lacan acts false because he speaks true, as if from his rigorous speech (yet quick to turn), he

could, ventriloquist-like, make the secret mirror of the unconscious reappear, symptom of a mastery in incomplete control.
Sorcerer without magic, guru without hypnosis, prophet without
god, he fascinates his audience with his impressive language
where, on the margins of desire, the great revival of an
enlightenment takes place. Lacan does not analyse, he associ-
ates. Lacan does not lecture, he produces resonances. At each
session of this collective treatment, the pupils have the
impression that the master speaks about them and for them in a
coded message secretly destined for each one.[12]

Could it be, then, that the unconscious only becomes manifest in
the performance? Any 'writing down' of this performance, any
attempt at capturing the secret of its power in a representation
would, it could be argued, contradict the notion of 'it' speaking.
On this basis, the reader of the published version of the seminar
would not have access to the (re)appearance of the unconscious; for
one could not come to understand the nature of the unconscious by
reading *about* it, but only by reading 'it' between the lines.

That the master himself was not satisfied that the unconscious
would be read between the lines of the published version of the
seminar, is suggested by the later Lacan's growing interest in a
possible mathematical presentation, not only of the nature of the
unconscious, but of all the fundamental aspects of his teaching.
The moebius strip, the Klein bottle, and borromean knots (see
Figure 1) are but some of the 'mathemes' used as a means of
transmitting the Lacanian doctrine.

To this concern about the problem of 'transmission' can be
added Lacan's interest in Wittgenstein. For the philosopher of

Figure 1   The borromean knot

language games had thought long and hard about the difficulties deriving from the difference between 'saying' and 'showing'. The realm of 'showing' is where what would otherwise require a metalanguage could be presented. With Wittgenstein, the limit to saying is reached when the question of defining language arises. Any definition – or general concept – inevitably becomes another example of language. In effect, the limits of language cannot be delineated within language. There is no more a metalanguage for Wittgenstein than there is for the psychoanalyst bent on making the poetry of the unconscious resonate for a public wider than the throng anxious to take up seats at the master's seminar.

In the mid-1950s, however, the need to combat the misreading of Freud carried out by ego-psychology meant that the complexities of the 'formalization' and the 'transmission' of Lacan's theory and teaching could remain secondary (as could the problems raised by Jean Laplanche concerning the status of the spheres of language and the unconscious and the link between them.)[13] At the time, it was necessary to prove that the privilege attached to the ego as a plenitude identical with itself was unfaithful to Freud's meaning. Freud's text, it was propounded, spoke about a divided subject, a subject resulting from *both* the unconscious and the pre-conscious–consciousness systems.

The unconscious as a purloined letter

For the Lacan of the fifties, then, a reading of de Saussure sharpened the emphasis on the notion that the unconscious could be seen fundamentally as a signifier pure and simple, without any particular meaning, and rather capable of taking on a plurality of meanings, thereby constituting subjects in their intersubjectivity. To 'teach' this truth, Lacan commented on 'The Purloined Letter', in a seminar which was pointedly chosen to head the French version of the famous *Ecrits*.[14] Let us consider Poe's story for a moment together with the use Lacan makes of it.

As is well known, the story, 'The Purloined Letter',[15] recounts the way Minister D— steals a letter of great importance to the Queen, right before her very eyes, and how Dupin, friend of the narrator, retrieves same. In purloining the letter, the Minister notices that the Queen does not wish to draw its presence to the attention of the King. As a result, Minister D— is able to get away scot-free with the letter and use its possession to blackmail the

Queen for political ends. The Queen, for her part, alerts the Prefect of Police to the theft and orders him to retrieve the stolen document. Having the mentality of one who is, to say the least, not a lateral thinker, let alone a psychoanalyst of Lacanian persuasion, the Prefect expects that in order to hide the letter it must be concealed in the most inaccessible (and predictable) hiding-place imaginable – in the hollowed-out leg of a table, for instance, or rung of a chair. The letter of course is in no such concealed place, but rather on display for all to see in a pasteboard letter rack hanging from a brass knob below the mantelpiece in the Minister's office. Hero of the story – to the extent that it is he who retrieves the letter and claims a handsome reward – Dupin realizes why all the detailed searching by the police has been in vain – experts as they are in this type of investigation. They have been looking in the wrong place: namely, where they would *expect* to find the purloined item, in some secret compartment detectable only with police 'expertise'. With this knowledge, Dupin, wearing dark glasses as a disguise, pays a visit to the Minister (with whom he had dealings in the past) and promptly notices the letter in the pasteboard letter rack, and, on the pretext of having forgotten his snuff box, pays the Minister a second visit. A disturbance in the street below, arranged by Dupin, entices the Minister to the window of his office, whereupon, our hero repurloins the letter from the purloiner (thereby repeating the Minister's act) and replaces it with a facsimile, where he writes the lines:

Un dessein si funeste,
S'il n'est digne d'Atrée, est digne de Thyeste.
(A design so deadly,
If not worthy of Atreus, is worthy of Thyestes.)

Other aspects of the narration should also be recalled. To begin with, the Prefect mentions very early on in the story that Dupin has 'odd notions'. In fact, the prefect has a 'fashion of calling everything "odd"',[16] especially if it does not fit his own way of thinking. This evokes the story of the schoolboy's game of 'even and odd' used by Dupin to illustrate, for the narrator, the strategy of thinking employed for retrieving the letter. Moreover, the Prefect says, almost at the same moment, that the whole thing seems to be '*very* simple indeed'. '"Simple and odd", says Dupin', thereby anticipating the kind of problem finding the letter involves. Of course, the Prefect is quite unaware of the significance of what he is saying, given as he is to assuming that the most complex solution will be the right one. Another point worthy of note is that both the Minister and Dupin are poets. And the Prefect takes being a poet only one step removed from being a fool. The Minister and the Prefect, therefore, are shown, right from the start, to have very different modes of thinking – so different, in fact, that clearly the Prefect will be unable to identify with the thinking of the Minister, a point quite crucial to Dupin's strategy.

What does the story show us about the unconscious as far as Lacan's commentary is concerned? In the first place, it is clear that it is not about a letter hidden in a 'conventional' sense, but about one that is hidden only because it is in a place too unexpectedly obvious for those who do not have eyes to see. For example, the Queen is perfectly well aware of the one who robbed her, and necessarily so if the Minister's blackmail is to work; the Minister, for his part, leaves the letter in full view of everyone, and Dupin – as if driven to continue the circuit – leaves lines from Crébillon in the facsimile which will readily identify him to the Minister. Indeed, everyone but the police and the King knows exactly what is going on; but they are none the less helpless to do anything about it.

If Dupin has understood that the thought of a poet is not the same as the thought of everyone, is he then absolute master of the situation? The answer is 'no', because Dupin reveals himself to be caught up in the very circuit of intersubjectivity founded on the play of 'even' and 'odd' for which the letter – irrespective of its contents – is the precondition. Thus the fact that Dupin wants to get *even* with the Minister keeps him within the circuit, while reference to the child's game of 'even and odd' opens up the question of how far any person can identify with the thought of another. The police, in the position of the ego-psychologist, are blind to the limits of the power of identification. In terms of Hegel's Master/Slave dialectic (still dear to Lacan at this time), any claim to mastery must be founded on a recognition of (the difference of) the slave. As poets, both the Minister and Dupin are purveyors of the full word, and it is this which establishes their difference from the other personages in the circuit, and possibly from each other. So while the story's phrase, 'the robber's knowledge of the loser's knowledge of the robber'[17] opens up the field of identification beyond the one-way caustic judgement of the police (a poet is but one remove from being a fool), a judgement blind to other as a subject, the significant move is to grasp that the intersubjective circuit always leads to the limit of reason. For even were I to recognize that the other recognizes me – or better: even if I were to recognize that the other recognises that I recognize him – still, the point at which our mutual recognition could be grasped in thought is inaccessible to us both; neither of us can grasp this point in thought, or identify with it, because it is outside the circuit of intersubjectivity produced by the chain of signifiers in language. Language is this limit of intersubjectivity. For its users, it has no outside: the absolute point of mutual recognition is inaccessible to consciousness.

Lacan sees this inaccessible point as the place of the unconscious – a place which hardly figures at all in western thought before Freud. This place – or this 'other scene', as Freud called it – can never appear as such in language, or indeed in any symbolic form whatsoever. It rather 'insists' (Lacan) in language as a precondition of poetry through: the presence or absence of punctuation; the spacing of letters – whether this be 'correct' or not; signifiers such as zero, and all sorts of diacritical marks which have no meaning or content in themselves, but which give meaning to other elements in the signifying chain. So it is that the 'Da, Da, Da' of the Upanishads, and of T. S. Eliot's, *The Waste Land* – which so intrigued Lacan[18] – gain their significance from the order in which they are said: 'Da: Datta; Da: Dayadhvam; Da: Damyata' (Give, sympathize, control).[19]

As Lacan's commentary also makes clear, 'The Purloined Letter' is both story (fiction) and the designation for an esential object in this story. This is important. For while the story sets the limits to the fictional reality described, the letter, in its turn, sets a limit to the story. In other words, the story takes place to the extent that the purloined letter governs the subjects in their intersubjectivity. The letter has no content (for the reader of the story), and so stands for, is the sign of, desire in general. The implication is that the letter could be substituted for any desired object – a diamond, perhaps – and the same circuit of events could be played out. A diamond, however, has a content; it is not a virtual object[20] like a letter which can function as a sign of desire, as a signifier of signification.

Poe's story, according to the tenor of Lacan's commentary, illustrates how desire and signification work in general, and how fiction is always a part of the human scene as the virtual object of desire, having no fixed or intrinsic content. And it seems that it has to be this way if the wide range of objects of desire is to be accounted for. Looked at from a slightly more psychoanalytic angle, every object of desire is a substitute for the real thing, or rather, the real object, which is the mother (more about which later). The real (object) cannot be signified, although it constitutes the basis of (is the cause of) signification as such. For, in Lacan's terms, the real is a plenitude, whereas language and signification can only ever refer to an 'absence', or 'lack' – without which there would be no desire. Desire emerges, Poe's story would be deemed to illustrate, when a value is attributed to one signifier above all others, and when all other signifiers only take on value in relation to this particular one. Accordingly, we recall that the Queen, and then the Minister, attribute such importance to the letter, that the former will go to inordinate lengths to get it back, while the latter sees that its possession alone is enough to achieve his political ends. Here is the way value is attributed to the letter as described by the Prefect of Police. The Queen has just been perusing its contents when the King, and then the Minister, enter the royal apartment:

> After a hurried and vain endeavour to thrust it in a drawer, [the Queen] was forced to place it, open as it was, upon a table. The address, however, was uppermost, and, the contents thus unexposed, the letter escaped notice. At this juncture enters the Minister D—. *His lynx eye immediately perceives the paper, recognises the handwriting of the address, observes the confusion of the personage addressed, and fathoms her secret.*[21]

The Queen attributes importance to the letter because she sees it – as we all must – as a real object. Only the (impossible) position outside the circuit, as we have seen, would allow her, or the other *dramatis personae*, to grasp the letter as a virtual object capable of infinite displacement. As Lacan says, the letter, as a signifier binding the subjects in the structure of intersubjectivity, has no proper, or fixed trajectory from which to deviate. In this sense, for each one, 'the letter is his (or her) unconscious'.[22] Or, as another version puts it: 'the unconscious means that man is inhabited by the signifier'.[23] And, Lacan adds, Poe's example of the large letters forming a name running across a map so that, in its obviousness, it remains concealed, constitutes a beautiful image of the unconscious.[24]

If the unconscious were a letter (and a virtual object), it would still be susceptible to taking on a plurality of significations, not successively, but simultaneously. It would thereby pose a problem for formalization and, particularly, for symbolization. But, according to Lacan's commentary, the unconscious is fundamentally symbolic. This is why so much attention is given to the letter. How precisely can the unconscious be symbolic? An answer to this question entails sketching out some of the main essentials of Lacan's psychoanalytic theory. This will also set the scene for understanding much of Kristeva's work.

The psychoanalytic triangle

Derrida[25] and Roudinesco note that Lacan's commentary on Poe served as a means of 'teaching', or illustrating psychoanalysis.[26] For the Lacanian enterprise, each *dramatis persona* (including, and especially, the letter) has the burden of psychoanalytic theory to carry. Hence the unconscious will not emerge for psychoanalysis by the literary quality of Poe's writing, but rather, psychoanalytic theory will reveal the unconscious in the writing itself.[27] The story, in other words, like the ego, would be part of the 'discourse of the unconscious', which *qua* discourse calls for psychoanalytic interpretation.[28]

The Queen in 'The Purloined Letter' is both the feminine in general, and the Mother. The King is the symbolic Father, in whose name arises the register Lacan calls the Symbolic: the realm of all language, symbolization and signification. As Mother, the Queen stands both for the Real, or what cannot be symbolized, and for death, which also poses a fundamental problem for symbolization. At a cultural, biological level, the reproduction of individuals (and thus the species) takes place in light of the interdiction against incest. The law against incest is the Law of the Father which ensures the possibility and continuation of social relations – that is, symbolic relations between subjects.

When the child is born, its first object is the mother. The mother, for the child, is an unmediated, unsymbolized object. No distance exists between mother and child, and there is even a certain resistance to separation which, in the case of the boy in particular, will be the basis of the unconscious desire to be reunited with the mother. The intervention of the symbolic (the father as its agent) brings about the separation of the child from the mother. This separation constitutes the subject through allowing the pain of this first fundamental separation, necessary for ego formation, to be symbolized as a lack or a feeling of castration – a feeling reinforced by the knowledge that the mother is different: she does not have a penis. Or, as Lacan prefers, it is the phallus, symbol of a lack or absence *par excellence*, which the woman bears – only an absence being capable of producing symbolization. In another version, Lacanian theory says that the phallus is what the woman/mother wants to have to complete her identity, and that the child is the phallus.[29] The child/phallus, therefore, becomes a substitute for the absent penis. Separation of the child/phallus from the mother is then re-experienced as a lack for which a substitute is sought, thus entailing the woman's further foray into the symbolic.

To return to Lacan's commentary, the letter in 'The Purloined Letter' is a signifier, a symbol of an absence, so that it is always there when it is missing, and not there when it is in its place. This is the implication of its being a virtual object and the equivalent of the phallus. To be separated from her letter entails the Queen's great consternation; for she is suffering the consequences of her lack. Because it is the phallus which makes one feminine or masculine, the possession of the letter by the Minister 'feminizes' him, as Lacan notes.[30] This is why Dupin finds the Minister exhibiting an air of nonchalance and ennui when he visits him in his apartment. For the Minister *has* the letter/phallus and consequently is not lacking in any way. In fact, he is at the point of dropping out of the symbolic circuit altogether – on the verge, in effect, of a psychosis. Hence the importance of Dupin's action, not only in retrieving the letter (seeing it, like the psychoanalyst where it was not), but more importantly for Lacan, in letting the Minister know that he had lost the letter by inscribing the verse from Crébillon in the facsimile. Only by experiencing his loss will the Minister be 'cured' of his psychosis and return to the symbolic order which is the precondition of social life. More broadly, the letter has to be returned to the law of the Father, in opposition to the unconscious desire of the subject to be reunited with the Mother, that is, according to Lacan, with death.

The unconscious as symbolic

If the unconscious is the phallus (letter) in this situation, then it would seem that it is fundamentally symbolic. More precisely, the unconscious would be the quintessentially symbolic in the symbolic

– the essence of the symbolic, as it were. It would be the symbolic as such speaking – a position beyond any single ego, but one speaking through everyone as an agent of language. This seems to be the outcome of the Lacanian notion that the unconscious is the discourse of the Other as the realm of the symbolic as such. '"It" speaks' can now be translated as 'the Other speaks': the Father, the phallus, the symbolic, desire, language, the unconscious, and, as one of Lacan's commentators has put it, culture[31] – these all speak in the subject. To be sure, the phallus as the signifier of an absence is evocative of death; but the idea of death comes to the subject though language itself. This signifier of death, therefore, is also a sign of life. Lacan, for his part argues that the bar to the real that the signifier sets up induces in the subject a sense of death. Thus, in 'Position de l'inconscient', Lacan writes: 'the signifier as such, in barring the subject in the first instance, allows the meaning of death to come home to him. (The letter kills, but we learn this from the letter itself.)'[32] What is this if not to say that the symbolic itself is a sign of death, and that it is through the symbolic that we grasp this fact? Is this to say, that we learn about the unconscious through the symbolic? An answer in the affirmative entails a re-evaluation of the sense in which 'it' speaks. For the latter proposition carries within it the very problematization of the notion that the unconscious can be grasped from the position of the symbolic. On the contrary, as Kristeva's work tends to suggest, the unconscious is precisely what is (potentially) disruptive of the symbolic, as death is disruptive of life. Whether or not we talk of the unconscious as disruptive of the symbolic, or as being – in keeping with the tenor of Lacan's thought – within the symbolic order itself, the problem remains as to whether the unconscious can be spoken *about*. In this regard, Derrida argues[33] that the letter (as mode of access to the unconscious in Lacan) cannot truly be the signifier it is deemed to be, if it can be spoken about. The signifier cannot be the signified of 'The Purloined Letter'. It is an all-or-nothing situation where we must decide whether the letter (and the unconscious) is indeed the signifier *par excellence*, or whether, like Wittgenstein we should remain silent on those things *about* which we cannot speak.

For Lacan, the unconscious is deemed to be a domain quite at odds with the notion of unity, identity, wholeness, and the signified. If the unconscious can be put into discourse, it is only as an empty figure devoid of content, albeit one not without a certain power to entice subjects into its sphere and become speaking beings. The ego-psychologist, on the other hand, is caught in the domain of self-identity constitutive of the ego and so is oblivious to the unconscious as a virtuality and the precondition of the (symbolic) ego. Consequently, in 'The Purloined Letter', the police are in the position of the ego-psychologist because they are always searching for the letter conceived as an enduring, self-identical, real object. They exemplify the 'realist's imbecility'[34] which does not take account of the limits of intersubjectivity founded on an imaginary identification – either with the other's ego, or with his reasoning. For the other, like the Minister and Dupin, may be a poet emitting words *full* of meaning. This point is somewhat incidental in Lacan's commentary, but it is still in keeping with the spirit of his thought here.

Speaking 'about' the unconscious

This, then, outlined in summary, is the fundamental turn Lacan brings to the theory of the unconscious. It involves a decentring of the ego not possible in ego psychology, or – more generally – in positivist thought. This theory of the unconscious involves pushing thought beyond the limits of communication towards the Freudian 'other scene'. We need to assimilate this in order to go further. At issue, though, is whether Lacan's discourse in the seminar is actually capable of bearing the weight of the consequences of a theory which both decentres the ego (gives precedence to the signifier over the signified in human thought), and uses literature and art to illustrate the basis of the Freudian discovery of the unconscious. For some strange reason, Lacan seems quite oblivious (and to say this is not simply to follow Derrida) to the implications of his approach to the literary text as an illustration for the notion of the unconscious as the discourse of the Other. To speak, for example, *about* 'The Purloined Letter' is to imply that this story is a signified. Theoretically, the signifier is the precondition of the story; but this can be said quite independently of Poe's tale itself. On the other hand, Lacan might object that although his commentary, showing 'The Purloined Letter' to be an exemplary instance of the working of the signifier, treats the story as a signified, the story's internal structure brings this reading to an impasse equivalent to a loss of the signified. The reader would now no longer know what the story was *about*, and yet might remain quite fascinated by the writing (telling). Even more: loss of the signified might produce a fundamental enigma and so induce the intuition that the story is 'about' the telling itself. Who could say, after all, what *Finnegans Wake* is about? And, after Joyce, what the writing of the 'New Novel' is about? For Kristeva, this enigma of the novel's signified becomes, as we shall see,[35] poetic language.

Lacan's writing, by contrast (that is, the transcription of the seminar), does not have the air of playing on the enigmatic, poetic aspect of Poe's writing, but seems almost to promise an answer to every enigma. And, even if psychoanalysis will be shown to be deeply implicated in the very possibility of language and signification, Lacan never gives a hint (in his style of presentation and mode of proceeding) that psychoanalysis is an impossible subject for elaboration. Although these indices are largely super-ficial in themselves, they become less so when considered in relation to a number of others to be found both in Lacan's commentary on 'The Purloined Letter', and in his reading of Shakespeare's *Hamlet*. Before considering Lacan's *Hamlet*, let us finally expand upon the problems of Lacan's seminar on Poe.

The letter as destiny (death) – and poetry

Lacan's commentary treats Poe's story *as* the veritable exemplifica-tion of the 'other scene'. For the tale would contain psychoanalytic truths (nature of language; notion of sexual difference; repetition automation; law of the Father, etc.), and also speak the (unconscious) destiny of humankind: 'No doubt the brazen creature [Dupin] is here reduced to the state of blindness which is man's in relation to the letters on the wall that dictate his *destiny*.'[36] The so-called 'primal' scene where the Minister purloins the letter (i.e., activates the signifier, whose trajectory is human life itself) – a scene which is the absolute (because real) other of the letter, and yet can only be known through the letter as fiction – this real, yet fictive scene means that the signifier is always already in flight. Its destination would be death as the destiny of human kind. This is the meaning Lacan attributes to Dupin's retrieval of the letter – for a time '*en souffrance*' – which returns it to its proper course: the Queen and death. Just as the Commander at the end of Molière's play pulls Don Juan to his death, so the purloined letter is returned to its proper course. Death now seems to mean: death of the signifier, death of the symbolic as such, and the end of the story.

This is why Lacan puts such emphasis on the lines from Crébillon which Dupin writes in the facsimile letter he leaves for the Minister coming right at the end of 'The Purloined Letter'. In changing '*dessein*' ('design') to '*destin*' ('destiny'), when he cites these lines,[37] Lacan makes his point clear: '"Un *destin* [emphasis added] si funeste . . .".' We now grasp that, for Lacan, the story is about 'a destiny so deadly . . .'. There is, though, a last twist. For in its being *written*, this destiny is also postponed, as Lacan does not fail to point out through reference to Scheherazade telling her story for a thousand and one nights.[38] 'Writing in order not to die', as Maurice Blanchot has put it.[39] This approach to the issue conforms to Lacan's view that we learn of death through the letter itself. In a sense, language is quite lucid on this point: 'Language delivers its judgment [*sentence*] to whomever knows how to hear it . . . .'[40] Thus, for Lacan, it is less that death insists in language (through disrupting the symbolic), and more that death is the message of language – a point which seems to bring language back to being fundamentally a means of communication.

Although both Dupin's and the Minister's status as poets does not seem to impinge upon the actual unfolding of the story, this factor alerts us to two important points. Firstly, that to be a poet is to be beyond the strategies of identification with the other that communicative language conventionally facilitates. Through poetry, indeed, one can have an inkling of 'difference' in language. Secondly, the displacement of scenes in 'The Purloined Letter' (what Lacan calls the 'repetition automaton') also dis-places the position of the author–reader.

The implications of this are taken up in Kristeva's work on Lautréamont, as we shall see, and so it will suffice to say now that the 'place' of the 'other scene' is the displaced author–reader. More generally, Lacan's rationalism seems to make him deaf to poetry – the music in letters, as Mallarmé said.[41] Such a deafness would render impossible access to the writing (*écriture*) of 'The Purloined Letter'. The purloining of the letter at the level of the 'manifest' content of the story seems, significantly, to keep Lacan riveted to the domain of the gaze, of sight, while he hardly attends at all to the vicissitudes of narration – what could be said to correspond to 'hearing'. This poetic level corresponds to what Kristeva calls the 'materiality' of language – a materiality disruptive of syntax and grammar, and thus of the message.

This materiality may be grasped by the question: Who, or what is speaking in Poe's short story? Is there a fixed centre of enunciation? Between the narrator, Dupin, the Prefect of Police, the letter, and Edgar Poe himself, who is really speaking? Might it not be that the *mise en scène* as such is speaking: this 'voice' – this plurality of voices – evocative of the unconscious? The materiality of the text, then, is this displacement of the voice in the word, a displacement which, when its music is perceived, becomes poetic language. This, at least, is Kristeva's thesis. It means that for the literary text, the dis-placed author–reader speaks (the reader identifies with the author's place which is embodied in the *mise en scène* of voices). The place of the author–reader would also be the 'place' of the unconscious. Even more: the literary, poetic text *is* the *mise en scène* of the unconscious. Such would be the way that literary 'discourse' avoids becoming a metadiscourse on the unconscious, a risk Lacan, in his analysis of *literary* texts, does not always avoid. Such, for example, is the case in Lacan's commentary on *Hamlet*.[42]

Psychoanalysing Hamlet

Like Poe's short story where the logic of the letter determines the way intersubjectivity unfolds, *Hamlet* too is a text where the displacement of a signifier structures the subjects in their intersubjectivity. Shakespeare's play would *illustrate* the fact that the subject of desire in psychoanalysis is dependent on the signifier, specifically on the phallus as the signifier of desire.[43]

From the beginning of his commentary, Lacan indicates that the signifier is not a mirror of 'interhuman relationships', but constitutes a 'topological system'. The 'essential co-ordinates of this topology' are what the play – via Lacan's commentary – illustrates:

> The story of *Hamlet* (and this is why I chose it) reveals a most vivid dramatic sense of this topology, and this is the source of its exceptional power of captivation.[44]

We shall have occasion to return to this notion that *Hamlet* illustrates certain psychoanalytic principles, for it distinguishes Lacan's approach to the literary text from that of Kristeva. For now, however, let us spell out the substance of Lacan's reading of Shakespeare's play.

Hamlet has 'lost the way of his desire', says Lacan.[45] And if the 'phallus is the privileged signifier of that mark in which the role of the logos is joined with the advent of desire', Hamlet must have lost the way of this privileged signifier. But not obviously. For the phallus is always veiled; it never appears as such; it is the signifier which signifies signification. It is revealed only in its effects, and is, as we know, 'that by virtue of which the unconscious is language'.[46]

Primordially, the phallus also stands, as we have noted above, for the loss of the mother as the subject's first object and for the mother's difference as one who does not have a penis. Hamlet's problem, Lacan's commentary suggests, is that he is only intermittently aware that his mother does not have the phallus, so that he only intermittently identifies with the (ideal) place of the Name-of-the-Father. The dead father, indeed. Hamlet's subjectivity thereby becomes a kind of defective signifier. For Shakespeare's hero has defectively entered ĩe symbolic order – the order of language – and is therefore unable to identify with his father, unable to love him entirely, or to make an ideal of him. Or, more exactly, Hamlet fails to make a perfect ideal of the Father's place. Lacan claims that the reason for this is that his mother's desire interferes with Hamlet's capacity to idealize, and therefore to love:

> This desire of the mother [the desire of the Other], is essentially manifested in the fact that, confronted on the one hand with an eminent, idealized, exalted object – his father – and on the other with the degraded, despicable object Claudius, the criminal and adulterous brother, Hamlet does not choose.[47]

Although Lacan does not say it, Hamlet possibly does not choose because he still has a foot firmly planted in his mother's camp. Hamlet, in other words, has not entirely 'left' his mother, and this is why he is always vacillating when it comes to avenging his father's death, and loving Ophelia. Ophelia is very important here. And Lacan stresses this importance by pointing out that she is the first person Hamlet meets after his encounter with the ghost. Hamlet does not speak, but stares vacantly at Ophelia's face, and then leaves her (II. i). Counterposing Polonius's view that 'This is the very ecstasy of love', Lacan speaks of Hamlet's complete 'estrangement' from Ophelia and his fellow beings.[48] 'Ophelia is after this episode', Lacan continues, 'completely null and dissolved as a love object.'[49] Ophelia, then, ceases, as Lacan notes, to be an object of desire, or to have the qualities of a woman at all.[50]

But even more pointedly, our analyst says, Hamlet's fate is mapped out by the symbolic – by the 'time of the Other'. Thus in the *playing out* of the Oedipal drama that Lacan after Freud sees *Hamlet* as being, the law is the law of the symbolic, the law of language to which the human being must submit in order to become a social being. The sudden death of Hamlet's father and King, however, causes a disturbance to this law because it creates, Lacan seems to say, a confusion in Hamlet's mind between his loyalty to the symbolic status of the King and his loyalty to his person. Hamlet's problem – brought on by the fact that he knows about the crime – is one engendered by the King's two bodies.[51] Hamlet knows about the crime and this induces his madness, both real and feigned. He tries to bring himself to kill the new King (his uncle), but is constrained precisely by Lacan's law of the Other: the law which also entices him to recognize that the King is more than his person. The King, thereby, occupies the place of the phallus:

> Hamlet always stops. The very source of what makes Hamlet's arm waver at every moment, is the narcisstic connection that Freud tells us about in his text on the decline of the Oedipus complex: one cannot strike the phallus, because the phallus, even the real phallus, is a *ghost*.[52]

Put another way, Hamlet cannot avenge his father's death because he is (unconsciously) caught up in the Oedipal circuit which entails that he also wants his father's death. Only the dead father, Lacan tells us after Freud can assume the position of the phallus and thereby ensure the continuation of the law. As opposed to Sophocles' Oedipus, Hamlet 'knows' about the crime that has been committed. He is now in the almost impossible position of the unconscious as such. Consequently, Hamlet has an impossible subjectivity, one that cannot be assimilated to the level of self-consciousness and which, for Lacan at least, is the reason for certain pathological symptoms becoming manifest.[53] *Hamlet* unconsciously raises – in addition to questions about the nature of man, and about whether 'to be or not to be' – the question about what it means to be a father. For Lacan, the play shows that the question of the father is inseparable from the question of the symbolic and the phallus as the signifier of all signification. As son of the symbolic father and the real mother, Hamlet as subject – that is, as both symbolic and real – 'is' and 'is not' simultaneously; and this means, in turn, that Hamlet is the subject of the logic of the signifier as virtual object: Hamlet 'is' when he is not (symbolic), and he is not (because he is the unsymbolizable real) when he is.

Like his commentary on 'The Purloined Letter', Lacan's commentary on *Hamlet* shows Shakespeare's play to be illustrative of the Freudian discovery of the unconscious; this is what the Oedipus myth in *Hamlet* is really about. As Shoshana Felman says in introducing the collection in which Lacan's piece appears, this is to imply that literature's role is one of subservience before the power of psychoanalysis: 'literature's function, like that of the slave, is to *serve* precisely the *desire* of psychoanalytical theory – its desire for recognition'.[54] Even for Lacan who went further than anybody in freeing psychoanalytic discourse from the logic of identity and biological and psychological determinism – even for him, psychoanalysis comes along to formalize what the literary/ artistic work only blindly dramatizes. The terms of the formula are: Shakespeare's *Hamlet* = S($\cancel{A}$), or the discourse of the unconscious,
where 'S' is the signifier, and 'A' is the *Autre* (Other), so that 'S' is the signifer of the Other as barred to the subject. Accordingly, the Other is barred to the subject because it is the very precondition of speech and language. The Other is therefore the 'locus' of a fundamental alienation. In the Other, 'it' speaks. This 'it' is not immediately knowable, but may be known secondarily through analysis. 'It' speaks in literature, desire appears there, and the unconscious, 'structured like a language' may become clearly known there – but only after analysis. In particular, psychoanalysis comes to provide the requisite formalization of the unconscious (for example, S ($\cancel{A}$) as the 'algebra' of the unconscious) as the space of the signifier (the 'x' (phallus)) and source of the essential (almost transcendental) deduction Lacanian psychoanalysis makes for language. The literary text does not 'say' this – only psychoanalysis does, arriving 'after the event'. Such would be the framework within which psychoanalysis assumes priority over literary and artistic endeavour in the struggle to grasp what is at stake in the effect of the unconscious in human life.

Art and subjectivity

Although working within psychoanalysis, Kristeva shows that literature and all forms of artistic endeavour fundamentally interpenetrate. Rather than being prior to the work of art (whether literary or not), subjectivity may be seen to be formed in and through art. Instead of choosing to produce this or that particular work as a result of what one is, 'the work of art, the production, the practice in which [the artist] is engaged extends beyond, and reshapes subjectivity. There is on the one hand, a kind of psychological ego, and on the other, the subject of a signifying practice.'[55] For many artists in the twentieth century, art has been a confrontation with psychosis – with the breakdown of the symbolic function. Here Kristeva goes on to explain that

> It's necessary to see how all great works of art – one thinks of Mallarmé, of Joyce, of Artaud, to mention only literature – are, to be brief, masterful sublimations of those crises of subjectivity which are known, in another connection, as psychotic crises. That has nothing to do with the freedom of expression of some vague kind of subjectivity which would have been there beforehand. It is, very simply, through the work and the play of signs, a crisis of subjectivity which is the basis for all creation, one which takes as its very precondition the possibility of survival. I would even say that signs produce a body. . . .[56]

Quite clearly, in light of the above remark, a work of art is not simply a displaced form of psychoanalytic truth, but is equally constitutive of psychoanalysis. Writing as art would thus not be a symptom (as Lacan would have it in relation to Hamlet), but the precondition of the symptom as such: the unconscious as writing, not in writing (Derrida).

Or again, as Felman reminds us, literature has provided psychoanalysis with a significant number of its key concepts: Oedipus, narcissism, eros, thanatos, sadism. Although these have figured largely in the formation of psychoanalytic theory, this is often 'forgotten' by psychoanalysis itself.[57] To paraphrase Lacan's remarks when talking about the Minister forgetting about the letter (signifier) in Poe's tale: psychoanalysis may come to forget literature, 'but literature, no more than the neurotic's unconscious, does not forget psychoanalysis. It forgets psychoanalysis so little that it transforms it more and more in the image of the writing which first offered itself for analysis.'[58] If, then, literature – and perhaps all art – is the psychoanalytic unconscious as both Kristeva and Felman have begun to suggest, artistic endeavour will come to be seen as illuminating and transformative of the psychoanalytic enterprise, as the latter has been of art.

Joyce and the limits of signification

Faced with Joyce's text, Lacan cannot avoid posing the question of its 'unreadable' and 'enigmatic' quality. *Finnegans Wake* is thus enigmatic because it may be read in many different ways.[59] It is the text of the *lapsus linguae* – slips over the signified – *par excellence*. Joyce's text thus *calls* for analysis, and in so doing, joins with analytic discourse. For analytic discourse is a reading of the signifier *other* than in terms of the signified – that is, other than in terms of a message being communicated.

However, if *Finnegans Wake* joins with psychoanalytic discourse through being infinitely analysable, might it not be that the literary object *par excellence* is what constitutes a limit for analysis and that, because of this, the literary object would have analytic effects. Thus *Finnegans Wake* as a plurality of voices is also language speaking poetically, simultaneously producing and pulverizing meaning. The unconscious here is *not* a discourse. Rather, it would be what puts the bond between subjects in their intersubjectivity at risk, but without violence.

Although we should recognize that Lacan's theory of the unconscious is at the limit of the thinkable, the representable, and the discursive as such, we should also recognize that it does not deal with a pre-discursive domain. In fact, in addition to there being no pre-discursive reality (which is not to say that the real is symbolizable – 'reality' being the environment of the ego and consciousness), Lacan says, too, that the unconscious is the *discourse* of the Other. Two crucial statements in *Encore* highlight the point to be made. Firstly, we see that there is no pre-discursive reality because human beings are signifiers:

> There is not the least pre-discursive reality, for the good reason that what makes a collectivity – what I have called men, women and children – is not at all like a pre-discursive reality. Men, women and children are only signifiers.[60]

Even more significantly, there is no pre-discursive reality because each 'reality' is a product of discourse:

> How can one return, if not by a special discourse, to a pre-

discursive reality? This is the dream – the dream at the heart of every idea of knowledge (*connaissance*). What is considered mythic is here as well. There is no pre-discursive reality. Each reality is founded and defined by a discourse.[61]

If reality and discourse are inseparable, how are we to interpret the famous, 'the unconscious is the discourse of the Other'? Given that reality is the special province of consciousness, the unconscious cannot be a 'reality' even though it it also a 'discourse'. Every reality is founded by a discourse, but not every discourse founds a reality. The avoidance of an excluded middle seems absolutely essential. Difficulties remain, however. For the Other, according to another of Lacan's well-known formulations, 'is the other sex',[62] that is, 'woman' about whom nothing can be said – except, of course, that she is 'not whole' (*pas toute*), and that 'there is always something in her which escapes discourse'.[63] But if the unconscious is what *escapes* discourse in 'woman', surely we are moving closer to the notion that the unconscious as such is *not* a discourse.

The unsymbolizable

The trouble is that although Lacanian theory opens the way towards the concept of a radically heterogeneous unconscious and the Other – in short, towards the consequences and effects of the inexpressible and unnameable – it never quite draws the full consequences from its formulations. As for Kristeva, she retains a suspicion that Lacan privileges the symbolic order, even when putting forth his theory of what cannot be symbolized. The unsymbolizable, Kristeva argues, vies in importance with the symbolizable. Derrida similarly suggests that every *sign* of difference is equivalent to its deferral.[64] Lacan's 'algebra', on the other hand, together with his mathematical images (the moebius strip, etc.), and his notion of 'mathemes', suggest very strongly that the unconscious – the discourse of the Other – might be another aspect of mathematical discourse. With Lacan, we may well be dealing only with the realm of pure abstraction, one evacuated of any content. The pertinence of the questions Kristeva poses when discussing the status of the Virgin in Freud's work stems, in part, from the insight that Lacan's approach tends to foreclose them:

> It is a question of the maternal role in the psychic economy, and more particularly, of the cleavage between the maternal

feminine, 'the black continent' resistant to representation on the one hand, and to the Symbolic paternal Law on the other. The question could be formulated differently. Is the archaic domain signifiable? In what way is the psychic representation of the archaic different from coded verbal expression? Or again: What is the exact status of unconscious representations in relation to verbal representations? Do different types of unconscious psychic representations exist?[65]

Such questions point to the direction Kristeva's enterprise has taken by comparison with Lacan's. In brief, while Lacan was concerned to trace the limits of the signifiable and bring it under the auspices of the symbolic order, Kristeva, by contrast, has been concerned to extend the limits of the signifiable, perhaps to the extent of relativizing the role of the symbolic order (see, for example, the notion of 'carnival', and *'chora'*, to which we shall return). While still respectful of Lacan's contribution to both psychoanalytic and literary theory – especially as concerns the Lacanian registers of the Real, the Imaginary, and the Symbolic – Kristeva has not given in to the tendency to privilege the *logic* of the signifier. Indeed, it is the realm of logic as such which does not escape Kristeva's analytic scrutiny. One or two points of importance for psychoanalytic theory seem, on the other hand, to have escaped Lacan's scrutiny leading to a certain blindness on a number of counts. Some of the factors which may have contributed to this blindness need to be examined. Elisabeth Roudinesco is a particularly rich source of insight here.

His Majesty's blindness

. . . neither the King nor the Police who replaced him in that position were able to read the letter because that *place entailed blindness*.

'Seminar on "The Purloined Letter"'

Les non-dupes errent.

Jacques Lacan

In illuminating aspects of the background to the 'master's' blindness, Roudinesco stresses that Lacan was not only an analyst, but also occupied the position of the King, a position highlighted by Roudinesco's description of him as an 'enlightened direct monarch'. 'His Majesty' is a designation for Lacan which Roudinesco's history of the psychoanalytic movement in France renders highly appropriate. What of the man, Lacan, however? In what sense do biography and history come together to help us understand the Lacanian 'return to Freud'?

Born of a bourgeois Catholic family, Lacan undertook a conventional medical degree in Paris, followed by training in neuropsychiatry between 1926 and 1930.[66] From the celebrated psychiatrist of the 1920s, Gaëtan de Clérambault, Lacan learned the art of observation, a training quite classical in its orientation. There was, as Roudinesco makes clear at various points, nothing of the marginal about him – rather, an impetus to make a mark in a traditional way. Hence, it is not such a surprise to find that Lacan urged prospective analysts to do a medical degree first, something not even Freud had insisted upon.[67]

While there seems to be little doubt that Lacan's work on paranoia in the 1930s, culminating in the publication of his thesis on Aimée,[68] was epoch-making and won the approval of the surrealists, the master's debt to the subject of his thesis, seemed to go unanalysed. That is, the degree to which Lacan himself experienced analytic effects, and consequently arrived at a new theoretical awareness through his study of Aimée's paranoia, seemed to go unanalysed. Roudinesco explains:

We can attempt a hypothesis: the analysis, which did not really take place on Loewenstein's couch [Rudolph Loewenstein, Lacan's analyst], took place for Lacan in another space. Close to a woman. Aimée, the criminal and paranoid, plays a fundamental role in Lacan's career. She offers him her speech, her life story, her writing, and her madness, allowing him to become the artisan of a new introduction of Freudianism in France. With Clérambault, Lacan learns to observe the insane. With Aimée, he gives up the idea of becoming Clérambault. At Saint-Anne, he begins to write, to transform himself and acquire the identity of a theoretician and psychoanalyst. If Clérambault is to Lacan what Charcot is to Freud, Aimée is to the same Lacan what Fliess is to Freud. She occupies the place of an analyst having the characteristic of resembling Schreber as much as Anna O. . . . There is always a woman behind every great man and, through this one, Lacan achieves a kind of spontaneous self-analysis which will perhaps prevent him from seriously returning to the couch of a male analyst.[69]

It is as though Aimée's case were the equivalent of the literary text – or work of art in general – which, at the same time as it is being produced, produces the subject. This is to say that perhaps Aimée holds the key to a conception of art Lacan did not see: art as formative and transformative, rather than as the unique illustration, representation, or imitation of truth. Lacan's writing of Aimée's case – where he proposes a *'writing'* (*'écriture'*) of madness,[70] and where he uses all the resources of fiction – this writing in its analytic effects, literally constitutes Lacan as subject/theorist/analyst. Lacan's writing of Aimée may then be counterposed to his reading of 'The Purloined Letter' and *Hamlet*: on the one hand, with Aimée's case, the writer-subject is put in question at the same time as he is in part constituted as a subject – there being no fixed subject prior to the literary-artistic moment; while on the other hand, with regard to Poe and Shakespeare, the analyst would appear to bring his psychoanalytic theory *to* the text. Quite simply, in the latter approach, Lacan the analyst rarely gives a hint of being put in question by the text.

Lacan's trajectory in the 1920s and 1930s, then, shows him ensconced in his milieu; he does not oppose its legitimacy, he rather wants to be its most successful son. The nature of this trajectory does not really change as we move into the 1930s. Rather than *create* the milieu around him, Lacan makes more of the opportunities it presents than anyone else. And so through Alexander Kojève's reading of Hegel in Paris in the 1930s, Lacan both acquires the Hegelian vocabulary so evident in his writings of the 1950s and early 1960s,[71] and at the same time learns how to give a new interpretation of a classic text, so that, through Hegel, Freud's concept of subjectivity will find its first major weapon in the battle to save it from the deformations of ego-psychology. Inspired at the same time by the work of Henri Wallon on the experience of the mirror in the maturation of the young of both humans and animals, Lacan develops his theory of the 'mirror stage' first presented at the International Congress of Psychoanalysis in 1936 at Marienbad.[72]

The mature Lacan of the 1960s, the guru of structuralism – the 'baroque' Lacan – is of course the avid reader of Lévi-Strauss on the idea of the universality of the interdiction against incest, and on the notion of the unconscious as the 'empty' set.[73] Saussure and Jakobson on the theory of the sign and figures of language, respectively, are subjected to a similarly avid reading. The former inspires Lacan's theory of the signified as being an effect of the signifier, while the latter provides Lacan with the figures of 'metaphor' and 'metonymy' to explain, in the first case, the working of the symptom as a substitution of one signifier for another, and in the second, the working of desire in the connection between signifier and signifier. Saussure's algorithm, $\frac{S}{s}$, even becomes the algorithm for the 'topography of the unconscious'.[74] Taking what he needs from diverse sources near at hand, not unlike Lévi-Strauss's *bricoleur*, Lacan brilliantly 'translates' Freud's text. He is searching for a way of presenting Freud's discovery of the unconscious as being radically different from anything that had gone before. What he often resorts to, however, are new formalizations. Formalization, after all, is in the milieu; to question the precise relationship between the unconscious and formalization would be to bring about an upheaval in the milieu – to such an extent, perhaps, that its very basis might be shaken.

And so, in the mid-1960s, Frege's concept of zero (the number not identical with itself, like the subject), brought to Lacan's attention by Jacques-Alain Miller, becomes the forerunner of the 'matheme'. The matheme, evocative of Lévi-Strauss's 'mytheme', is, as Roudinesco explains, 'the writing of the signifier, of one, of the trait, of the letter, that is to say, writing which cannot be said, but which can be transmitted'.[75] We note, then, that the matheme is above all tied to the goal of formalization. Without the latter, as Lacan saw it, the ineffable could not be presented in its integrity. Thus the mathematically inspired figure of the borromean knot – a figure without a localizable point (see Figure 1, p. 37) – emerges in the early 1970s as an additional means of presenting the 'form' of the unconscious. Indeed, not only does psychoanalytic discourse become more formalized, but also the very notion of the unconscious. To illustrate this, it is only necessary to note that mathematization alone touches the real for the Lacan of *Encore*, and that the real, as well as being the mystery of the body speaking, is also the mystery of the unconscious.[76] In short, the unconscious is fundamentally *formalizable*. In another place, Lacan says, quite unambiguously, that the formalizable subject of the signifier and the subject of the unconscious are one and the same.[77]

With the work of Frege, Cantor, Boole, Gödel, and Russell much debated in the late sixties, together with the problem of the ineffable raised in Wittgenstein's philosophy, Lacan was again ready to turn the milieu to his advantage, and produce mathematical figures to serve as the vehicle for transmitting psychoanalytic theory. By 1973, then, gone were the days when the baroque style of the seminar would introduce the audience to a pure experience of the word (and the unconscious?) quite separate from any formalization. The baroque Lacan was close – but without acknowledging it – to introducing his audience to the ineffable 'melody' of the word. Perhaps the 'music' of language remained unexplored, not only because Lacan, like Freud before him, did not like music, but also because the idea of 'music and letters' was not yet sufficiently *au courant*. For in 1973 Julia Kristeva was yet to publish *La Révolution du langage poétique*. Whatever the case, it is clear, as we shall see, that the issue of the relationship between logic, formalization, and the 'music' in language, constitutes the point of departure for the Kristevan *oeuvre*.

Notes

1 Reproduced as Jacques Lacan, 'The Freudian Thing, or the meaning of the return to Freud in psychoanalysis' in *Ecrits: A Selection*, trans. Alan Sheridan (London, Tavistock, 1977), pp. 114–45.

2 See Pierre Fidida, 'A propos du "retour à Freud"' in *Nouvelle Revue de Psychanalyse* ('Regards sur la psychanalyse en France'), no. 20 (Autumn, 1979), p. 112, note 2.

3 For a description and interpretation of the two psychoanalytic styles in question through the prism of different approaches to the notion of 'woman' and femininity, see Elisabeth Roudinesco, *La Bataille de cent ans: Histoire de la psychanalyse en France. 2. 1925–1985* (Paris, Seuil, 1986), pp. 511–30.

4 Some of the main recent texts in French on Lacan are: Catherine Clément, *Vie et légendes de Jacques Lacan* (Paris, Grasset, 1981) – in English as *Lives and Legends of Jacques Lacan*, trans. Arthur Goldhammer (New York, Columbia University Press, 1983); Joel Dor, *Introduction à la lecture de Lacan* (Paris, Denoel, 1985); Jeanne Granon-Lafont, *La Topologie ordinaire de Jacques Lacan* (Paris, Point Hors Lignes, 1985); Philippe Julien, *Le Retour à Freud de Jacques Lacan* (Paris, Erès, *c.* 1988); Bertrand Ogilvie, *Lacan, Le Sujet* (Paris, Presses Universitaires de France, 1987); François Roustang, *Lacan: de l'équivoque à l'impasse* (Paris, Minuit, 1986); Roudinesco, *La Bataille de cent ans*; Jacques Sédat, *Retour à Lacan?* (Paris, Fayard, 1981).

Some of the main recent texts in English on Lacan are: Bice

Benvenuto and Roger Kennedy, *The Works of Jacques Lacan: An Introduction* (London, Free Association Books, 1986); Shoshana Felman, *Jacques Lacan and the Adventure of Insight* (Cambridge, Mass., Harvard University Press, 1987); Juliet Flower MacCannell, *Figuring Lacan: Criticism and the Cultural Unconscious* (London and Sydney, Croom Helm, 1986); Jane Gallop, *Reading Lacan* (Ithaca, New York, Cornell University Press, 1985); John P. Muller and William J. Richardson, *Lacan: A Reader's Guide to 'Ecrits'* (New York, International Universities Press, 1982); Ellie Ragland-Sullivan, *Jacques Lacan and the Philosophy of Psychoanalysis* (Urbana and Chicago, University of Illinois Press, 1986); Stuart Schneiderman, *Jacques Lacan: the Death of an Intellectual Hero* (Cambridge, Mass., Harvard University Press, 1983); Joseph H. Smith and William Kerrigan (eds), *Interpreting Lacan* (New Haven and London, Yale University Press, 1983); Martin Stanton, *Outside the Dream: Lacan and French Styles of Psychoanalysis* (London and Boston, Routledge & Kegan Paul, 1983).

5 See below, Chapters 4, 5, and 6.

6 Jacques Lacan, *Encore*, p. 126. Literally translated *lalangue* means a particular national language such as English or French. Lacan uses *lalangue* to signal that his interest is not of a conventional linguistic nature, but rather that of the analyst concerned with the unconscious resources of language (*la langue*).

7 ibid.

8 'Man speaks, then, but it is because the symbol has made him man' in Jacques Lacan, *Ecrits: A Selection*, p. 65.

9 The study of paranoia being fundamental to Lacan's early career: see Jacques Lacan, *De la psychose paranoiaque dans ses rapports avec la personnalité suivi de Premiers écrits sur la paranoia* (Paris, Seuil, 1975).

10 See Jacques Lacan, *Le Séminaire, livre II: Le moi dans la théorie de Freud et dans la technique de la psychanalyse* (Paris, Seuil, 1978), p. 207. See also Roudinesco, *La Bataille de cent ans*, p. 312.

11 Roudinesco, *La Bataille de cent ans*, pp. 571–3.

12 ibid., p. 306.

13 See Jean Laplanche, 'Postscript' in *Yale French Studies* (French Freud), no. 72 (1972), pp. 176–8 – and particularly p. 178, where Laplanche states: '*The Unconscious*, we said, rather than a language, *is the very condition of language*' (Laplanche's emphasis).

14 See Jacques Lacan, *Ecrits* (Paris, Gallimard, 1966), pp. 11–61; in English, 'Seminar on "The Purloined Letter"', trans. Jeffrey Mehlman in *Yale French Studies* (French Freud), no. 48 (1972), pp. 38–72.

15 Edgar Allan Poe, 'The Purloined Letter' in *Selected Writings*, ed. David Galloway (Harmondsworth, Penguin, 1975), pp. 330–49.

16 ibid., p. 330.

17 ibid., p. 332.

18 See Jacques Lacan, 'The function and field of speech and language in psychoanalysis' in *Ecrits: A Selection*, pp. 106–7.

19 See T. S. Eliot, *Collected Poems, 1909–1962* (London, Faber & Faber, reprinted 1983), p. 85, note to line 401 of *The Waste Land*.
20 For a commentary on the 'letter' as virtual object, see Gilles Deleuze, *Différence et répétition* (Paris, Presses Universitaires de France, 3rd edn, 1976), pp. 134–6.
21 Poe, 'The Purloined Letter', p. 332. Emphasis added.
22 Lacan, *Le Séminaire, livre II*, p. 231.
23 Lacan, 'Seminar on the "Purloined Letter"', p. 66.
24 ibid.
25 See Jacques Derrida, 'Le Facteur de la Vérité', in *La Carte Postale: de Socrate à Freud et au-delà* (Paris, Aubier-Flammarion, 1980), pp. 453–4.
26 See Roudinesco, *La Bataille de cent ans*, p. 302, where it is noted that Lacan's text first appeared, significantly, under a clinical rubric in the journal, *La Psychanalyse* (*Mélanges cliniques*) no. 2 (1956).
   Also, Roudinesco points out on a number of occasions (see p. 532) that Lacan was not interested in literature as such, but rather used it to confirm his doctrinal position.
27 The basis of Derrida's position here is that writing *is* the unconscious. See Jacques Derrida, 'Freud and the scene of writing' in *Writing and Difference*, trans. Alan Bass (Chicago, University of Chicago Press, 1978), pp. 196–231, esp. p. 226 on the trace producing the space of its inscription.
28 See 'The ego (*moi*) is itself one of the significant elements of common discourse which is the discourse of the unconscious' (Lacan, *Séminaire, livre II*, p. 245).
29 Lacan, *Ecrits: A Selection*, p. 289.
30 Lacan, 'Seminar on "The Purloined Letter"', p. 66.
31 See Juliet Flower MacCannell, *Figuring Lacan*, pp. 156–7 and *passim*.
32 Lacan, 'Position de l'inconscient' in *Ecrits*, p. 848.
33 Derrida, 'Le Facteur de la Vérité', p. 455.
34 Lacan, 'Seminar on "The Purloined Letter"', p. 55.
35 See our Chapters 4 and 5.
36 Lacan, 'Seminar on "The Purloined Letter"', p. 72.
37 ibid., p. 71.
38 ibid.
39 Maurice Blanchot, *L'Espace littéraire* (Paris, Gallimard, 1955), pp. 111–12.
40 Lacan, 'Seminar on "The Purloined Letter"', p. 53.
41 Kristeva notes, in this regard, that neither Freud nor Lacan liked music. See Julia Kristeva, 'Il n'y a pas de maître à langage', *Nouvelle Revue de Psychanalyse* ('Regards sur la psychanalyse en France'), no. 20 (Autumn, 1979), p. 139.
42 Jacques Lacan, 'Desire and the interpretation of desire in *Hamlet*' in Shoshana Felman (ed.) *Literature and Psychoanalysis: The Question of Reading: Otherwise* (Baltimore and London, The Johns Hopkins University Press, 1982), pp. 11–52.

43 See, in particular, ibid., p. 28.

44 ibid., p. 11.

45 ibid., p. 12.

46 Lacan, *Ecrits: A Selection*, p. 288.

47 Lacan, 'Desire and the interpretation of desire in *Hamlet*', p. 12.

48 ibid., p. 21.

49 ibid., p. 22.

50 ibid., pp. 22–3.

51 See Ernst H. Kantorowicz, *The King's Two Bodies: A Study in Medieval Political Theology* (Princeton, Princeton University Press, 1957).

52 Lacan, 'Desire and the interpretation of desire in *Hamlet*', p. 50.

53 'Clinical' as well as 'pathological' are Lacan's terms. See pp. 21–2.

54 Shoshana Felman, 'To open the question', in Felman (ed.) *Literature and Psychoanalysis*, p. 6. It is interesting to note, however, that, with Lacan's reading of 'The Purloined Letter', Felman elsewhere remarks that the literary factor (*'la chose littéraire'*) is not lost in the interests of psychoanalysis. Rather, Lacan's reading would show that Poe throws a new light on Freud's 'Beyond the Pleasure Principle'; literature would thus also inform psychoanalysis. See Shoshana Felman, 'La chose littéraire, sa folie, son pouvoir' (interview with Philippe Sollers), *Tel Quel*, no. 81 (Autumn, 1979), p. 38. Be this as it may, a conception of literature as fundamentally 'poetic' would seem to preclude it being conceived as a mechanism of illumination. Opacity might well be the essence of the 'literary thing'.

55 Perry Meisel, 'Interview with Julia Kristeva', *Partisan Review*, vol. LI, no. 1 (1984), p. 131.

56 ibid., pp. 131–2.

57 See Felman, 'La Chose littéraire, sa folie, son pouvoir', p. 39.

58 Lacan, 'Seminar on "The Purloined Letter"', p. 65.

59 Lacan, *Encore*, p. 37.

60 ibid., p. 34.

61 ibid., p. 33.

62 ibid., p. 40.

63 ibid., p. 34. See also, ibid., p. 68.

64 At least this is so if the sign is conceived as a sensible plenitude. Difference would be the very precondition of the sign, and thus unsignifiable. See Jacques Derrida, *Of Grammatology*, trans. Gayatri C. Spivak (Baltimore and London, The Johns Hopkins University Press, 1976), pp. 62–3, and *passim*.

65 Julia Kristeva, 'La Vierge de Freud', *L'Infini*, no. 18 (Spring, 1987), p. 23.

66 Roudinesco, *La Bataille de cent ans*, p. 120.

67 ibid., p. 226. Jean Laplanche was one analyst Lacan encouraged to do medicine.

68 See note 9.

69 Roudinesco, *La Bataille de cent ans*, pp. 134–5.

70 ibid., p. 127.

71 See in particular, 'The subversion of the subject and the dialectic of desire in the Freudian unconscious', in *Ecrits: A Selection*, pp. 292–324.

72 A revised version was given at the sixteenth International Psycho-analytic Congress in Zurich in 1949. See *Ecrits: A Selection*, p. xxiii.

73 See Claude Lévi-Strauss, 'The effectiveness of symbols', in *Structural Anthropology*, trans. Claire Jacobson and Brooke Grundfest Schoepf (Harmondsworth, Penguin, 1972), pp. 186–205.

74 Lacan, *Ecrits: A Selection*, p. 163.

75 Roudinesco, *La Bataille de cent ans*, p. 567. See also Lacan, *Encore*, p. 108: 'Mathematical formalization is our goal, our ideal.'

76 Lacan, *Encore*, p. 118.

77 ibid., p. 129.

3

Towards the semiotic

> I would say that one will always be able to do good criticism in
> *C* major.
>
> Roland Barthes

Savour, subtlety, finesse – 'modesty' (to use Kristeva's term): these
words point (but inadequately!) to the writing of Roland Barthes.
'Modesty' is the term Kristeva applies to Barthes' analyses of the
'irruption within the neutral truth of science of a subject of
enunciation'.[1] This is an irruption calling attention to the
'objective genesis' of neutral scientific truth. Modesty emerges –
writing emerges – at the precise point where the very possibility of
speaking is under consideration. When the 'I' which speaks is
shown to be part of language ('I is another' – Rimbaud), there, in
that place – equivalent to the *topos* of the subject – writing appears.

Roland Barthes and his writing have a special place in
Kristeva's intellectual and personal trajectory. 'He is the precursor
and founder of modern literary studies', wrote Kristeva in 1971.[2]
Emile Benveniste, professor of General Linguistics at the Collège
de France for almost forty years from 1937, holds a similarly
special place. As Kristeva often remarks throughout her work, it
was Benveniste who confided to her that there were only two great
French linguists: Mallarmé and Artaud.[3] At an intellectual, if less
personal level, Georges Bataille is also a very important figure for
Kristeva.

The above remarks aim to introduce a reflection in this chapter
on some influences on Kristeva's work. Along with Barthes,
Benveniste, and Bataille, I shall also discuss the influence of

Saussure's anagrams, together with the fact of Kristeva's being, to some extent, an outsider in Paris, someone in exile, as she described it in 1977, a foreigner experiencing and inducing a '*dépaysement*' (bewilderment, disorientation, feeling of strangeness and unfamiliarity). 'Writing is impossible without some kind of exile', said Kristeva.[4] What these influences converge upon is the path towards the theory of the semiotic: the theory of the 'music' of language. Such influences would mark out the other pole of Kristeva's intellectual universe – the pole running parallel to psychoanalysis.

Of course, consideration of these influences could appear arbitrary without some explanation. Why leave out Roman Jakobson, Philippe Sollers, Claude Lévi-Strauss, Mikhail Bakhtin, or, for that matter, Hegel? The answer is that these last-mentioned figures are quite explicitly central to Kristeva's theorizing on language, art, and subjectivity, whereas this is not the case for each of the thinkers to be treated in this chapter, or for the topics of the anagrams, exile, or being a foreigner. With regard to Barthes, Benveniste, and Bataille, in particular, their influence is at the same time seminal and between the lines. It is most of all this aspect of being 'between the lines' that I would like to address in this chapter.

Roland Barthes

If Kristeva's first published work in France[5] is on Mikhail Bakhtin's literary writings, Roland Barthes' seminar is the place where this first substantial part of the Kristevan *oeuvre* would be presented. Roland Barthes is not there in the writing, but he is, in part, its precondition. Or perhaps it is more accurate to say that Barthes is there, but only in a displaced form.

Similarly, Kristeva will not take up Barthes' theories as such in her work, but it was Barthes' writings, from *Le Degré zéro de l'écriture*[6] (1953) onward, which opened up the whole terrain for studies in semiotics. Roland Barthes, then, is Kristeva's Parisian mother, as it were; there is nothing Oedipal here.

With all his genius as a stylist, Barthes' sentences work, in their classical limpidity, to provide the reader with a pleasure in reading. Barthes thus writes about the myth of writing as transparent,[7] but oh, so transparently! The author of *The Pleasure of the Text*[8] himself provides pleasure. An important difference here is that between *plaisir* (pleasure), and *jouissance* (enjoyment, bliss, loss of self as in orgasm). The pleasure of the text is, in the final analysis, the pleasure of understanding. 'It is bound up with the consistency of the self, of the subject which is confident in its values of comfort, of expansiveness, of satisfaction . . . .'[9] To be sure, it is certain that the pleasure derived from Barthes' writing cannot be contained – as he also recognized – within the confines of the self. In exceeding that self, in going 'beyond' consciousness, pleasure becomes an indescribable jouissance. Barthes' texts thereby very visibly become writing.

Nevertheless, at one extreme of the scale between 'pleasure' and 'jouissance', there are texts which, in their unreadability, are unreservedly texts of jouissance. And so if the text of a 'classical' reading is a text of pleasure, the avant-garde text would be one of jouissance. The text of jouissance (the text *as* jouissance) is the text of writing, the opaque text – referring us to the level of language as such. Kristeva will come to make the text of jouissance the focus of her theory of the operation and genesis of avant-garde writing in the nineteenth and twentieth centuries. Barthes' writing is the undeniable backdrop to this Kristevan project.

Bound by a mixture of delight and friendship to the classical realist texts of pleasure (cf. Balzac's *Sarrasine*), no one more than Roland Barthes unhinged realism from its referent, or 'reality'. Revealing the conventions of verisimilitude became fundamental to this 'unhinging'. For Barthes, bourgeois culture is constituted, in part, as a resistance to this unhinging.[10] When seen as the producer of the signified – whether or not this be the referent – language is revealed to be fictional in its essence. This is not to deny the pleasure of the seduction involved when verisimilitude leads us to suspend disbelief and the imagination becomes the scene of the drama itself. The ultimate verisimilitude, quite clearly, is the language of communication; for this is also language's ultimate transparency – the denial of its existence – just as the eye is non-existent in seeing, or the ear in hearing. Barthes, then, committed himself to the study of language as essentially fictional. As a set of masks providing the simulacrum of reality, language is inescapably an illusion because it is constitutive of our social being. How do individuals cope with this illusion of the mask? Barthes' response is that it all depends on the culture and the society concerned. In Japan, for example, the Bunraku dolls, where the manipulators remain visible throughout the performance, signal the other face of language, of writing. The manipulators, according to Barthes, are the code of the art made visible. In the western art of theatre, however,

> the actor simulates action, but his acts are never anything but gestures: on stage, nothing but theatre, yet a theatre ashamed of itself. Whereas *Bunraku* (this is its definition) separates action from gesture: it shows the gesture, lets action be seen, exhibits simultaneously the art and the labor, reserving for each its own writing.[11]

With the Bunraku dolls, Japanese culture shows itself to be willing to present the mask of language for what it is. Theatre is seen as theatre, rather than in terms of verisimilitude. Western art forms, however, especially those emerging since the eighteenth century, are locked into the conventions of verisimilitude; that is to say, the west prefers to treat the mask – to use my own terminology[12] – as a disguise. It is the disguise which, unlike the mask, does not give itself out for the illusion that it is. Consequently, there is something deceptive in a disguise; hence, Barthes' reference to 'shameful' theatre in the above quotation.

For Kristeva, Barthes' unveiling of the conventions of language is the indispensable bridge to an analysis of the very limits of language and the symbolic order. What precisely occurs on the edge of language as a code of the symbolic? This is one of Kristeva's most pressing questions. In effect, if Barthes' writing evokes a pleasure of the text, this pleasure opens the way for Kristeva's studies of the often disruptive jouissance of language's barely coded, and barely theorizable side.

Perhaps nothing gives more insight into Roland Barthes' place in Kristeva's work than his use of the term 'amateur'. The amateur is not simply someone who does something for its own sake, for enjoyment, and who, thereby, experiences a certain liberation – whether this be from the rat race of society, or, more profoundly, from one's own ego. Rather, there is an amateur disposition which reveals any activity as inseparable from the constitution of subjectivity. For the amateur, no part of the subject is outside the constitution and/or dissolution of the symbolic. The amateur, then, recognizes that, potentially, nothing is insignificant. For the writer/critic, this means that not only is the published text significant, but everything from the type of pen and paper used, to the desk, lighting, and space for writing, together with the timetable for writing (the organization of the day, or even the hour) also has its interest. In short, the amateur in writing is recognizably constituted by writing's materiality. 'Amateur' in Barthes' lexicon, thus also means 'materialist'. This is why Barthes analysed, in the last lectures he gave at the Collège de France, the writer's material accoutrements: what Flaubert and Proust ate; the writer's drugs and medicines (Proust drank seventeen cups of coffee a day); the clothing (Rousseau took to Armenian dress); the house, and space of work: Proust's room, Kafka's work-table, etc. The focus, in fact, is on everything that is 'insignificant' or 'minor', and supposedly *outside* the order of writing.

Similarly, in his 'chronicle' in *Le Nouvel Observateur*,[13] Barthes attempted to develop, and spoke about developing, a 'minor' style of writing, one that would be adequate to describing the so-called trivial facets of his existence, of his being. The amateur is, in a sense, the writer *par excellence* because, for this person, the difference between writing and being is minimal. For the one who only writes in order to be published – who tailors writing to publication – writing is only an object of exchange, an object which can at best be a mirror (representation) of the individual ego.

The amateur is a materialist only in the sense that what was deemed to be outside language and the symbolic is now revealed to be within writing. The amateur, therefore, is not simply interested in the insignificant – the supposedly banal preconditions of art for its own sake – but shows us that there is no material dimension that is not also a form of art, of writing. There is no writing separable from the subjectivity – from the person, if one likes – of the writer. This is not because an author is the origin of writing, but because without writing, as a fundamental experience within the symbolic, there would be no author. As a result, the amateur in Roland Barthes' work is the precursor to Julia Kristeva's view that art is constitutive of subjectivity, just as it points towards Kristeva's notion of the body in language in her theory of the 'semiotic'.

Emile Benveniste

Modesty as an effect of writing is also how Kristeva describes the work of the French linguist, Emile Benveniste. As with Roland Barthes, Kristeva has publicly declared the importance for her of Benveniste's friendship. Suffering the terrible affliction, for a specialist in language, of aphasia, it was Benveniste who wrote on a sheet of white paper with a trembling hand the enigmatic letters, 'THEO', when Kristeva visited him in hospital towards the end of his life.[14] Roland Barthes, too, felt this close bond of respect and friendship for Benveniste. Indeed Barthes' perception was that with Benveniste a specific relation between the body and writing became manifest in modesty and in a style both 'burning and discreet', with a 'total absence of intellectual vulgarity' and much 'tact'.[15] Thus, through modesty, and the presence of the body in his text – much as he worked to render it absent – Benveniste corresponds to Barthes' 'amateur'. This is, most assuredly, the quality Kristeva appreciated in Benveniste. There is, though, much more. For not only did Benveniste's discreet praise of Mallarmé and Artaud as linguists mean that a great linguist had acknowledged the well-founded nature of Kristeva's intellectual trajectory, but a particular aspect of Benveniste's writings in linguistics assumes a particular importance for Kristeva. This is the theory of subjectivity in language, studied from the perspective of the act of utterance, the enunciation (*énonciation*).

Analysed from the perspective of subjectivity, English (due to an empirical bias?) does not have a term equivalent to the French *énonciation* as it differs from the notion of an already completed utterance, statement, or proposition: the *énoncé*. In English, 'enunciation' can mean 'speech-act' or the act of utterance, as well as 'a distinct statement or declaration: the words in which a proposition is expressed' (*Chambers Twentieth Century Dictionary*). As has often been pointed out,[16] the distinction in French between the *sujet de l'énonciation* and the *sujet de l'énoncé* is one that is only rarely made in English. Rather, the subject of the completed statement has assumed a privileged place – even in linguistics. Because this distinction is fundamental for the work both of Benveniste and Kristeva after him, I intend to leave the terms *énonciation* and *énoncé* untranslated when the two forms of discourse are at issue.

In several essays dealing with subjectivity in language, Benveniste focuses on the status of pronouns, and in particular those of the first and second person: *I/you*.[17] These pronouns, Benveniste argues, are not only the means by which the human being is constituted as a subject, but also have a special role in marking an act of language. In short, the 'I/you' complementarity has no meaning at the level of the subject of the *énoncé*, but only at the level of the subject of the *énonciation*. Benveniste does not put it in precisely these terms; however, a little reflection soon shows that this is the underlying implication of his argument. For example, in defining the 'reality' to which 'I' or 'you' refers, Benveniste says that they refer 'uniquely' to a 'reality of discourse':

> *I* cannot be defined except in terms of a 'locution', not in terms of objects as a nominal sign is. *I* signifies 'the person who utters the present instance of discourse containing *I*'. This instance is unique by definition and has validity only in its uniqueness.[18]

Before commenting on this passage, we may recall that Benveniste defines 'discourse' as referring to the semantic level of language, while the 'semiotic' dimension refers to the significance of the sign. A sign exists when it is recognized by the linguistic community to have signifying power. Basically, the sign is the material base of discourse. A sign can have its existence registered in a dictionary – even though its meaning can only be fully established differentially in discourse.[19] This is to say, therefore, that a sign can be partially analysed at the level of the *énoncé*. Its meaning can be posited independently of any context. At least this is often the way linguistics proceeds today. It operates at the level of the sentence, and thereby at the level of the subject of the *énoncé*.

The meaning of pronouns, by contrast, cannot be grasped independently of the act of their being produced: the level of the *énonciation*. It is at this level that two things are accomplished: firstly, it constitutes the dimensions of time and place in discourse; and, secondly, it posits the speaking being in language: the subject of the *énonciation*. In other words, Benveniste's approach moves us towards the realization that the true subject does not precede language, thus reducing the latter to an apparatus of representation: rather, it is constituted by language. Such an approach also foreshadows Kristeva's concern to move away from a conception of the subject in language which simply reduces subjectivity to the self-conscious ego: 'We know that the concept of "language" (*langue*) had to yield before that of "discourse" in order to permit the introduction, on the one hand, of modal relations, and on the other, the subject of the *énonciation* and the antinomy, language (*langue*) – discourse', wrote Kristeva in 1971.[20] By 1977, Kristeva clearly states that Benveniste is the first – with the possible exception of Charles Morris and his concept of 'pragmatic' – to show rigorously an act of discourse taking place at a specific instance.

This has the following implications: that the subject of the *énonciation* is more fundamental for the constitution of subjectivity as such than the concept of the subject of the *énoncé*, but that, nevertheless, the former level does not refer to a 'concrete', 'singular' reality outside language. Furthermore, the subject of the *énonciation* does not have a name because the discursive instance is a 'pronominal instance', that is, a place in the discursive chain occupied by the locution. Finally, the inseparability of 'I' and 'you' ('I' presupposes, and cannot exist without 'you') means that the subject of the *énonciation* is 'dialogical' in its essence, and is to this extent produced by a 'fundamental scission in the linguistic function'.[21] As divided, the subject of the *énonciation* evokes the psychoanalytic subject, although Kristeva is also quite right to say that for psychoanalysis, there is a basic discrepancy between the subject of the linguistic message (whether of the *énoncé* or the *énonciation*) and the psychoanalytic subject, the subject of the '"accidents of discourse" (lapses, metaphors, metonymies, etc.)'.[22]

Benveniste's work would thus offer a way in which linguistics might remain close to Lacan's psychoanalytic theory of the subject. For Kristeva, the notion of 'discursive instance' becomes particularly fruitful in analyses of texts like Diderot's *Le Neveu de Rameau* – 'where the hero mimes 36 roles all at once, without any fixed identity'[23] – and, as we shall see later,[24] Lautréamont's *Les Chants de Maldoror*. In these analyses, Kristeva seeks to show that a poetic effect is achieved through a pluralization of the place assumed by the subject of the *énonciation*. This 'pluralization' will come to play an important part in Kristeva's theory of the subject in process.

As a final point illustrating the importance of Benveniste's writing, we may recall a passage from the eminent linguist's essay on Freud and the function of language in psychoanalysis.[25] There, Benveniste's insight is that negation in language is always a negation of something that has already been said, in one form or another. In effect, both affirmation *and* negation are part of the linguistic universe. The negative in language is no less language for all that. At the level of the self-conscious ego, on the other hand, negation is often taken to be equivalent to absolute otherness, a reality in some way outside language. Negation in language, therefore, is a kind of affirmation, where we are still dealing with what Kristeva will define as the sphere of an already-constituted 'judging subject'.[26] Kristeva's work examines the basis of the formation/production of the judging subject in the 'signifying process', and in so doing, moves beyond the affirmation–negation opposition to the process of negativity. Although differing from Benveniste's precise interpretation of Freud on this point, the problematic opened up by Benveniste's researches becomes a crucial point of departure for the development of Kristeva's theory of the semiotic both as negativity and as the indispensable precondition of the symbolic realm – the realm of meaning, judgement, and representation.

Georges Bataille

The field that Georges Bataille's work opens up had perhaps been hinted at by Pascal: Man prefers the hunt to the capture. Put another way: the means become an end in themselves. In Bataille's philosophical universe, the notion of 'means' as an end in itself becomes 'nonproductive expenditure'.[27] But we are jumping ahead of ourselves. We first need to consider the notion of productive expenditure.

According to Bataille, humanity seeks to conserve itself through utilitarian activities of all kinds. It has, in fact – particularly in the west – devised a prudent economy of expenditure which would ensure the reproduction of the species in all its facets: individual, social, cultural, political, etc. Actions done within this economy must be justified in terms of the end in question. Here, expressing the Father's interests – equivalent to social responsibility – is the only pleasure allowed. This, then, is Bataille's economy of 'productive expenditure'. It corresponds, to a large extent, to the economy of the modern-day western economist. It assumes that the sole aim of the species is to find the optimal means of survival and reproduction.

Opposed, in a certain sense, to the economy of productive expenditure is the economy of unproductive expenditure with an emphasis on 'loss'. Here, neither the danger of death, nor the horror often arising from such expenditure, is avoided. Within western bourgeois society, the full realization of nonproductive expenditure is often veiled behind other kinds of activities – those, for instance, of living in luxury, mourning, war, sport, arts, perverse sexual activity, etc.[28] Unproductive expenditure gives full reign to the pleasure principle, is governed by a logic of destruction and is, according to Bataille, the basis of true poetry:

The term poetry, applied to the least degraded and least

intellectualised forms of the state of loss, can be considered synonymous with expenditure; it in fact signifies, in the most precise way, creation by means of loss. Its meaning is therefore close to that of *sacrifice*.[29]

'Sacrifice' is a crucial term in Bataille's theory of social life,[30] and serves to introduce an important dimension of Kristeva's writings. Before elaborating here, however, we note that with the production of poetry that is, for Bataille, worthy of the name, the whole life of the poet is 'engaged'. 'The poet frequently can use words only for his own loss. . . .'[31] Implied in such a conception is the notion that poetry, at least in part, escapes the strictures of the symbolic order, and may in fact disrupt it. This same notion opens up the terrain of Kristeva's reflection on the *semiotic* (to which we shall return).

The concept of sacrifice mentioned above is, for Bataille, intimately bound up with the *sacred*. Sacrifice, in effect, is the sacred transgression of the Law. Consequently, if the profane world is a world of interdictions, the sacred world is that of the festival, intoxicating religious ritual, and dance.[32] The sacred world, indeed, is the world of unproductive expenditure. Of equal importance here is the insight that with sacrifice, the sacred and the profane coincide: the sacrifice is both murder, and the sign of the interdiction against murder.

For Kristeva, the general trajectory of Bataille's analysis of expenditure and sacrifice opens the way – along with the work of Lévi-Strauss – to a reconsideration of Freud's discussion of the constitution of society in works such as *Totem and Taboo*. Kristeva will find, in fact, that the constitution of society can only be grasped in all its profundity with reference to the act of murder at the basis of the law. To be sure, it is precisely this violent dimension which the symbolic order (Bataille's 'profane' world) recognizes only grudgingly – in the rhythm and intonation of language, for example.

Generally speaking, Bataille's work constitutes a refusal to be silent about the profoundly ambivalent nature of all social life. For the principles of productive and nonproductive expenditure imply that with the greatest restraint comes the possibility of an excess without limits; that the interdiction is bound up with violence; that purity is tied to horror; that good is bound to evil, life bound to death: the pleasure of expenditure leads to death. This expenditure is what will constitute jouissance in Kristeva's theoretical universe.

The terms just specified, however, should not be understood simply as binary oppositions; it is not necessarily the case that for every affirmation, there is a corresponding negation. On the contrary, what is at stake are domains which are heterogeneous, and therefore disruptive of each other because there is no communicative link between them. It thus makes no sense to ask why the gambler, religious fanatic, or poet (that is, anyone bent on some form of dangerous excess) does not think of the consequences – why they do not, in short, stop themselves in light of the prospect of death. For the logic of excess (if it has a logic) has no connection with the kind of rationality implied in this question: it is precisely what is beyond the logic of means–end rationality. To think otherwise is to miss the full import of the heterogeneity that is here in play. It is just such a conception that Kristeva seems to be looking for in her effort to theorize Freud's death-drive in terms of Hegel's concept of negativity. Negativity, indeed, comes to be the pivotal concept in Kristeva's discussion of the relationship between the semiotic as embodied in poetic language, and the symbolic as embodied in the Law of the Father. Negativity, then, and not negation, would also open the way to an understanding of the nature of the repression as both constitutive and disruptive of the social order.

The domain Bataille opens up points, as we have seen, to a profound link between individual excess and the social order. For Bataille, it is never the case that such excess can be separated from the very nature of society. Artistic endeavour, therefore, although in important respects heterogeneous to the social order, does not leave this order unaffected by its presence. Perhaps in contrast to Bataille's move to separate the principle of productive from nonproductive expenditure, Kristeva attempts to show that while it is important to see that the two principles of economy are conceptually quite distinct, neither exists independently of the other, each is imbricated in the other, so that there is no artistic practice outside a productive economy, any more than the productive economy is free from a nonproductive dimension. A full elaboration of just such a problematic is to be found in the second half of Kristeva's *Revolution in Poetic Language*, where the avant-garde text is theorized within the context of a social and economic formation.

Like Barthes and Benveniste, then, Bataille too contributes to delineating the broad theoretical and practical landscape within which Julia Kristeva will work.

Anagrams

Ferdinand de Saussure's theory of anagrams in poetic language is often cited throughout Kristeva's *œuvre*, but only rarely commented upon at any length. It is, however, this aspect of poetry – and language at large – that signals an insight equal in importance for Kristeva to that of Saussure's theory of the sign as composed of both signifier and signified. How is it that the concept of the anagram becomes so important to Kristeva? We begin our answer to this question by referring to James Joyce's great work, *Finnegans Wake*.[33]

Even if a reader finds the story of *Finnegans Wake* obscure, it is hard to imagine that a little attention to the text (the words and letters on the page) would not result in the recognition of the repetition of certain letters in more or less anagrammatic form, that is, in a marked form. Consider, for example, the letters 'H', 'C' and 'E', the famous sigla for . . . well, nearly everything. Thus, a short way into the novel, we find: 'the sigla H.C.E.' 'which gave him those normative letters the nickname Here Comes Everybody'.[34] Before this reference, the letters in question had appeared in the following form: 'Howth Castle and Environs' (p. 3). The letters are clearly visible in their upper-case form – a form appearing throughout the novel on too many occasions to enumerate fully. Very briefly, here are some other forms: '*H*ic *c*ubat *e*dilis' (p. 7). '*H*oo *c*avedin *e*arthwight' (p. 262); 'the *H*arbourer-*c*um-*E*nheritance' (p. 264), and so on. This is only a fraction of the permutations which become visible once a determined effort is made to follow the trails set.[35] *Finnegans Wake* thus alerts us to the possibility that every text is constructed along similar anagrammatic lines, but often less visibly because the message tends to blot out the materiality (the letter) of the text. Indeed, every text is at least double. And in this regard an interesting sequence of appearances of HCE in Joyce's text illuminates precisely what is at issue. The sequence begins with the evocation of the word 'hesitancy', misspelled by the betrayer of the Irish political leader, Parnell, as 'hesitency' 'his hes hecitency Hec' (p. 119); 'His hume. Hencetaking tides (p. 261); 'hectoendecate' (p. 273); 'hiscitendency' (p. 305); 'Hek' (p. 411); 'HeCitEncy' (p. 421); 'heckhisway' (p. 577). Crucial to this sequence is the term from the philosophy of Duns Scotus, 'haecceity' (*hek-sé 'i-ti*). 'Haecceity' evokes an infinitely disseminated singularity. In other words, haecceity would be HCE not simply repeated, but disseminated throughout *Finnegans Wake*: a dissemination (Here Comes Everybody) which is also a here (*'Hic'*), a place, a *'Bibelous hicstory'* (p. 280): 'Hear! Calls! Everywhair!' (p. 108).

In those parts of his notebooks dealing with researches into the underlying rules governing poetic composition,[36] Saussure tries to make explicit the way that the poetic text comes into being. The rules of poetic production, according to Saussure, will be those of the anagram, 'the words under words', or 'the text in the text', to use Starobinski's phrases. Saussure imagines that he is on the way to discovering how the individual poet *used* language in the past in order to produce poetic effects. Thus, if the text were doubly articulated, suggests Saussure, it would be because the conscious creative talents of the poet made it so – albeit in accordance with certain formal principles which Saussure initially attempted to discover in ancient Latin poetry. Saussure's project was to elaborate, inductively, a theory explaining the structure and operation of a whole range of progressively more complex anagrammatic forms. A cursory recognition of letters and phonic patterns revealing another word, or words, in addition to the manifest text, would thus only be a starting point. Thus, the *'locus princeps'*,[37] or initial set of tightly organized and demarcated words would have the general form of a *'mannequin'* (sometimes a line of poetry) within which a *'syllabogramme'* would be concentrated. Saussure calls the combination of 'syllabogramme' and 'mannequin', a *'paramorphe'*[38] – or roughly a different composition from the same letters. The 'words under the words', or what Saussure calls a 'hypogram', could then be formalized if Saussure had been right in his speculations.

While this increasingly complex collection of rules and linguistic figures perhaps only serves to highlight the unlikelihood of these ever being at the conscious disposition of the poet,[39] Saussure's research on anagrams, moves firmly in the direction of the pluralization of language so visible in Joyce. As Kristeva says:

> Saussure's *Anagrams* are to be situated amongst those theories which look for signification through a signifier dismantled by action as an insistent meaning in action. As if denying his own theory of the sign, Saussure discovers the *dissemination* throughout the text of what he believes to be the name of a leader or a god. This action of the signifier that we have called 'paragrammatic',

breaks up definitively language as an opaque object, opening it up to this double foundation that we mentioned at the beginning: the engendering of the geno-text.[40]

In her work of the late 1960s, therefore, Kristeva uses the term 'paragram' (also used by Saussure) rather than 'anagram' because she is intent on emphasizing the idea that language is, in its essence, doubly constituted: it has a material base which insists poetically (that is, materially, as the geno-text, or as 'music') in the textual message or in the text as a vehicle of communication. 'Paragram' rather than 'anagram', then, because the poet is not only creating poetic language, but is equally created by this language. This is to say that Kristeva takes Saussure's *Anagrams* as an important point of departure in order to go beyond the psychologism (and the notion of poems as denotative) Saussure himself was not able to avoid at the level of his explicit theoretical formulations. For Saussure, the anagram/hypogram in the hands of the poet–writer *gave* language a double dimension; for Kristeva, the paragram serves to show that language *qua* language is always already essentially double.

'Paragram' thus points beyond the letter as such to the phonic pattern of language, that is, towards its 'volume' which 'breaks up the linearity of the signifying chain'.[41] In part, the paragram is the 'Echoland' (see 'Hush! Caution! Echoland!' (p. 13) of *Finnegans Wake*). Thus: 'whispering his ho (*he*re *k*een [hek] again and begin again to make soundsense and sensesound kin again). . .' (p. 121) Here is seen the 'soundsense and sensesound' that the Kristeva paragram would highlight. Consequently, in reading Philippe Sollers' novel, *Nombres*, Kristeva highlights the often doubly suppressed 'sensesound' of the letter. In focusing on the term (*vocable*) '*voix*' (voice), for example, Kristeva shows that it 'insists' in: '"*fluide*" (fluid), "*voyelle*" (vowel), "*vol*" (theft), "*ondulation*" (undulation), "*note*" (note)'.[42] The 'v's and 'f's repeated in other words continue to evoke *voix*, just as *voix* is dissolved into other 'signifying differentials' such as '*vois*' ('*je vois*', I see), '*pouVOIR*' (to be able to), and '*violet*' (violet). The latter word begins another series: '*violé*' (violated, raped), and '*viol*' (rape), etc. In this way the 'engendering' of the text is rendered visible – an engendering which takes place not simply at the level of a communication, but at the level of the sounds and graphic marks of signifiers functioning differentially.

Saussure's researches constitute only a preliminary step for Kristeva's work on the materiality of signification. Nevertheless, the *Anagrams* are important in the task of unlimiting literary studies from the narrow and one-dimensional view of the text as transparent: as the vehicle of a communication necessarily based on stereotypes, and thus comfortably familiar.

Exile, foreigner, and cosmopolitan

Exile, as a reality and a practice, has provided a fertile, if often invisible aspect of Kristeva's theoretical writing. Indeed, in an interview in 1986, Kristeva indicated that her interest in psychoanalysis resulted, in part, from being in exile from her native Bulgaria.[43] This, however, is only one form of exile. At least two other forms are important: being an exile as a woman, and living in exile as a way to intellectual vitality and imaginativeness. At a more visible political level, the exile is often a foreigner in a new land, and Kristeva has also written about this in advocating an ethic of cosmopolitanism. Let us now examine each of these aspects in more detail.

Although a Bulgarian living in Paris, the pain of separation from her country of birth has, for Kristeva, also had an extremely positive side to it. To begin with, it prompted a reflection about the link between this situation and the constitution of an individual psychic structure. It raised the possibility that, apart from political or social reasons, some people choose to be exiles 'because they have never felt at home anywhere'.[44] In fact, a whole problematic exists in Kristeva's writing which indirectly addresses the issue of separation (from the mother). More succinctly: exile is not simply political or social, but can also occur *in situ* as the result of a particular psychic structure.

In 1977 Kristeva referred to another form of exile:

A woman is trapped within the frontiers of her body and even of her species, and consequently always feels *exiled* both by the general clichés that make up a common consensus and by the very powers of generalisation intrinsic to language.[45]

A woman, as excluded from the hegemonic rationalism of modern society may, nevertheless, come to provide a unique insight into that rationalism. In other words, with alienation also comes an insight unavailable to men. Indeed, a woman is always 'singular', condemned to be so, in effect; she is never present in the social stereotypes which reduce 'difference' to another version of the same. Kristeva herself feels this exile as a woman; but she also calls upon it in her reflections on the nature of poetic language and the avant-garde text. Perhaps from the (non) place of a woman's exile, Kristeva can 'see' the way this exile impinges precisely upon the language that every human being speaks. For its effects are to be felt in the very materiality of this language.

As to the notion of the link between exile and intellectual work, Kristeva asks, 'How can one avoid sinking into the mire of common sense, if not by becoming a stranger to one's own country, language, sex and identity?' And she adds: 'Writing is impossible without some kind of exile.'[46] In this sense, exile constitutes a necessary *dépaysement* which would enable a 'ruthless and irreverent dismantling of the workings of discourse, thought, and existence . . .'.[47] Here, it is clear that intellectual vitality is seen by Kristeva to depend on not falling into a dogmatic slumber where what is familiar forms the basis of what is deemed to be interesting and important. On the contrary, her writing calls on us to experience familiarity as extraordinary and disturbing. Like Paolo Freire, Kristeva is not interested in singing 'lullabies' to her audience;[48] rather, she seeks to challenge people as she herself has been challenged by the experience of exile.

Exile thus means: to open up new possibilities, to be able to confront new challenges; but most of all, it means coming to terms with 'difference' and the 'other' – not destroying them, either by violence, or indifference. Kristeva's writing, therefore, is neither difficult nor inaccessible, but the product of an exile without which thinking is no longer possible.

In her most recent book,[49] exile assumes even larger proportions as the theorist of poetic language reflects on her own status as a foreigner in France, and on the status and images of the cosmopolitan in European cultural history. Exile produces the foreigner who must make a new beginning in a decidedly non-maternal environment. Being an outsider and suffering the psychological and social trauma that this often entails, leads to the call for a cosmopolitanism that would recognize everyone as having universal rights *qua* human being – a cosmopolitanism founded on the insight that, in the last analysis, foreign-ness is in us: we are strangers to ourselves – *étrangers à nous-mêmes*. Foreign-ness is our unconscious other caused by a failure of repression (we shall return to this).

Such is the crux of Kristeva's thesis in *Etrangers à nous-mêmes*. Although, as in an earlier reflection on the same theme,[50] the psychoanalytic explanation ultimately assumes decisive importance with an analysis of Freud's notion of the *unheimlich* (uncanny),[51] the text in question proceeds almost for its entirety without the fully elaborated psychoanalytic exploration to which Kristeva's other books have accustomed us. It is almost as though the approach here were governed by a personal motive, a feeling generated by being a foreigner oneself. Although foreign-ness and its synonyms – otherness, unconscious, difference, feminine – constitute the dynamic of all innovative intellectual work, *Etrangers à nous-mêmes* makes this factor unusually explicit. Or, as Kristeva puts it, being a foreigner involves a separation from one's origins – from the mother(land) – and the assumption of an orphan status. The foreigner becomes rootless, a wanderer in exile, living different guises, taking on different personas in a life of the mask. Identity has become tenuous, and although this has its potentially creative side, it is also the source of anxiety. Socially speaking, the foreigner as an outsider must face up to the reality of submitting to conditions (for example, as 'guest' worker) that he or she may find undignified. In addition, of course, language has often ceased to be the easy instrument of communication it was felt to be in the maternal setting, and functions instead as a mark of foreign-ness – even (at least in France) when used with great virtuosity.

On the other hand, despite the anxiety provoked by a potential loss of identity, despite not being listened to and having to accept the worst jobs – especially to begin with – the foreigner experiences everyday life with an intensity evocative of the events of a true biography. Foreign-ness effectively becomes an escape from the boredom and banality of the 'everyday'. The familiar becomes unfamiliar – other, foreign – even superreal. Doubtless this is why Kristeva – like Joyce, Beckett, and so many others – has written so well about the 'mother' tongue from her position as exile and foreigner. She is hypersensitive to the maternal, the familiar, and the same. Such may well be the source of her legendary 'difficulty': what she is talking about is so close to us that it becomes difficult to grasp intellectually.

Kristeva is writing within a society (or is it a nation? or are these the same thing?) where the foreigner has long been discussed, debated, and analysed. At various times, thinkers such as Montaigne (1533–92), Montesquieu (1689–1755), and Diderot (1713–84) defended rights of the foreigner by way of a conciliatory cosmopolitanism.[52] It was, after all, Montesquieu who said in the famous lines quoted by Kristeva that, 'the citizen's duty is a crime when it makes one forget one's duty as a man'.[53] But has not the recent history of the nation-state, the prejudice against foreigners, and the valorization without precedent of *particular* values made cosmopolitanism into little more than an anachronism? Maybe this is what a particularistic perspective would lead one to believe, but it does not conform to the reality – signalled by Marshall McLuhan and before him, Kant – of the world as a 'global village'. Indeed, even at the end of the eighteenth century – let alone at the end of the twentieth – Kant could write that:

> Since the earth is a globe, [men] cannot disperse over an infinite area, but must necessarily tolerate one another's company. And no-one originally has any greater right than anyone else to occupy any particular portion of the earth. The community of man is divided by uninhabitable parts of the earth's surface such as oceans and deserts, but even then, the *ship* or the *camel* (the ship of the desert) make it possible for them to approach their fellows over these ownerless tracts, and to utilise as a means of social intercourse that *right to the earth's surface* which the human race shares in common.[54]

Given the reality of contact between human beings all over the globe, the Kantian view is that every person has a duty to give, and every stranger has a right to receive, hospitality as a *human* right. Cosmopolitanism thus becomes the only truly viable ethic when human dispersal over the globe is finite.

 - Kristeva's analysis in *Etrangers à nous-mêmes* proceeds in the knowledge that what Kant first explicitly recognized, is even more obvious at the end of the twentieth century. Tourism, migrant labour, and modern mass communications alone ensure that it is no longer possible, even if it might once have been desirable, for human beings to remain entirely isolated – whether as individuals, groups or nations – from each other, and locked into a cocoon of particularity. To be a foreigner has become the normal state of affairs for a citizen at the end of the twentieth century.[55] Given such a situation, cosmopolitanism once again becomes the necessary universal principle for regulating human relations.

Glimpses of cosmopolitanism can, Kristeva suggests, also be seen early in European history with the Stoic's concept of *oikeosis*, or universal conciliation. With the Paulian *Ecclesia*, a community of foreigners emerges, while St Augustine's notion of *caritas* emphasizes the union of man with man – i.e., stranger with stranger. *Caritas* is infinite: a treasure which does not reduce in the spending of it; it is also the principle which most clearly conflicts with the political exigencies that form the basis of the civil and juridical code, the rules which determine who is a foreigner and thus who will be excluded from the rights of citizenship. In sum, politics today defines who is to be classified as a foreigner, while in the past a religious approach often transcended the political definition of human beings.[56]

At the beginning of the modern era, in the Renaissance, Dante the exile begins a tradition of exploring difference and otherness in imagination. For the reality of his native Florence of which he has been forcibly deprived, Dante, in the *Divine Comedy*, substitutes an entirely imaginary universe peopled by the widest range of characters possible. This cosmopolitanism of the imagination finds its echo, first of all in Rabelais, and then later in Swift, Poe, Joyce, and Henry James.

With the Enlightenment, the cosmopolitanism of the imagination gives way to a cosmopolitanism as a real mode of interacting with others: a universal respect for diversity is put before every particular interest. Diderot's *Le Neveu de Rameau (The Nephew of Rameau)* offers a model of cosmopolitanism captured in an *alter ego* where modern man would become a foreigner to himself. Diderot, influenced by dialogical, menippean discourse,[57] presents foreign-ness in a polyphony of voices and positions. The polyphony of *Le Neveu de Rameau* thus places the notion that one is always the same under threat. Here, says Kristeva, is the disarticulation of identity which each of us is: foreign-ness is thus in us – this is the ultimate insight of Diderot's writing, and Kristeva clearly acknowledges her debt to his genius on this point.

If Diderot shows that foreign-ness is in us, that it is the unrecognized component of identity, it will be Freud who ultimately draws many of the fundamental implications for human subjectivity. With him, we are able to ask the question: how can we tolerate foreigners if we cannot see that we are foreigners to ourselves? In this regard, Freud was able to show how the other (foreigner) is my own unconscious, that what is strange was formerly familiar – in particular, my attachment as an infant (without speech) to my mother. What is now strange and foreign has been repressed, but maybe only partially so that the return of the repressed (the basis of drive activity[58]), re-emerges as something unfamiliar, 'unhomely', 'uncanny' – *unheimlich*. Death, the feminine, the drive – pretexts for the uncanny – at the same time constitute the basis of the repressed, the basis of the both fascinating and repellent otherness constitutive of every subjectivity. This dimension of the repressed must be confronted if a viable cosmopolitan ethic is to come to govern our lives in the global village in this *fin de siècle* twentieth century.

Such is the way that Kristeva finds that the politically sensitive issue of the status of the foreigner in France eventually ties in with her more explicitly psychoanalytic concerns. In this sense, foreignness is another term leading into the nature of the unconscious and the drive activity forming the basis of the Kristevan elaboration of the semiotic. *Etrangers à nous-mêmes* thus has the hallmark of being the partial culmination of a personal odyssey which began in political exile from Bulgaria, and continued as foreign student and theorist of the semiotic. The latter, as *chora*, is an extremely provisional articulation, having in fact no particular place of its own, being rather *foreign* to all forms of positing and representation. It is, however, not so much that Kristeva is an exile and herself a foreigner, and that *therefore* she comes to develop a theoretical perspective beyond the familiar and the same, but that in the act of theorizing foreign-ness in its various forms, she at the same time constitutes herself as a subject formed (like all of us) through foreignness. Kristeva's writing and theorizing are thus geared to taking in charge the strangeness formative of our identities as subjects of life – and of death.

Notes

1 Julia Kristeva, 'How does one speak to literature?' in *Desire in Language*, p. 116. Here, in fact, we are dealing with the *sujet de l'énonciation* to which we shall refer a little later. See also Julia Kristeva, 'Comment parler à littérature', in *Polylogue*, p. 49.
2 Kristeva, 'How does one speak to literature?', p. 93.
3 See, among other places, Kristeva, 'Mémoire', p. 45.
4 Julia Kristeva, 'A new kind of intellectual dissident', trans. Seán Hand

in Toril Moi (ed.), *The Kristeva Reader*, p. 298.

5 See Julia Kristeva, 'Le Mot, le dialogue et le roman', *Critique*, no. 239 (1967), pp. 438–65, reprinted as 'Word, dialogue, and novel', in Kristeva, *Desire in Language*, pp. 64–91, and Moi (ed.), *The Kristeva Reader*, pp. 34–61.

6 In English as *Writing Degree Zero*, trans. Annette Lavers and Colin Smith (New York, Hill & Wang, second printing, 1977).

7 See *S/Z*, trans. Richard Miller (New York, Hill & Wang, 1974).

8 Trans. Richard Miller (New York, Hill & Wang, 1974).

9 Roland Barthes, *Grain of the Voice: Interviews 1962–1980*, trans. Linda Coverdale (New York, Hill & Wang, second printing, 1986), p. 206. Translation modified.

10 See 'The reluctance to declare its codes characterizes bourgeois society and the mass culture issuing from it: both demand signs which do not look like signs.' Roland Barthes, 'Introduction to the structural analysis of narratives', in *Image–Music–Text*, trans. Stephen Heath, Fontana Communications Series (Glasgow, Fontana/Collins, 1977), p. 116.

11 Roland Barthes, *Empire of Signs*, trans. Richard Howard (New York, Hill & Wang, fourth printing, 1986), p. 54. Translation modified.

12 See John Lechte, 'Woman and the veil – Or Rousseau's fictive body', *French Studies*, vol. XXXIX, no. 4 (1985), pp. 423–4 and *passim*.

13 See Roland Barthes, 'Pause', *Le Nouvel Observateur*, no. 750 (1979), p. 78. In English as 'Last chronicle: Pause', trans. John Lechte in *Meanjin*, no. 3, Melbourne (1982), pp. 369–70.

14 Kristeva, 'Mémoire', p. 45.

15 Barthes, *Grain of the Voice*, p. 214.

16 See, for example, Stephen Heath, 'Translator's Note' in Barthes, *Image–Music–Text*, pp. 8–9.

17 Emile Benveniste, *Problems in General Linguistics*, trans. Mary E. Meek, Miami Linguistics Series, no. 8 (Coral Gables, Florida, University of Miami Press, 1971), p. 217.

18 ibid., p. 218.

19 Emile Benveniste, *Problèmes de linguistique générale, II* (Paris, Gallimard, 'TEL', 1973), p. 64.

20 Julia Kristeva, 'Du sujet en linguistique', *Languages*, no. 24 (1971), reprinted in *Polylogue*, pp. 287–322; the passage is on p. 321. Also see Benveniste, *Problems in General Linguistics*, p. 67.

21 Julia Kristeva, 'La Musique parlée ou remarques sur la subjectivité dans la fiction à propos du "Neveu de Rameau"', in Michèle Duchet and Michèle Jalley (eds), *Langue et langages de Leibniz à l'Encyclopédie* (Paris, UGE, 1977), p. 160.

22 ibid., p. 162.

23 ibid., p. 163.

24 See below, Chapter 5.

25 See Benveniste, 'Remarks on the function of language in Freudian

Context and influences

theory', in *Problems in General Linguistics*, pp. 65–75, and in particular, pp. 72–3 on negation.

26 Kristeva, *Revolution in Poetic Language*, p. 28. See also Kristeva's discussion of negation in terms of Frege's philosophy in ibid., pp. 119–24.

27 Georges Bataille, 'The notion of expenditure', in *Visions of Excess: Selected Writings, 1927–1939*, trans. Allan Stoekl, with Carl R. Lovitt and Donald M. Leslie, Jr (Minneapolis, University of Minnesota, second printing, 1986), pp. 116–29.

28 ibid., p. 118.

29 ibid., p. 120.

30 See, for example, Georges Bataille, *L'Erotisme* (Paris, Minuit, 1957), p. 29 and *passim*.

31 Bataille, 'The notion of expenditure', p. 120.

32 Bataille, *L'Erotisme*, pp. 76–7.

33 London, Faber & Faber, 1939.

34 ibid., p. 32.

35 A point demonstrated with regard to religious themes by Philippe Sollers and Jean-Louis Houdebine, 'La Trinité de Joyce', *Tel Quel*, no. 83 (1980), pp. 36–88.

36 See the presentation of Saussure's notebooks on anagrams by Jean Starobinski in his *Les Mots sous les mots: Les anagrammes de Ferdinand de Saussure* (Paris, Gallimard, 1971). This text contains, amongst other things, the substance of three important articles by Starobinski on the anagrams published between 1964 and 1969. These are: 'Les anagrammes de Ferdinand de Saussure', *Mercure de France*, (February, 1964), pp. 243–62; 'Les Mots sous les mots', in *To Honour Roman Jakobson* (The Hague, Paris, Mouton, 1967), pp. 1,906–17; 'Le texte dans le texte', *Tel Quel*, no. 37 (1969), pp. 3–33.

37 Starobinski, *Les Mots sous les mots*, pp. 50–2.

38 ibid., p. 51.

39 As Starobinski says: 'Saussure's error (if there is an error) would also be an exemplary lesson. It would teach us how difficult it is for the critic to avoid taking his own findings for the rule followed by the poet.' (ibid., p. 154).

40 Julia Kristeva, 'L'Engendrement de la formule', pp. 292–3.

41 Kristeva, *Revolution in Poetic Language*, p. 152.

42 Kristeva, 'L'Engendrement de la formule', p. 309.

43 Edith Kurzweil, 'An Interview with Julia Kristeva', *Partisan Review*, vol. LIII, no. 2 (1986), p. 216.

44 ibid.

45 Julia Kristeva, 'A new type of intellectual dissident', trans. Seán Hand in Moi (ed.), *The Kristeva Reader*, p. 296.

46 ibid., p. 298.

47 ibid., p. 299.

48 Neal Bruss and Donald P. Macedo, 'Toward a pedagogy of the

question'. Conversations with Paulo Freire, *Boston University Journal of Education*, vol. 167, no. 2 (1985), p. 8.

49 See Julia Kristeva, *Etrangers à nous-mêmes* (Paris, Fayard, 1988).

50 Julia Kristeva, 'Le Nouveau monde solitaire' in *Le Genre humain 11* ('La société face au racisme') (Autumn–Winter, 1984–5), pp. 207–14.

51 See Sigmund Freud, *The 'Uncanny'* in *The Standard Edition of the Complete Psychological Works of Sigmund Freud* (hereafter *SE*), trans. James Strachey, vol. XVII (London, The Hogarth Press, reprinted, 1964), pp. 217–52.

52 Kristeva cites the following works (among others):
Michel de Montaigne, *Essais* (Paris, Presses Universitaires de France, 1965).
Montesquieu, *Mes Pensées, Oeuvres Complètes* (Paris, Gallimard, 'Bibliothèque de la pléiade', 1949), vol. I, pp. 974–1,574.
Analyse du Traité des devoirs, ibid., pp. 108–11.
Denis Diderot, *Le Neveu de Rameau, Oeuvres Romanesques* (Paris, Garnier, 1962), pp. 395–492.

53 Montesquieu, *Analyse du Traité des devoirs*, p. 110, cited by Kristeva in *Etrangers à nous-mêmes*, p. 193.

54 Immanuel Kant, 'Perpetual Peace, a philosophical sketch', in Hans Reiss (ed.), *Kant's Political Writings*, trans. H. B. Nisbet (Cambridge, New York, Melbourne, Cambridge University Press, reprinted, 1980), p. 106. Kant's emphasis.

55 Kristeva, 'Le Nouveau Monde solitaire', p. 207.

56 See Kristeva, *Etrangers à nous-mêmes*, p. 141.

57 See below, Chapter 4, for an explanation of 'dialogical' and 'menippean'.

58 See below, Chapter 5.

Part Two

A reading of Kristeva's œuvre

PART TWO

A Theory of Knowledge Units

4

Writing, dialogue, infinity

... literature ... unique, impossible nomination which brings into being every subjective experience in its infinite state.

Séméiotiké

Writing

Julia Kristeva arrived in Paris from Bulgaria at Christmas time 1965, the holder of a French government bursary. As she herself has said, her education in Bulgaria had been both francophile and francophone:[1] 'La Marseillaise', Voltaire, Victor Hugo, and Anatole France (authors tolerated in Bulgaria) had not only served her as manuals of the French language, but also as manuals of morality.[2] However, this somewhat orthodox entry into the French language and culture belied the disruptive blow that Kristeva's semiotic theory of language, signification, and textuality was destined to bring to the orthodoxies of linguistics, formal logic, and philosophy. And this, almost immediately from the time of one of her first major publications in Paris in 1967.[3] Not the traditional works in French culture, but rather the more or less modernist texts of Céline and Blanchot which were in Kristeva's bag on her arrival in the land of Descartes, thus serve as a more accurate sign of the young Bulgarian's imminent intellectual trajectory.

This will be a trajectory that begins to explore the ways in which the productivity of the text, or 'semiotic practices'[4] – its poetic and, some would say, ephemeral and elusive dimension – can be written about at all. Too much (scientific) formalization, and the poetic or musical side of language becomes imperceptible. Without words or concepts of some kind, however, our appreciation, or even

91

awareness of the musical, material – in a word, poetic – dimension of language remains intuitive, speculative, or maybe leads us into mysticism. Whatever the case, the task now is to provide an analysis and interpretation of Kristeva's work of the 1960s and early 1970s. We shall see how the issue of the formalization of poetic language is of prime concern for Kristeva's writing at this time.

Formalization

While the notion of textuality as 'dialogical' and infinite will become the main theme of our discussion, the question of formalization – especially with regard to literature or textuality[5] – illuminates the dynamic of Kristeva's early work. In its most general sense, 'formalization' refers to the presentation, in signs and symbols of all kinds, of what would otherwise be irrevocably lost. What is truly inexpressible, unrepresentable, unthinkable, and unknowable is lost in this general sense. Strictly speaking, it is hardly possible, without contradiction, to give an example of this loss, but our experience in the first months of life, the exact origin of human society and language, and an absolutely unique event (for which there could be no document) might provide an approximate idea of what is at stake. Any further reflection along these lines would lead us into the world of Heidegger's philosophy.[6] And while this would not be without interest, it is only tangential to Kristeva's concerns in the late sixties.

What stimulated Kristeva's intellectual development with regard to formalization was, firstly, the fact that she had come from a political environment where the impetus towards transcending existing limits to formalization in literature and the arts was frowned upon, and favour given to a mode of humanism which extolled the human spirit, consciousness, ideological purity, and a socio-historical explanation of artistic endeavour; or, as in the case of Pereversev's 'refutation' of Russian Formalism,[7] art and literature had to be seen as the direct expression of the means of production.[8] In the final analysis, the move against so-called formalism in the Eastern bloc countries becomes an indirect and personal reason as to why Kristeva developed, with enthusiasm and vigour, a number of the concepts (e.g. 'dialogic', 'carnivalization') found in Bahktin's writing – Bahktin having been originally a member of the Formalist group. After almost a decade of exile in

France, the importance for Kristeva of the political realities of Eastern Europe (the same realities which led to the suppression of the work of the Formalists) is expressed with uncharacteristic personal intensity in her theoretical text on Sollers' novel *H*:

> To put it bluntly, I speak in French and about literature because of Yalta. I mean that because of Yalta, I was obliged to marry in order to have a French passport and to work in France; moreover, because of Yalta I wanted to 'marry' the violence that has tormented me ever since, has dissolved identity and cells, coveted recognition and haunted my nights and my tranquility, caused hatred to well within what is usually called love, in short, has raked me to death. Consequently, as you may have noticed, I have no 'I' any more, no imaginary, if you wish; everything escapes or comes together in theory, or politics, or activism.[9]

While it would be a mistake of some magnitude to see 'Yalta' and 'exile' reflected or expressed in her theoretical writing, it is reasonably clear that this personal aspect played a part in setting Kristeva's work on its unique theoretical course.

The second important stimulus to Kristeva's intellectual trajectory with regard to the question of formalization concerns her perception, in the mid-1960s, of its limits with regard to language and literature. Here, there are at least two significant aspects.

Firstly, Kristeva considered certain features of Formalism – especially in its later, high-structuralist mode – not only too reductionist (hence, her early attraction to the work of Roland Barthes) and in need of being made more dynamic,[10] but also too tolerant of traditional binary oppositions. With regard to the notion of the sign, this meant accepting the (ultimately metaphysical) distinction, 'symbolic/non-symbolic' recalling the ancient division, 'spirit/matter' and serving to inhibit the scientific study of the so-called spiritual realm.[11] Furthermore, Kristeva emphasizes the importance for her of the linguistic term 'anaphora': a semantic supplement of language without any *structural* connection.[12] This is not all. The etymology of the term is also called upon. Anaphora connotes that element which unites language to its outside, thereby breaking down the sharpness of the opposition, language/reality, but without reducing the one to the other. It is the 'non-structured', the 'non-spoken', what is 'silent and mute' – the 'non-written'. Anaphora thus challenges the notion that the sign exists at a fixed remove from the realm of material practice.[13] But in addition, by evoking (etymologically) the idea of a 'carrying back' in space, and what is 'fixed in the memory', we are put in touch with the 'volume' of language.

Secondly, and equally importantly for the Kristeva of *Séméiotiké*, existing modes of formalization in mathematics and science generally showed themselves to be severely limited when it came to formalizing literary and textual production. According to Kristeva, this was particularly so with regard to poetic language which exists on the hither side of representation and (more obviously) the language of communication. The latter can be formalized in grammar and syntax, or even logic; but poetic language cannot be contained within the aforementioned strictures because it is inseparable from language's materiality. As Kristeva saw it, existing modes of formalization in linguistics were unable to cope with this materiality (productivity), primarily because linguistics, and even early semiotics, had determined that language's material- ity was beyond their scope. Here, we may recall that any mode of formalization that relies on principles inherited from Aristotle will always produce an 'outside' beyond its own legitimate limits. This can be illustrated by referring to the characteristics of formalization in mathematics, characteristics thought to be sacrosanct before Georg Cantor brought about an upheaval in its foundations at the close of the nineteenth century.[14] These principles of formalization may be summarised as follows:

(a) The axiomatic method (an existing set of proven axioms are the point of departure for the development of new axioms).

(b) Existence as free from contradiction so that the law of identity holds, i.e. $a \equiv a$.

(c) The law of the excluded middle: $a = b$, *or* $a \neq b$, there is no third way.

(d) The decidability of every mathematical or logical problem (i.e., we would be able to make a decision about (c) above).

Some, like Bertrand Russell, went so far as to say that the 'laws' of identity, contradiction, and of the excluded middle are 'Laws of Thought'.[15]

Kristeva's early work challenges the above characteristics of formalization as applied to textuality because they become too restrictive: they do not account for either the nature of the product (text) or, more importantly, the 'productivity' of that product. Overall Kristeva's work – especially through the impetus of psychoanalysis – contests the view that the conditions of formalization are 'Laws of Thought'. It is precisely one of the features of poetic language, for example, that it embodies contradiction. Life *and* death, being *and* non-being, good *and* evil, etc., can exist simultaneously in a text. A text does not (simply) obey the rules of logic, or grammar, or the characteristics of mathematical formalization; or at least it does a great deal more: this is what Kristeva begins to show us in her early writings.

The writing of the text: 'Grammé' and 'Sémîon'

Grammé

By the indications given so far, the text is going to be a vehicle of contradiction: it may break the law of identity and not 'be' identical with itself. In 1967, precisely at the time when Kristeva was developing a theory of semiotics that would account for the specificity of the text and thus of literature, Jacques Derrida published *De la grammatologie* (*Of Grammatology*). Derrida was at that time loosely associated with *Tel Quel*, the journal in which Kristeva's important essay on paragrams would be published in the following year.[16] Derrida's basic argument in *De la grammatologie* is that writing is a kind of totality which is not identical with itself *qua* totality. For writing, in the (literally) expanded sense in which Derrida uses it, 'contains' an inside and an outside within itself. Such a conception thus opposes the traditional definitions of writing (in linguistics, history, and philosophy) as secondary to the spoken word and a simple representation of it, or as an *aide-mémoire* – a secondary mark serving as a reminder of a primary experience. For Derrida, the notion of writing as secondary in relation to what is primary is nothing other than one more binary opposition within a long series which has characterized thought within the tradition of western metaphysics.[17] Instead, Derrida proposes that writing – understood in the broadest (and not simply the colloquial) sense – breaches the barrier between inside and outside and thus (potentially) between all such binary oppositions. Writing is deemed to cover the whole field of linguistic signs and can 'look at itself' because it is neither a simple unity nor limited to what may be imagined by any particular subject:

What can look at itself is not one; and the law of the addition of the origin to its representation, of the thing to its image, is that one plus one makes at least three.[18]

In other words, writing undermines the 'law of identity' because it is, in effect, both one *and* other simultaneously.

During the halcyon days of the structuralist endeavour in the sixties, theorists frequently referred to Ferdinand de Saussure's notion that language has two basic structural features: firstly, that the relationship between the signifier (word, acoustic image) and the signified (meaning, concept) is arbitrary, and, secondly, that language is a series of differences 'without positive terms'. Derrida, however, noted that despite Saussure's insight into the nature of language, the latter still held to the narrow, colloquial view of writing as purely phonetic and secondary to speech. Speech (the voice) was thus the true model of language for Saussure, and for the tradition of western metaphysics beginning with Plato. For Derrida, on the other hand, to hold to such a view amounted to violating the very principles of 'arbitrariness' and 'difference' deemed to be fundamental to language as such. Derrida further noted that to sustain the notion of difference in itself, quite separately from identity, required that a new term be coined: *différance*. This neologism, simultaneously combining the notions of 'differ' and 'defer', and containing a silent 'a' as a reminder of its irreducible graphic aspect, would serve to convey the idea of language as always already 'double': an inscription made up of both temporal and spatial aspects. *Différance*, in short, would be the *interval* (spatial and temporal) of writing as inscription.[19]

At a more 'scriptural' level, we may ask whether there is a concept, term, or category that would allow us to grasp what is really essential to writing, that would come closest to revealing the *mark* of writing as such? To be sure, the mark of writing is the graphic mark itself, or *grammé* from the Greek for a line, which reminds us of *gramma* meaning 'letter'.[20] But, 'letter' does not quite reveal what is at stake unless it is recognized that a letter (mark) cannot have an identity (or be what it is) without being implicated in its 'other', the non-mark, or spacing. Thus, writing is, in short – as a fusion of *grammé* and *gramma* – fundamentally an inscription; but this means that there has to be an *act* of inscription: for example, making a mark on a surface, or against a background in space. Consequently, we see now that both spacing and the act of inscription are essential to writing's constitution, but it is precisely these aspects which cannot be accommodated to the 'law' of identity. The latter leads to the reduction of letters and words as such to writing. The very 'reality' of writing, however, is the 'trace' (to use Derrida's term) of the act of writing's coming into being. This trace cannot be imagined or made an object of knowledge in the traditional scientific or philosophical way because it is the very condition of writing, and thus of science and philosophy also. When Derrida's work was first talked about, and then translated into English in the mid seventies, people found it all the more baffling because, at that time, consciousness, or even the ego as the locus of consciousness, still maintained a relatively unchallenged and privileged position in the sphere of knowledge. In other words, what could not be conceptualized, objectified, represented, or simply imagined, tended to be disqualified from entering the field of discussion.

'*Grammé*' thus has led us to consider writing as 'trace'. But this trace is not just a mark like a footprint in the sand; it is, according to Derrida, also the *other* of this mark: it is the insensible imprint, an 'arche-trace' (from the Greek *arké*, meaning a founding and controlling principle) which is contradictory and therefore 'not acceptable within the logic of identity'.[21] This arche-trace is never present as such in writing or a text; for to be *present* is always to be present to consciousness, and thence to the law of identity – the very ideas that are here being brought into question. As Derrida points out, the trace is inseparable from its absence, or erasure. Have we simply said, then, that the (arche) trace is merely the opposite of the present empirical mark which is part of writing in the colloquial sense? The answer is that we have not, because to do so would imply that the trace is only the other term in a binary opposition, whereas writing (in the broadest sense) as trace, is the condition of the possibility of writing as a totality not identical with itself: the difference between inside and outside, presence and absence, and even between the part and the whole, is dissolved. *Grammé* understood as trace is perhaps that 'element' of writing which makes it a totality. Mention of the difference between part and whole here foreshadows our later discussion of the infinite in relation to Julia Kristeva's work. For it is to some extent the somewhat paradoxical (for consciousness) relation of the part as equal to the whole, or totality, which is revelatory of the nature of poetic language.

As with a number of French philosophers of the early sixties,[22]

Derrida's philosophy is, in part, a settling of accounts with phenomenology, and with the work of Husserl and Heidegger in particular. If phenomenology had emerged as the most elaborated philosophy of consciousness, reflexivity, and, most significantly, subjectivity, Derrida's originality consisted in 'going beyond' phenomenology via the (to the phenomenologist) very impersonal, if not alienating, sphere of writing. It was, from Kristeva's own indications,[23] this focus on writing as such by a philosopher which made Derrida's work so interesting to writers such as Sollers and other intellectuals associated with *Tel Quel*. Derrida's work served both as a stimulant to further thought about what had gone before and as a guiding light for things to come. Nevertheless, in certain respects, Kristeva seems to go in quite a different direction to that of the grammatologist. For instance, while Derrida had been at pains to point out that 'Writing can never be thought under the category of the subject',[24] Kristeva was concerned to develop a theory of the speaking subject aimed at taking account of the nature of language in all its aspects.

Though not denying that there is an important difference between Derrida and Kristeva here, Derrida's work on writing in the late sixties proves to be illuminating as far as Kristeva's writings of the same period are concerned, precisely because of the notion of the *grammé*. For just as *grammé* shakes the hold of the logic of identity in relation to writing and opens it up so that the possibilities as well as the limits of the text can be indicated, so Kristeva brings about a similar opening with her project of 'semanalysis'. This project moves the orientation of semiotics away from the study of meaning as a static sign-system,[25] and towards the analysis of meaning as a 'signifying process'.[26]

Focus on the signifying process here points to a semiotics not limited by the presuppositions inherent in the sign (see, for example, the opposition, 'symbolic/non-symbolic' mentioned above). The sign is static, fixed, objective – on the side of the product rather than productivity, and this is why Kristeva, in *Séméiotiké*, says that rather than a semiotics, or a semiology of the sign, she is interested in carrying out a semanalysis – namely, 'the critical analysis of the notion of the sign', a 'science constructed as a critique of meaning, of its elements and its laws . . .'.[27] Or again, a semanalysis would be a 'scientific theory of signifying systems'.[28] Only a semanalysis can adequately analyse the text because it goes beyond the sign in order to analyse 'what *cannot* be thought by the whole conceptual system which is currently the foundation of intelligence, because it is exactly the text which designates its limits'.[29] No doubt semanalysis paves the way for '*la sémiotique*' (semiotics of the sign) to give way to '*le sémiotique*' (the pre-symbolic). But let us now rather focus on the notion that semanalysis is also an analysis of the French '*sème*', or the Greek '*Sémeîon*, meaning 'sign'.

Sémeîon (sème)

The '*sémeîon*' in Kristeva's hands, like the '*grammé*', goes 'beyond' the limitations of a linguistics ultimately indebted to Husserl's transcendental ego. This may be explained as follows. In order to account for the nature of meaning in language, the linguistics and the semiotics of the sixties, even in the wake of the development of structuralism, had continued to treat language as a discrete object, or product. For it was upon this supposition that a systematic and positive description and theory of meaning *for a knowing subject*, depended. Consequently, for the homogeneous subject of consciousness, language had to be treated *as though* it were a static object. The 'outside' of language became its non-systematizable, dynamic, and even non-formalizable aspect – the aspect of 'play, pleasure or desire'.[30] This is the aspect of the body's imprint in language, a body bound up with a potentially transgressive (because *un*-scientific) *practice*. Kristeva was thus beginning to argue in her first major publications dealing with the nature of semiotics, that the place of the body (the 'outside' of language according to conventional linguistics), should not only become the legitimate concern of semiotics as such, but perhaps even become its *raison d'être*. In a fundamental way, the nature of meaning is distorted if it is reduced to what is possible within the conventional framework of communication. The body, moreover, is the *place* where we 'are' as speaking beings; it is the place of the material support of the language of communication. In this sense, the latter can be represented (indeed, it is inseparable from representation); the body cannot be. Or rather, it 'appears' in language in a way comparable to Derrida's arche-trace in writing. Or again it appears 'anaphorically', if we take into account our earlier remark about anaphora pointing beyond the sign for Kristeva.[31]

The body as outside the domain of the sign cannot be represented in the conventional language of communication. It is rather located at the level of the text, the level seen by Kristeva in *Séméiotiké*, as the precondition of representation. Body and textuality thus exist together. And as Kristeva's work develops in the 1970s this insight comes to be made ever more explicit. In 1969, however, conventional linguistics still holds a certain sway, and acts as a kind of horizon in relation to which Kristeva's theory of semanalysis takes shape. From a linguistic perspective, the body partially evokes the difference between the subject of the *énonciation* and the subject of the *énoncé*, we discussed in Chapter 3. The subject of the *énonciation*, although still indebted to the notion of the transcendental ego, opens the way to the idea of the subject of the *act* of speaking, writing, etc. – to the notion of a subject *in actu*. In fact, the *énonciation* may disrupt the *énoncé*, or at least leave its imprint in it.

Emile Benveniste and Roman Jakobson were linguists who began to point to the way that the *énonciation* leaves its imprint in the *énoncé*. Thus the personal pronouns, 'I' and 'you', which Benveniste studies,[32] together with Jakobson's work on 'shifters'[33] – the class of words like the demonstratives ('here', 'there', 'this', 'that', etc.) whose meaning is a product of context – evoke the imprint of the *énonciation* in the *énoncé*. In other words, the meaning of the shifter is entirely in the act of stating itself.

But a linguistics of the *énonciation*, however, is only the starting point. Kristeva, especially at the time of *La Révolution du langage poétique*, will come to absorb and expand upon this aspect of the work of Benveniste and Jakobson, and will speak, in 1979, of the 'imperialism of the *énonciation* and *énoncé*.'[34] Right from the start – and despite the conventionally linguistic tone at some points – semanalysis will focus attention as much on the conditions of the production of meaning, as on the (static) meaning produced. As with the shifter, but far more radically, the indices of productivity are now seen to impinge upon the meaning in the product itself. Indeed, it is productivity that makes possible the very difference between *énonciation* and *énoncé*.

As the trace is the basis of writing before writing (i.e., before the separation of speech and writing), so the *sème* is the basis of, as Kristeva puts it, 'the "other scene" of the production of meaning prior to meaning'.[35] More generally, this notion of meaning *as* production will come to be called in French, *la signifiance*, a term which cannot be translated satisfactorily into English as 'significance' because the latter suggests the presence of meaning as communication and representation. What Kristeva intends is that we should see a link between the *signifiance* and the materiality of language – even if this materiality is often only available for analysis in the text of communication: in the sound and rhythm of words, and in the graphic disposition of the text on the page – those aspects which come to occupy such a prominent place in the writings of a Mallarmé or a Joyce. We shall elaborate on the concept of *signifiance* in the following chapter. For now, it is sufficient to note that for Kristeva at the end of the sixties, semanalysis becomes the study of 'the types of *signifiance* in the text'.[36] Here, semanalysis will bring to light the heterogeneity of language, rather than the homogeneity of the conventional linguistic model. Similarly, it will illuminate the 'subject in process' – a bodily subject in the sense announced earlier, the subject as practice in fact, and not the stereotypical subject of consciousness. Finally, and most importantly, semanalysis will reveal practice as transgressive because 'the moment of transgression is the key moment in practice' to the extent that practice is bound up with the transgression of systematicity: 'i.e., a transgression of the unity proper to the *transcendental ego*'.[37]

Before moving on to examine the notions of the 'dialogical' text and transgression in more detail, let us note that the key to a clear understanding of what has been discussed turns around the relativizing, or the 'de-centring' of consciousness, and thence, the ego and representation. Within western culture it is difficult *not* to take consciousness for granted. It is at the level of consciousness (centred on the ego), furthermore, that we are most resistant to disturbing of the 'law' of identity. Once the latter is not taken so much for granted, however, the difficulty of reading Kristeva – although still substantial – at least begins to diminish for the reader of good faith.

Dialogue

Epic (myth) and novel

Poetic language founded on *signifiance*, and thence 'text' (both production and product), cannot be contained within the conventional strictures of formalization consisting of the 'laws' of identity, contradiction, the excluded middle, and decidability. As Kristeva succinctly wrote in 1967: 'It is therefore impossible to formalize poetic language according to existing logical (scientific) procedures without distorting it.'[38] This serves notice that the hegemony of scientific formalization founded on the logic of identity, will come to be challenged in Kristeva's work. Kristeva's most explicit attempt to develop a logic appropriate to the nature of poetic language occurs in her theory of paragrams.[39]

By way of introduction to the concept of 'paragram', we first consider the differences between the epic and the novel in order to enable us to see that, in general, these are founded on two different logics, with the logic of the novel coming to form the basis of the formalization of poetic language.

Kristeva's analysis of the differences between the epic and the novel forms the basis of her *Le Texte du roman*.[40] Although not published until 1970, the substance of this book was developed as a doctoral thesis directed by Lucien Goldmann in 1966–7. The concerns of *Le Texte du roman* were therefore elaborated prior to those of any other of Kristeva's publications. Even the issues of 'dialogue' and 'ambivalence' in the novel as they are to be found in the 1967 essay 'Word, dialogue and novel' were, to all appearances, foreshadowed in the context of the above-mentioned thesis.[41] Also, in its more formal and systematic presentation, as in the treatment of, and interest in, transformational analysis (see Chomsky), this 1970 text is clearly a precursor to Kristeva's more theoretically elaborate approach in, for instance, 'Pour une sémiologie des paragrammes'. *Le Texte du roman* appears less theoretically elaborate than work published earlier, partly because it is still more or less anchored within the framework of the logic of identity even while it is bringing the latter into question. This means that the reader is often still on reasonably familiar ground, especially as Kristeva's point of departure is largely contained in the work of major Anglo-American philosophers (especially of logic), and theorists of language.[42] More than is the case with Derrida, Kristeva in her early work, focuses on developments in Anglo-American thought.

As to its content, *Le Texte du roman* combines a study of Antoine de la Sale's (1385–1460?) *Jehan de Saintré* published in 1456 ('the first French novel written in prose'[43]), with an outline of the important historical and cultural co-ordinates and societal changes (change from thought based on the symbol to that of the sign, rise of the book, and changes in the status and image of 'women') that played a part in the emergence of the novel as a specific form of semiotic activity. Rather than resort to the old concept of 'genre' established by rhetoric, Kristeva introduces the notion of 'ideologeme' which defines a current historical mode of textual organization. The ideologeme has always already penetrated a text: it is the specific mode of textual organization partly formed by socio-historical and cultural forces outside the text. However, these are not to be understood as being primarily ideological, as it would be the ideologeme which is in fact the precondition of ideology. The ideologeme rather corresponds more closely to the semiological (non-representative) level of the text. In Antoine de la Sale's *Jehan de Saintré*, Kristeva discerns a transition from the ideologeme of the symbol to that of the sign. An elaboration on the nature of this transition and its elements will provide us with an excellent background to the theory of poetic language.

According to Kristeva, the second half of the Middle Ages (the thirteenth to the fifteenth century) is the period where thought based on the ideologeme of the symbol merged with that based on the sign. In particular, the epic, myth, or folktale – in fact, all modes of textual organization which are 'closed', homogeneous, and static – are based on the ideologeme of the symbol. The sign, on the other hand, contrasts with the symbol by being 'open-ended', heterogeneous, and dynamic. More specifically, within the field of the symbol, opposites are *disjunctive*, i.e., non-reconcilable: if the hero of the epic embodies goodness, he will never exhibit any trace of turpitude. In the epic, etc., 'the symbol assumes the symbolized (universals) as irreducible to the symbolizer (its markings)'.[44]

The sign which challenged the symbol from the thirteenth to the fifteenth century (without the latter disappearing entirely) is characterized by *non-disjunction*: opposites, alterity, and negation can often appear in the same figure, or identity: the mocked sovereign, the defeated warrior, the unfaithful wife, the evil priest, etc. In effect, the ideologeme of the sign allows the sign to refer to the complexity of 'existence'. In doing so it ushers in a potential challenge to both the symbol and to the logic of identity. For indeed, in the text based on the symbol, one in which the elements are structurally predictable, the dominant mode of inference is syllogistic, that is, logical in Aristotle's sense. Conversely, in the sign-based novel – or more correctly, novelistic discourse – the 'totality' is never entirely analysable because it does not constitute a closed or unified whole: it thus challenges the syllogism and Aristotelian logic.

In the epic and folk-tale, too, human individuality is limited: the characters tend to embody one side of a binary opposition (e.g. 'good' or 'bad'), so that for example in the tale, 'Little Red Riding Hood', Little Red Riding Hood is good (innocent), and the wolf is entirely bad. Such symmetrical oppositions reflect the static nature of the tale's story, fixed in space but outside time.

The novel, predictably, has a different nature. It is more like the text *as* narration, or a discourse for which time is a fundamental element, than it is *a* story. In effect, time gives the novel its dynamism, so that no content can exhaust its structural base.

Taken to its highest form of development, the novel moves closer to becoming a pure discourse, where the story becomes inconspicuous in relation to the act of narration/writing itself. The 'purer' the novel form the more verisimilitude, the 'message' being transmitted, and the logic of the syllogism cease to be pertinent to what is being presented to the reader. As examples, we can keep in mind the novels of Swift, Dostoyevsky, and, ultimately, Joyce.

Kristeva argues, too, that the dynamic structure of the novel can be grasped by what she calls a 'potential infinity'[45] which enables the novel to be described as open-ended and polymorphic. Polymorphism renders verisimilitude inconsequential. For verisimilitude depends on making decisions regarding the 'truth' and 'falsity' both of statements and of the novel as a whole. The logic of polymorphism, however, is an 'undecidable' logic,[46] in the sense that it is impossible to decide whether or not each statement is either true or false. Thus, Kristeva writes that,

> The 'truth' of textual productivity is neither provable nor verifiable – which would mean that textual productivity pertains to a domain other than that of verisimilitude. The 'truth' or the pertinence of scriptural practice is of another order; it is undecidable (unprovable, unverifiable) . . . .[47]

We may observe that the transformation of the ideologeme of the symbol occurs when it is permeated by the ideologeme of the sign. The novel, therefore, is this becoming-sign-of-the-symbol – or as Kristeva has called it, 'intertextuality'. This term, which Kristeva claims has been misunderstood, does not refer then to the references in one book to other books, but to the interpenetration of two or more signifying practices. To reveal the process of intertextuality requires the study of various utterances in the text. In *Le Texte du roman*, this includes an analysis of the utterance (as either disjunctive or non-disjunctive), of the presence/absence of indices of the author, and of the indices of the reader/addressee. Of particular interest, is what Kristeva calls, after Bakhtin, 'dialogue' and 'carnival' (transgression). It remains to examine each of these in turn; for they are of strategic and continuing importance for Kristeva's work, particularly to the end of the 1970s. Before doing so, though, I conclude my remarks on *Le Texte du roman* by noting that in it the theory of paragrams is foreshadowed, together with the idea of poetic language as fundamentally 'double', and founded on the logic of 'One and Other'.[48] According to *Le Texte du roman*, the ideologeme of the sign becomes in its turn a limitation, in the twentieth century, to the ideologeme of 'writing': the condition of possibility of poetic language. Indeed, the novel before Joyce has yet to free itself completely from being the expression of an entity (psychological, or intellectual) existing prior to it. As a result, the novel can still be given a 'realist' interpretation and judged in terms of verisimilitude because it remains affected by the logic of the symbol and of identity still animating the sign.

Dialogue and carnival

What supposedly hastens the transposition of one ideologeme into another is a process of 'carnivalization'. Carnival in general may be understood as a make-believe overturning of the law and existing social norms. But Kristeva – again following Bakhtin – means by carnivalization something more subtle than a make-believe reversal of existing social relations: carnival as parody, for example. On the contrary, the carnival is a genuine transgression, not simply a mirror reversal of things as they are which cannot be predicted by the existing law. The carnival is not just the other side of the law, but includes the law within itself. Carnival is a specific kind of 'double':

> The scene of the carnival introduces the split speech act:
> the *actor* and the *crowd* are each in turn simultaneously subject and addressee of discourse.[49]

This double, Kristeva designates (as already mentioned) 'One and Other'; it becomes a totality which is not identical with itself and cannot be represented, for it includes representation within its bosom, as it were. As we shall see, the logic of the carnival (0-2) will form the point of departure in the effort to formalize poetic language.

For the moment, let us note that Kristeva shows, in her discussion of Bakhtin's work,[50] that the 'concept' of carnival is taken over by him and modified in order to better describe the structure of Dostoyevsky's novels. Accordingly, Bakhtin suggests that Dostoyevsky's fiction is 'polyphonic' in structure; that is, like the carnival it includes its other (voice) within itself. Thus with a text like *The Brothers Karamazov*, Bakhtin points out that 'the other's discourse gradually, stealthily penetrates the consciousness and the speech of the hero'.[51] For Bakhtin, discourse, or the 'word' (as Kristeva prefers here), should not be understood as the word of communication studied by linguistics, but is rather the 'dynamic milieu' in which the exchange (dialogue) takes place. In terms of linguistics, the word for Bakhtin is translinguistic; or, in Kristeva's terms, it is the intersection of meanings rather than a fixed point, or a single meaning. While parody, irony, and satire are, for instance, clear examples of the word in Bakhtin's sense (we must resort to the translinguistic/semiotic dimension in order to interpret them), Dostoyevsky's work leads us to the same kind of insight by way of the dialogical word – a word as we have noted, penetrated by the word of others: it includes the other of itself within itself. This is a polyphonic word in the sense that polyphony, too, has no fixed point but is the interpenetration of sounds. Polyphony is multiple, not singular; it includes what would be excluded by a representation of it.

Essentially, Bakhtin reads Dostoyevsky in the spirit of carnival with its double logic. This means, amongst other things, that justice cannot be done to Dostoyevsky's writing by reducing it to a story with characters as is typical of the closed structure of the epic, and fundamental to what Bakhtin called a 'monological' text. Most simply understood, a monological text, by virtue of being identical with itself, may be reduced, more or less without violence, to a single (mono-), homogeneous, and relatively uniform logic. Hence, a monological structure lends itself very easily to an ideological appropriation; for what is essential to ideology is the message conveyed, and not the *way* the message arises and is articulated within the milieu of the word. For Bakhtin, Tolstoy's works are most often monological in this sense.

In 'Word, dialogue and novel', Kristeva sums up Bakhtin's significance for semiotics and, at the same time, sharpens our focus regarding the issues involved, by indicating that the most important sense of 'word' in Bakhtin's criticism is as the 'ambivalent' word – one appropriated from another without losing its meaning, but bearing the mark of this appropriation. For instance, in *The Brothers Karamazov*, it is not simply the words themselves which create meaning, but the contextual relationship between them (e.g., Ivan's 'poem', 'The Legend of the Grand Inquisitor', and Smerdyakov's confession).

The ambivalent word draws attention, then, to the *mise en scène* of the word, and thence to the writer(W) (see Diagram 1) . We note here that the writer is not equivalent to any ideological position in the dialogical novel, as this would turn it into a monological text. On the contrary, the writer is, in the carnivalesque text, a blank space, a form without a content, if one prefers. This blank space, Kristeva argues, is the condition of possibility of the subject of narration(S) and an addressee (reader)(A). The author is anonymous in fiction, and this anonymity may be symbolized in Kristeva's approach by 'zero'. What takes the place of the author's identity, such as it might exist in a monological text, is the content of narration itself, particularly the third-person pronouns, or proper name (N). Zero now no longer exists as such and is replaced by 'one' (the other of zero). This narration of course is the object of the addressee (reader) who transforms the subject of narration into an author. 'S', however, may also be the speech/word of characters. As such, it, like any other speech, divides up into the difference between the subject of the *énonciation* (Sa) and subject of the *énoncé* (Se). The positions of a writer and reader are summarized by Kristeva in the following diagram:[52]

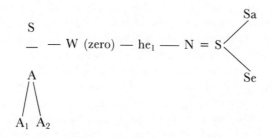

Diagram 1

In the diagram, 'S' and 'A' are transformations of each other: the writer is included in what the reader reads, but the reader is presupposed in what the writer writes. Not that either the position of the writer or reader can easily be represented, for they are irrevocably double. Indeed, in the act of reading, the writer is rather, in French, an *instance*: an agency which always *insists* or leaves an 'imprint' throughout the text.

To conclude this discussion, we note that writing is also a reading, and vice versa. This does not mean that the psychological individual is a writer and reads his/her own text; nor is the reader this psychological individual. Rather, we should now speak about a writing or a reading function. Such an approach means that the text itself (understood as both production and product) is the starting point for talking about writing and reading at work in literary criticism in the past of the realist variety. Presupposed by such criticism, is the notion that a book is written simply by the psychological author, and that therefore a text is essentially a reflection of the psyche of this author (who has also been God). This is not the level at which Kristeva is working. Moreover, as soon as the author/writer becomes essentially a psychological entity, the logic of identity (which excludes the logic of the carnival) comes to dominate every interpretation, and every analysis. To repeat a point made above: for Kristeva, textuality in the profoundest sense is *not* the expression of an entity which is prior to it.

The logic of the carnival paves the way for Kristeva's further consideration of the formalization of poetic language in her work on a theory of paragrams done mainly in 1968. Those features of carnivalization which are pertinent in this regard are the following:

The logic of the carnival is not a 'true' or 'false' logic (0-1), but is the 'correlational' logic of 'One and Other' or 'true *and* false' (0-2). Carnival is a transgression – but not in the sense of the negation of what is constituted by the existing law; for the latter is premised on just such a negation. Here, Kristeva sometimes refers to the libertine novel as being entirely predicted by the laws of censorship. A carnivalization might occur, on the other hand, when the libertine novel itself 'seriously' included a proposal for its being censored within its own discourse. Then it would become moral *and* libertine simultaneously. Nothing can represent the carnival as the embodiment of both truth and falsity; for representation is founded on the true-or-false logic of identity. Carnival is a transgression, then, because it shakes thought based on the logic of identity to its foundations.

To understand exactly what is at stake in carnivalization, we must recognize that all monological (0-1) discourses – discourses which operate according to the laws of representation and identity – cannot assimilate otherness, negation, opposition – contradiction, in a word. Such discourses include: theology, science, philosophy, 'everyday' language – all those depending, in fact, on definition and the exclusion of falsity. These discourses are bi-valent (either one *or* the other), homogeneous, and subject to the law of 'One'. 'One' is a whole and, in principle, a perfect unity or identity which excludes difference.

Kristeva is now led to ask whether a bi-valent logic can adequately comprehend the logic of ambivalence – whether, indeed, it is possible to include poetic language (especially as it is found in the poetry of Mallarmé or Lautréamont) within bi-valent logic. Two 1968 essays ('Poésie et négativité' and 'Pour une sémiologie des paragrammes') on paragrams,[53] take up the issue of the relationship between bi-valent and ambivalent, or poetic logic. Kristeva is exploring, in both essays, the possibility of developing a mode of analysing poetic language which would be able to cope with contradiction as it appears in specific texts. In short, the logic of carnivalization needs to be given theoretical force in literary-cum-textual studies. What is most striking about Kristeva's work at this point is the competence with which it is presented, the intense singlemindedness with which it is pursued, and finally, its intricate rigour. No resources are spared: existing theories of logic are invoked and, at one point, quantum mechanics – for the concept of the 'unobservable'.[54] Although the uninitiated reader will find difficulty in following all the moves Kristeva carries out in these essays, the basic project is a relatively straightforward and coherent one. It now remains to highlight some of the important aspects of this project.

The logic of poetic language

First of all, we see that poetic language, like carnival, is simultaneously a particular speech-act, or particular logic, and its implicit negation.[55] This 'double' aspect of poetic language Kristeva calls 'paragrammatic'. 'Paragrammatic writing' (*'écriture paragrammatique'*) is the movement between: the real and the non-

109

real; being and non-being; speech (*parole*) and non-speech, etc. Between these terms there is a 'non-synthetic union', symbolized by 'A Q B', equivalent to the very logic of ambivalence that we talked about above. The poetic signifier, then, both refers and does not refer to a referent. An example of this ambivalence may be seen in the following lines cited by Kristeva from Baudelaire's poem, 'Une Martyre' 'A [Woman] Martyr'.[56]

> Au milieu des flacons, des étoffes lamées
> Et des meubles voluptueux,
> Des marbres, des tableaux, des robes parfumées
> Qui traînent à plis somptueux,
>
> Dans une chambre tiède où, comme en une serre,
> L'air est dangereux et fatal,
> Où des bouquets mourants dans leurs cercueils de verre
> Exhalent leur soupir final . . . .

(Literal translation:

> In the middle of perfume flasks, of lamé fabrics
> And voluptuous furniture,
> Of marbles, of pictures, of perfumed dresses
> Which trail in sumptuous folds,
>
> In a warm bedroom where, as in a greenhouse,
> The air is dangerous and fatal,
> Where dying bouquets in their glass coffins
> Exhale their final breath . . . .)

On one level, says Kristeva, these lines refer to objects just as non-poetic speech does; but then, with phrases like 'meubles voluptueux' (voluptuous furniture) and 'bouquets mourants' (dying bouquets), the referential status of the names of objects is negated. For from the position of non-poetic speech, furniture is not voluptuous, and dead bouquets do not deserve a coffin as human beings might do. And so it is not that poetry is metaphoric and rhetorical, and that prose (assuming for the moment that this distinction between poetry and prose can be sustained) is literal and referential with the object outside the text in its sights, but rather that poetic language, founded on the logic of ambivalence, also embodies prosaic speech. It is true of course that within everyday (non-poetic) language the poetic potential that Kristeva is analysing is also to be found. A reading of Joyce virtually removes all doubt about this. Why, then, is the logic of poetic language not perceived in the language of everyday life? The answer Kristeva gives in 1968 is that the conceptual tools of analysis available for interpreting poetic language are dominated by the bi-valent logic of the sign (0-1) – the logic of the language of communication and everyday life. Poetic language cannot be contained with the laws of this logic. On the contrary, it is not observable or manifest like non-poetic language, but is 'unobservable'.[57] In general, 'unobservable' means that poetic language is not localizable in words, or unities of words, because it is the 'undulation' (Mallarmé), or the very movement, of language as such.

Kristeva shows how poetic language 'transcends' the laws of logic as these are conventionally understood in the language of communication. Thus, in poetic language, the repetition (of words, etc.) does not lead to a tautology or pure redundancy, as we saw with the 'yes' of 'Molly's monologue'.[58] Mallarmé's poem 'L'Azur', where 'l'azur' is repeated four times in the last line, and Edgar Poe's 'The Raven' where the words 'never more' are repeated throughout, serve Kristeva as examples of how the law of 'idempotence' does not apply because poetic language is not a meaning to be thought, but presents itself as the production of meaning.

Consequently, the laws of Aristotelian logic can be seen to be, at least in part, laws of equivalence and identity: the statement, 'Peter hits Paul' is equivalent in meaning to the statement, 'Paul is hit by Peter.' Such a possibility comes within the law of commutativity.[59] Another aspect of this law is that even though the disposition of the statement on a page may vary, the meaning does not change because grammar is not affected. The forms of equivalence just cited do not apply to poetic language as may be illustrated by Mallarmé's poem 'Un Coup de dés' ('A Throw of the Dice'). For the Mallarméan poem is composed of a combination of italics, and upper- and lower-case characters, which form words and phrases distributed across two pages to form, perhaps, a calligram of waves.[60] Due to this very mode of presentation, words are combined in a range of ways, but rarely, as Kristeva notes, [61] to form a grammatical statement. Rather, the way the words are distributed across the page focuses the eye on the volume (space) of writing without this being reducible to an *observation*. In this way, Mallarmé shows that it is inappropriate to try to come to grips with his poetry from the standpoint of communicative language. The lines from 'Un coup de dés' cited by Kristeva in her discussion of poetry and negativity are worth reproducing here, as this will serve to foreshadow our later exposition of the 'semiotic' (*'le sémiotique'*) as it emerges in Kristeva's close analysis of aspects of Mallarmé's *oeuvre* in *La Révolution du langage poétique*:

UN COUP DE DÉS
JAMAIS
   Quand bien même lancé dans des
circonstances éternelles
     du fond d'un naufrage
soit
  que
    l'Abîme
blanchi
    étale
      Furieux
        sous une inclinaison
          plane désespérément
            d'aile
             la sienne. . .[62]

(Literal translation (almost impossible because the syntax is entirely fluid):

A THROW OF THE DICE / NEVER / *Even though thrown into eternal / circumstances / from the bottom of a shipwreck* / whether / the Abyss / whitened / becalmed / furious / under an incline / hovers despairingly /
on wing / hers / . . .)

Meaning in non-poetic language can be a question of interpretation, or point of view. Very often it happens in fact (cf. readings of Marx) that there are numerous interpretations of the same text, so 'the' meaning of a particular discourse is seen to be polysemic. Such a view, however, does not rule out the possibility that a text's meaning conform to the logical law of 'distributivity', where words like 'each' and 'every' can indicate that the units of a number (insight) whether taken individually, or as a whole, come to the same unique meaning (number). A text's meaning would then be the agglutination of all particular meanings. Polysemy, according to Kristeva is also possible in poetic language, but it is not its uniqueness.

If, therefore, the logical laws of equivalence, etc., are not the basis on which the nature of poetic language can be described, how are we to proceed, given that the communicative language is really the only one available for the task in hand? Kristeva's tentative answer here is to employ the concept of 'orthocomplementarity' from the mathematician, Dedekind.

Orthocomplementarity simply refers to the attempt to make the division between 'true'(1) and 'false'(0) more subtle. Thus, if we imagine that 0-1 constitutes the vertical axis, X,Y, and Z are orthocomplements which make the pluridimensional and indeterminate aspect of signification 'visible'.

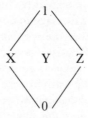

Diagram 2[63]

In Diagram 2, the axis 0-1 represents the reading of a literary/ poetic text according to the rules of logic and the language of communication. But when Gerard Manley Hopkins writes, 'Breathe, body of lovely Death' ('The Wreck of the Deutschland'), it could be said that death does not have a body – or at least, a body also evokes life. And if (by way of illustration) we modified the line's performative status, so that it read: 'Keep breathing, body of lovely Death' – at two levels we then have the (implied) notion that death is life, which is 'false' (0) according to the logic of everyday language. When seen as part of poetic language, on the other hand, the problem of whether the notion is true or false does not arise, or rather the question of truth alone is not important. What is important is the effect of the relationship between the words as such – the effect of their materiality, we could say. Another famous line from the same poem by Hopkins makes this point even more strongly:

113

His mystery must be *instressed, stressed*. . .

('The Wreck of the Deutschland' – emphasis added)

'Instress' approximates, as Hopkins says, 'the recasting of speech into sound-words, sound-clauses and sound-sentences'.[64] This, together with 'pitch', forms the basis of rhythm in poetry (and in prose becoming poetic). Pitch and the sound of words are, in Hopkins, 'beyond' the 'true' and the 'false' of speech, a beyond which becomes the X,Y, and Z of orthocomplementarity. 'Instress' does not have to be seen as something akin to God's mysterious presence in the text,[65] but can be understood as a new kind of meaning irreducible to a 0-1 logic.

As regards the discussion of the text and poetic language, our focus has been on the horizontal axis of text and context. Kristeva, however, also reflects on the position of the subject in relation to the sign: the vertical axis of textuality. Indeed, here a sender might be thought to be sending a message to a receiver. More specifically, through whom or what does the speaking subject emerge in *poetic* language? According to Kristeva, poetic language in fact heralds the dissolution of the subject as identical with itself, and foreshadows a generalized negativity seen, in certain respects, to be reminiscent of Buddhist philosophy where 'a "zerologic" subject, a non-subject comes to assume the thought which cancels it out'.[66] This subject does not depend on any sign: it is simply an 'empty' space – a 'paragrammatic space'.[67] This is the space of the movement of the constitution of subject, language, and text, which can only be grasped at the level of their deconstitution.[68]

The infinite

Paragrammatic space is also a particular kind of 'totality', one which introduces us to poetic language as a 'real infinity'[69] in Georg Cantor's sense of the term in set theory.[70] The theory of the infinite, quite notably, relates – as much in the Anglo-American tradition of philosophy as elsewhere – to the unrepresentable place of what will become Kristeva's subject in process in the mid-1970s – a dynamic subject in movement and in the throes of production, in contrast to the punctual, phenomenological subject of consciousness – the, in the end, endlessly representable, psychological subject. The concept of the infinite will emerge, too, in Kristeva's analysis of Mallarmé's poetry,[71] and in her discussion of the state as a fiction in the social context which gave rise to the avant-gardes in writing, music and painting in the late nineteenth century. Before saying more on this theme, I want to examine the theory of the infinite by referring to British philosophy and its concerns at around the turn of the century.

We may begin here by recalling Bertrand Russell's famous letter to the philosopher and mathematician Gottlob Frege in 1903, stating that the notion of a class which is a member of itself, leads to a contradiction. One of the more popular illustrations of this is that of the barber who shaves everybody in a village who does not shave himself. Does the barber shave himself or not? Of course the answer is 'no', because the barber does not shave people who shave themselves, so he cannot shave himself. But if he does not shave himself, he comes into the category of those whom he shaves, therefore he shaves himself. And so the barber, according to the rule laid down, must both shave himself *and* not shave himself, which is a perfect contradiction. As Russell mentions in his *My Philosophical Development*,[72] the form of this problem, or paradox, was known to the Greeks. Epimenides, the Cretan, said: 'All Cretans are liars.' The problem is to know if Epimenides was, or was not, lying when he uttered the words because it is impossible to decide whether or not to include Epimenides in the category of people about whom he is speaking, namely, the Cretans. The paradox, or contradiction, is only avoided if Epimenides is not included in the group of Cretans.

The strategy of excluding the class of things being spoken about from the class doing the speaking, or containing the point of enunciation, was typical of the reaction of many mathematicians and logicians to the emergence of Georg Cantor's set theory and the theory of the infinite, as these were first developed in his 'Foundations of set theory' of 1883.[73] Cantor's work inevitably focused on the foundations of mathematics and logic, which many mathematicians preferred, and still prefer, to ignore. Some, like Russell, attempted to work out a way of overcoming, or eliminating the contradictions involved,[74] in order that perhaps, finally, everything could be placed on a firm and rigorous (i.e., entirely formalized) basis once again.

In the theory of the infinite as Cantor outlined it,[75] the dominance of a potential, or empirical infinity – represented by a theoretically unending series of natural numbers $(1,2,3,4,5...n)$ and symbolized by 'ω' – had to be challenged successfully.

Cantor, in fact, had to convince other mathematicians that there could *be* a number that was a real infinity. Cantor called this number a transfinite number, and he said that there could be more than one of them. Such a transfinite number is not obtained by means of 'empirical' calculation – which is in principle how one would proceed if a potential infinity alone constituted the infinite – but by an 'act of nomination', as Jean-Louis Houdebine puts it.[76] Such a nomination alludes to the infinite as *act*-ual (real because related to an act; cf. the act of writing), to be grasped as *in actu*. In other words, the infinite is the naming of the infinite totality of finite units. Cantor's symbol for this was ω (omega). The infinite constitutes a limit exterior, and not interior, to what it delimits. In no sense, then, can the infinite be grasped in terms of finite units. However, according to Cantor these finite units presuppose the unrepresentable infinite – i.e., it is *in actu*.

More pertinent to Kristeva's work is the notion that the infinite confutes Euclid's theorem that the whole is always greater than its parts. By contrast with Euclid, Cantor showed that an infinite set is to be distinguished from a finite set in that the former has a part which is equal to itself. As Philippe Sollers puts it, with the infinite in writing 'the first words, the first series of words, of a collection where each word *counts* (that is to say becomes a figure raised to the power of the voice), already contains the collectivity of which it is a part'.[77] The part becomes equal to (has the power of) the whole in contradistinction to a simple representation of the whole (e.g., if the whole is language) which would risk becoming just another part.

References to the infinite occur throughout Kristeva's *oeuvre*, and particularly with regard to the relationship between part and whole. Thus, right from the early essay on paragrams, we find Kristeva writing, first of all with regard to set theory, that:

> poetic language is a formal system whose theorization can be a matter for *set theory* . . .[78]

and then with regard to the elements of the collection of sets that

> poetic signification obeys the principles designated by the *axiom of choice*. This stipulates that a univocal correspondence, represented by a class, exists which gives to each of the non-empty sets of the theory (of the system) one of its elements.[79]

Consequently, one can *simultaneously* choose one element in each of

116

the non-empty sets: this is the basis on which each element of a book carries the whole of the poetic message[80] – or, as Kristeva states near the beginning of the essay on paragrams just cited under the heading of 'Poetic language as infinity': 'It is only in pl [poetic language] that the "totality" (I prefer this term to that of "infinite") of the code which the subject has at its disposal is practically realized.'[81] Here we see that the infinite *is* the totality in relation to which 'One and Other' (being and non-being, positive and negative, etc.) is interior.

The infinite as lyrical – and one can recall here Hopkins' 'instress' – appears in Kristeva's *Tales of Love*, as the following passage on the Biblical 'Song of Songs' illustrates:

> the lyrical meaning is contained in each of the minimal elements of the text, which thus condense, in microcosmic fashion, the totality of the message. A metaphor, and perhaps even a simple invocation, a tonality of speech, are endowed with the semantic power of the whole.[82]

Here we see that in 'The Song of Songs' the lyricism of each part of the lover's message contains the whole of which it is a part. More generally, Kristeva argues that love is equivalent to the whole (message), or is a power equal to the whole, because it is never *localizable* – just as castration and jouissance are never localizable.[83] The logic of the paragram is situated precisely at this level. It, too, is not localizable in the explicit representation of the text, but is the product of a textual practice which can be seen as the equivalent of a whole of which it is at the same time a sub-set. Or as Kristeva says, poetic language, as paragrammatic is seen by semiotics as a '*real infinity* impossible to represent'.[84]

In *Powers of Horror* the infinite is implicit in the notion of abjection which finally finds its way into modern writing as the confusion of boundaries (moral, linguistic, psychic, etc.). The lyricism of Céline's style is seen by Kristeva to support abjection as the flow of opposites into one another.[85]

From a different perspective, the infinite features in Kristeva's *Revolution in Poetic Language* as part of her discussion of the state as the entity claiming to be the embodiment of the whole of society, especially in late nineteenth century Europe. Thus in a section entitled 'L'illusion de l'Etat d'être l'ensemble de tous les ensembles' ('The illusion of the state being the set of all sets'),[86] we read that,

The state is, in all rigour, only a collection of all finite sets. But for this collection to exist, and for the completed sets also to exist, the infinite must exist; the two propositions are equivalent.[87]

On this basis, the very existence of society would have a stake in the infinite: the individual as constituted by and through poetic language, the individual as an unrepresentable singularity, would be *equal* to the whole.

Overall, the infinite calls on us to make a conceptual leap. For, quite literally, a break exists between the finite and the infinite, and it is embodied in the difference, as Cantor said, between the notion of a potential infinity and a *real* infinity. 'Leap', 'imagination', and even 'freedom' (cf. the freedom encapsulated in poetry) are approximate terms in this context – the same context in which Kristeva's work is situated. But rarely, if at all, has the force of this truth been registered, even by assiduous readers of her writing.

As far as literature is concerned, 'the audacity is to name the infinite in its very innumerability, inscribed in the flesh of everyday speech'. For each speaking singularity is both 'the place of the infinite's emerging and of an enigmatic, hallucinated listing. . .'.[88] Kristeva's work is tied up with such an as yet unnoticed audacity. This gives her writing on the feminine (amongst other things) its pertinence and originality.

But rather than talk about the infinite as such, let us talk, as Houdebine has suggested, about an 'infinitist problematic' ('*problématique infinitiste*').[89] In particular, this problematic would include an analysis and elaboration of this space of singularity which is the subject as it appears poetically in language. This space is the 'place' (not localizable) from where we speak, write – in short, *act*; it is the place of practice, Kristeva will argue in *Revolution in Poetic Language*. In brief, to focus on the infinitist problematic is to dislodge consciousness from its ascendancy in – especially – the Anglo-American philosophical tradition. But it is also to do more than that. For the infinite in mathematics, and the links that mathematics has been seen to have with logic and language (cf. Russell) *in* that very tradition, are a profound indication of how Kristeva's work can be seen to have organic links with the very tradition of thought supposed by some to be foreign to hers. It is a tradition which has more than contributed to the misrecognition of Kristeva's 'audacity'.

Notes

1 Kristeva, 'Mémoire' p. 42.
2 Kristeva does not fail to note the unfavourable comparison Bulgaria makes with the 'cosmopolitan' tradition of France. See ibid.
3 See Julia Kristeva, 'Le Mot, le dialogue et le roman'.
4 For an illuminating early outline of Kristeva's concerns in this regard, see her 'L'Expansion de la sémiotique', in *Séméiotiké*, pp. 43–59.
5 See Julia Kristeva, 'Le Texte et sa science', in *Séméiotiké*, pp. 7–26.
6 For example, Heidegger says:

> Are we in our existence historically at the origin? Do we know, which means do we give heed to, the essence of the origin? Or in relation to art, do we still merely make appeal to a cultivated acquaintance with the past?
> For this either–or and its decision there is an infallible sign. Holderlin, the poet – whose work still confronts the Germans as a test to be stood – named it in saying:
>
> > *Schwer verlässt*
> > *was nahe dem Ursprung wohnet, den Ort.*
>
> > Reluctantly
> > that which dwells near its origin departs.
>
> > 'The Journey', verses 18–19

Martin Heidegger, 'The origin of the work of art', in David F. Krell (ed.), *Martin Heidegger, Basic Writings* (London, Routledge & Kegan Paul, 1978), p. 187.
7 See Kristeva's presentation of Bakhtin's poetic theory in the French edition of Bakhtin's text, Mikhail Bakhtine, *La Poétique de Dostoievski*, trans. Isabelle Kalitcheff (Paris, Seuil, 1970), pp. 5–21.
8 ibid., p. 8.
9 Julia Kristeva, 'The novel as Polylogue', in Julia Kristeva, *Desire in Language*, p. 161.
10 Kristeva, 'Mémoire', p. 43.
11 Kristeva, 'L'Expansion de la sémiotique', p. 46.
12 Kristeva, 'Le Sens et le mode' (on Roland Barthes' *Système de la mode*), in *Séméiotiké*, pp. 60–89; p. 81.
13 ibid., pp. 48 and 82.
14 See Joseph Warren Dauben, *Georg Cantor, His Mathematics and Philosophy of the Infinite* (Cambridge, Mass., Harvard University Press, 1979), pp. 1–5, and *passim*.
15 Bertrand Russell, *The Problems of Philosophy* (London, Oxford University Press, reprinted, 1973), p. 40.
16 See 'Pour une sémiologie des paragrammes' (1967).
17 See Derrida, *Of Grammatology*, trans. Gayatri C. Spivak (Baltimore and

London, Johns Hopkins University Press, 1976), p. 71.

18 ibid., p. 36.

19 Jacques Derrida, 'Différance' in *Margins of Philosophy*, trans. Alan Bass (Chicago, University of Chicago Press, 1982), pp. 1–27.

20 See, ibid., p. 34, note 9.

21 Derrida, *Of Grammatology*, p. 61.

22 See the work of Michel Foucault, Jean-François Lyotard and Gilles Deleuze, and see Vincent Descombes, *Modern French Philosophy*, trans. L. Scott-Fox and J. M. Harding (Cambridge, New York, Melbourne, Cambridge University Press, 1980), pp. 75–7.

23 Kristeva, 'Mémoire', pp. 44–5.

24 Derrida, *Of Grammatology*, p. 68. Kristeva begins to develop a critique of grammatology in later work. See Kristeva, *Revolution in Poetic Language*, pp. 140–6.

25 See Julia Kristeva, 'The system and the speaking subject', in Moi (ed.), *The Kristeva Reader*, p. 28.

26 ibid.

27 Kristeva, *Séméiotiké*, p. 19.

28 ibid., p. 22.

29 ibid., p. 24.

30 Julia Kristeva, 'The system and the speaking subject', p. 26.

31 See above, pp. 93–4.

32 See Emile Benveniste, *Problems in General Linguistics*, trans. Mary E. Meek, Miami Linguistics Series, no. 8 (Coral Gables, Florida, University of Miami Press, 1971), pp. 217–30.

33 See Roman Jakobson, 'Shifters, verbal categories and the Russian verb', in *Selected Writings*, vol. II (The Hague, Mouton, 1971), pp. 130–47.

34 Julia Kristeva, 'Il n'y a pas de maître à langage', p. 129.

35 Julia Kristeva, 'Semiotics: a critical science and/or a critique of science', in Moi (ed.), *The Kristeva Reader*, p. 84.

36 Kristeva, *Séméiotiké*, p. 9.

37 Kristeva, 'The system and the speaking subject', p. 29. Kristeva's emphasis.

38 Kristeva, 'Word, dialogue, and novel', in Moi (ed.), *The Kristeva Reader*, p. 41.

39 See Kristeva, 'Pour une sémiologie des paragrammes', but also the equally important, 'Poésie et négativité' in *Séméiotiké*, pp. 246–77.

40 *Approche sémiologique d'une structure discursive transformationnelle* (Mouton, The Hague, 1970, second printing, 1976).

41 See Kristeva, *Le Texte du roman*, pp. 87–97, 104, 117–19, 162–76.

42 See the following: in linguistics: Chomsky, Halliday, Harris, Halle, Katz, and Fodor; in logic: Kneale and Kneale (*The Development of Logic*); in philosophy: Peirce, Quine, Robinson, Taski, and Wittgenstein.

43 Kristeva, *Le Texte du roman*, p. 22.

44 Kristeva, *Desire in Language*, p. 38.

45 Kristeva, *Le Texte du roman*, p. 75.

46 ibid., p. 76.

47 ibid.

48 ibid., p. 90.

49 Kristeva, *Desire in Language*, p. 46.

50 See Kristeva, 'Word, dialogue, and novel'.

51 Mikhail Bakhtin, *Problems of Dostoevsky's Poetics*, trans. Carlyl Emerson (Manchester, Manchester University Press, 1984), p. 222. Also see the French edition of this work. Mikhail Bakhtine, *La Poétique de Dostoievski*, p. 288.

52 Kristeva, 'Word, Dialogue, and Novel' in Moi (ed.), p. 46. Diagram modified.

53 See above, note 39.

54 See in Kristeva, 'Poésie et négativité, pp. 258–9 and note 15 referring to H. Reichenbach, *Philosophic Foundations of Quantum Mechanics* (Berkeley, California University Press, 1946) for the concept of the 'unobservable'; for references to G. Birkoff, *Lattice Theory* (New York, American Mathematical Society, 1940), see p. 263; for Dedekind's structure of orthocomplementarity, see pp. 265–6.

55 Kristeva, 'Poésie et négativité', p. 264.

56 ibid., p. 252.

57 See ibid., pp. 258 ff.

58 See 'Molly's monologue' in Joyce's *Ulysses* cited in our Introduction, p. 5.

59 Symbolically: X.Y $\equiv$ Y.X; XUY $\equiv$ YUX. See Kristeva, 'Poésie et négativité', p. 260. See also Bertrand Russell, *My Philosophical Development* (London, Allen & Unwin, 1985), p. 70 for summary of these laws.

60 See, for example, the calligrams of waves inspired by the graphic disposition of Mallarmé's 'Un coup de dés' produced by Ernest Fraenkel in his book, *Les Dessins trans-conscients de Stéphane Mallarmé: à propos de la typographie de 'un coup de dés'* (Paris, Nizet, 1960). See designs 25–8.

61 Kristeva, 'Poésie et négativité', p. 262.

62 See ibid., p. 261 and Stéphane Mallarmé, 'Un coup de dés' in *Oeuvres Complètes* (Paris, Gallimard, 'Bibliothèque de la Pléiade', 1945), pp. 57–60.

63 Kristeva, 'Poésie et négativité', p. 266.

64 Gerard Manley Hopkins, 'Rhythm and the other structural parts of rhetoric – verse' in Humphrey House (ed.), *The Journals and Papers of Gerard Manley Hopkins* (London, New York, Toronto, Oxford University Press, 1959), p. 273. Also recall Joyce's 'soundsense and sensesound'.

65 See, for example, W. H. Gardener and N. H. MacKenzie, 'Editorial Notes' in Gardener and MacKenzie (eds), *The Poems of Gerard Manley Hopkins* (Oxford, London, New York, Oxford University Press, 4th paperback edn, reprinted, 1978), p. 258.

66 Kristeva, 'Poésie et négativité', p. 273.

67 ibid., p. 274.
68 See Kristeva's paraphrasing of the statement by Jacques Lacan in ibid.
69 Kristeva, 'Pour une sémiologie des paragrammes', p. 180.
70 See Joseph Warren Dauben, *Georg Cantor* . . ., pp. 219–39.
71 See Kristeva, *Revolution in Poetic Language*, pp. 226–34.
72 See Russell, *My Philosophical Development*, p. 59.
73 See G. Cantor, *Contributions to the Founding of the Theory of Transfinite Numbers*, trans. P. E. B. Jourdain (New York, La Salle, 1955 – republication of 1915 edition).
74 See Russell, *My Philosophical Development*, pp. 60 ff.
75 As well as works on set theory, my main reference here is Jean-Louis Houdebine, 'L'Expérience de Cantor', *L'Infini*, no. 4 (Autumn, 1983), pp. 87–110.
76 ibid., p. 100.
77 Philippe Sollers, 'Lettre à Marc Devade' in exhibition catalogue *Marc Devade, Peintures 1979-1981* (Paris, éd. Peinture, 1981), cited in Houdebine, 'L'Expérience de Cantor', p. 109.
78 Kristeva, 'Pour une sémiologie des paragrammes', p. 189.
79 ibid.
80 ibid.
81 ibid., p. 178.
82 Julia Kristeva, *Tales of Love*, p. 92.
83 See Daniel Sibony, 'L'Infini et la castration', *Scilicet*, no. 4 (1973), pp. 75–133.
84 Kristeva, 'Pour une sémiologie des paragrammes', p. 180.
85 See Kristeva, 'Those females who can wreck the infinite', in *Powers of Horror*, esp. p. 162.
86 This section is to be found in the as yet untranslated part of *La Revolution du langage poétique*, pp. 379–83.
87 ibid., p. 379.
88 Houdebine, 'L'Expérience de Cantor', p. 109.
89 See ibid., p. 105.

5

The semiotic in
poetic language and history

We view the subject in language as decentring the transcendental ego, cutting through it, and opening it up to a dialectic in
which its syntactic and categorical understanding is merely the
liminary moment of the process . . . .

Julia Kristeva, *Revolution in Poetic Language*

Governed by the insights of psychoanalysis, Kristeva's writings
become, particularly after 1973, concerned with an elaboration of a
theory of the subject in language and the signifying process in
general. Just as the signifying process is inextricably bound up with
the constitution of society (the symbolic and society being
inseparable), so society itself is part of history. In effect, Kristeva
shows, as we shall see, that the nineteenth-century European
avant-garde might never have occurred were it not for such events
as the emergence of nationalism and the Paris Commune of 1871.
On this basis, then, it would be quite incorrect to see literature, as
the vehicle of poetic language, as isolated from history and society;
rather, textual practices have to be seen to be – at least in part –
the basis of history and society. Such is one of the telling theses put
forward in Kristeva's mammoth *Doctorat d'état, La Révolution du
langage poétique*. It is a somewhat neglected thesis in Anglophone
countries, possibly because it is more fully elaborated in the
untranslated last third of the text in question.[1]
    From a slightly different angle, the text as productivity which
featured so strongly in Kristeva's work in the early 1970s, now
becomes integrated into the notion of writing as 'negativity', and
thence as 'rejection' – a writing which constitutes the subject in

123

process as exceeding the limits of the punctual, static, transcendental subject of phenomenology.[2] The subject in process is a subject of flows and energy charges, of jouissance[3] and death. It is what emerges in light of Kristeva's theory of the 'semiotic' in contradistinction to the 'symbolic'.[4] These two terms above all encapsulate the constituent elements explaining the revolution in poetic language that has hardly failed to touch all the arts. To introduce some of the dynamics of the 'semiotic' and the 'symbolic', we shall briefly digress and consider Jackson Pollock's painting, 'Blue Poles'. Here is one spectator's meditation on that work.

Painting rhythm

I stand before 'Blue Poles'.[5] At a distance of three metres, I can hardly take in the extremities of the work; in fact I am lost in the maze of dancing vermilion set off by 'waterfalls' and 'webs' of dripping cream, yellow, white, and aluminium. Fine and thick lines – swirling endlessly, when one is close – are punctuated by the 'poles' of cobalt which have the appearance of being about to dance – some perhaps into the 'forest' of line, others perhaps to the left or to the right extremity of the brass frame. Then again, these 'poles' could be coming out to meet and encircle me. I stand transfixed; for the 'I' is lost for a moment in the painting; there seems to be no outside – only the paint which captures me in its movement – in its rhythm. Now the painting is simply this enchanting rhythm of contrasts: the vermilion is shooting lightly, delicately into the dark recesses and then reappearing in the light of the cream so that it is set off by the light and the dark. At various points cream has a full centre and exploding edges – much like a fireworks display. In this case, the poles would be illuminated by the bursting light around them. These poles are clearly marked out. They are, if one likes, a raw boldness highlighting the infinite intricacy of the aluminium and the white. The pole second from the right, however, is almost cut in half – by cream in particular, but also by vermilion and aluminium. Glass (not detectable in any photograph) is embedded in the lower extremity of this pole, making a contrast between line and surface perceptible. The dancing line indeed finds its resistance in the paint and glass of the surface. Near the top and the bottom of the same pole, slivers of cream, like barbed wire, cross the cobalt blue.

Blue Poles by Jackson Pollock (1952). Reproduced courtesy of the Australian National Gallery, Canberra

The pole third from the left has, it seems, lost its upper quarter – and then it becomes clear that no pole is left untouched by the horizontal rhythms of colour – even to the extent that the cobalt itself joins in the ecstatic movement and traverses its own verticality. The poles are thus in the throes of being exceeded by the horizontal rhythms. Their firmness, clarity, and order is about to be overcome. I feel pleasure at this prospect. The poles are now becoming lost in the rhythms of energy. Clarity and order are under threat; all forms of limit – the frame, the represented object, the name of the work, etc. – are being exceeded. In other words, my effort to interpret Pollock's painting is being exceeded.

I recall the famous photographs by Hans Namuth of Pollock painting.[6] The artist is seen approaching the canvas stretched on the floor of the barn studio. He moves in from one side, then another, or moves in from above. In one photograph, Pollock's baton and the arm holding it are a mere blur poised above the rhythms of black on the canvas below. In at least two other photographs, the whole of Pollock's body is a blur of movement dancing around the perimeter. Then again Pollock is seen stepping into the work, standing back on the outside, bending deep over one corner, stooping to add a touch at the edge, standing almost erect letting the paint fall, walking, chin jutting forward, to another spot, standing still in contemplation . . . . In short, by comparison to the relative stillness of the artist working before a conventional easel, Pollock working is the movement of which so many of his paintings are a trace.

We know from Namuth and Lee Krasner that Pollock had a markedly introverted personality: 'The Pollocks were generous despite limited means. The meals were delicious. The conversation, stimulated by Lee, was always good. Jackson never talked much, and never expounded on theories of art.'[7] It is as though Pollock's shyness gave way to explosions of rhythm and movement in painting, as though silence gave way to a transcending of limits which would render painting ambiguous. Lee Krasner is extremely illuminating in this regard when she says that:

With the larger black-and-whites he'd either finish one and cut it off the roll of canvas, or cut it off in advance and then work on it. But with the smaller ones he'd often do several on a large strip of canvas and then cut that strip from the roll to make more working space and to study it. Sometimes he'd ask, 'Should I cut

126

it here? Should this be the bottom?' He'd have long sessions of cutting and editing . . . . Working around the canvas – in the 'arena' as he called it – there really *was no absolute top or bottom*. And leaving space between paintings, there was *no absolute 'frame'* the way there is working on a pre-stretched canvas. Those were difficult sessions. His signing the canvases was even worse. I'd think everything was settled – tops, bottoms, margins – and then he'd have last minute thoughts and doubts. *He hated signing. There's something so final about a signature* . . . .[8] (emphasis added)

Krasner's remarks suggest Pollock as a person of rhythms and flows, one who is distinctly uneasy before the prospect of the punctual and the limit. Pollock's aim seems to have been to leave his paintings entirely open-ended, without boundaries of any kind (no frame). This would be Pollock's battle against the symbolic father, but a father of order who must be present, at least minimally, if art is not turned into the chaos of psychosis. This, at any rate, is what Julia Kristeva's interpretation of psychoanalysis would tell us.

This brief digression into Pollock's work serves to introduce many of the issues arising from Kristeva's work in the mid- to late 1970s – in particular, the difference between the semiotic (*le sémiotique*) and the symbolic. Let us now summarize, in this regard, some of the pertinent aspects of my remarks on Pollock and 'Blue Poles'.

To begin with, the rhythm and movement of colour dominate representational or symbolic elements: in 'Blue Poles' the frame is put in question, and the title has only a tenuous link with the painting. As a result, the place of the spectator is rendered tenuous and ambiguous because the limits of the painting are ambiguous: perspective, order, and representation are challenged. In sum, the painting is predominantly a release of controlled drive energy – a fact confirmed by the perception of rhythm, and strongly evoked in the photographs of Pollock in movement while painting. Kristeva herself has called the non-geometric, non-symbolic space of Pollock's paintings 'semiotic'.[9]

The 'semiotic' and the 'symbolic'

While Kristeva's book *Séméiotiké* brought together studies based on the geno-text, or the non-phenomenal aspect of language and textuality, the idea of language presented by the discipline of linguistics is the point of departure. For example, even in the transitional piece, 'L'Engendrement de la formule' ('Engendering the phrase'), the subject remains exterior to the *engendering* of meaning and the significance of the geno-text. In short, if a subject is in question, it is still almost exclusively symbolic. For 'being neither structured nor structuring, the geno-text does not know the subject. Exterior to the subject, it is not even its nihilist negative.'[10] Although the lengthy analysis of Sollers' *Nombres* in 'L'Engendre-ment de la formule', together with references to Mallarmé's 'Un coup de dés' begins to undermine the sovereignty of the symbolic subject,[11] Kristeva is only concerned to affirm here that the text is more than the punctual presentation of meaning in words – the 'pheno-text' – and has to be understood to include the engendering of meaning – the 'geno-text'. So if the punctual is pluralized in *Nombres*,[12] the subject is yet to be seen as this process of engendering – as will be the case with the concept of the semiotic – Kristeva's aim being to challenge the (then) conventional view of language as an exclusively formal device for communicating meaning. On the other hand, 'L'Engendrement de la formule' foreshadows the theory of the semiotic in the way the pronoun 'I' is no longer seen as being divided into 'mind' and 'body', but as making the body as jouissance the material, unrepresentable support of language: 'this "I" has one possible place: that of the main axis which pulverizes every body thinkable by a narcissistic and metaphysical subject . . .'.[13] The semiotic, then, is bound up with the body as jouissance. But most of all, the body as jouissance comes to be seen, in the lengthy theoretical introduction to *Revolution in Poetic Language*, as the locus of drive energies in the *chora*:

> a nonexpressive totality formed by the drives and their stases in a motility that is as full of movement as it is regulated.[14]

The *chora* is a kind of place, or receptacle. It is not easy to make this element intelligible because it is not, strictly speaking, repre-sentable. What may be represented, conceptualized, thought of, imagined, made clear and explicit, and is above all a product of *réglementation* and order, is part of the symbolic order or simply, the symbolic. The ego and its narcissism are part of the symbolic. To speak about the *chora* at all is paradoxical, given that to do so is to give it a place in the symbolic. The *chora* is a mobile and 'extremely provisional articulation constituted by movements and their ephemeral stases'.[15] The *chora* is a semiotic, non-geometrical space where drive activity is 'primarily'[16] located. As I see it, the *chora* is akin to a provisional concentration of energy, or an equally provisional pole of attraction. It is in no way any kind of position. In particular the *chora* is the locus of the drive activity underlying the semiotic. The drives being both positive and negative, creative and destructive, set up both stases and attacks against these. In short, the drives set up a continuous tension of energy charges and their dissipation. The importance that the drives assume in Kristeva's work from 1974 onwards cannot be overemphasized. For it is the drives above all which become the preconditon of the subject in process. More will be said about the drives and their stases in psychoanalysis in a moment; but firstly, let us get a general picture of Kristeva's theoretical framework.

The *chora* is connotative of the mother's body – an unrepresent-able body. The mother and the body as such in fact go together for Kristeva. The mother's body becomes the focus of the semiotic as the 'pre-symbolic' – a manifestation – especially in art, of what could be called the 'materiality' of the symbolic: the voice as rhythm and timbre, the body as movement, gesture, and rhythm. Prosody, word-plays, and especially laughter fall within the ambit of the semiotic. Chronologically, the operations of the semiotic can be observed in children before the acquisition of language in Lacan's 'mirror stage'. The unarticulated sounds a baby makes are thus not entirely insignificant and arbitrary, even if they have no specific (symbolic) meaning. These sounds, rarely manifest without any form of control whatever, thus constitute the pre-symbolic *signifiance*. *Signifiance*, Kristeva argues, is always present in the operations of the symbolic – such as in the everyday language of communication. For in all such speech-acts, timbre, rhythm, gesture, etc., are perceptible, but rarely noticed due to the dominance of the communicative function of language. Art – for example, poetry – can draw attention to the semiotic/pre-symbolic in language through exaggeration, or possibly just through the very act of presenting a poem *as* a poem, a novel *as* a novel, a film *as* a film etc., and thus within a symbolic framework of some kind. Any *presentation* of the semiotic will consequently involve *some* degree of ordering or *réglémentation*.

Ordering, here, amounts to a distancing of the subject from the material in question. As we hinted in Chapter 2, such a distancing is the mark of the symbolic which, in the mother–child–father triad, is a place occupied by the father. The father's clearly defined place corresponds to the mother's body as the unrepresentable *chora* – a kind of non-place, symbolically speaking. Within the triad, the symbolic intervenes in the relationship between mother and child. This intervention by the symbolic (the more marked to the extent that the mirror stage has begun) is experienced by the child as a separation from the mother. Consciousness, the ego, and identity are all premised on the intervention of the symbolic in the mother–child relation. Such indeed would be the basis of psychoanalytic theory of Lacanian inspiration. Kristeva, however, unlike Lacan in certain ways, has endeavoured to bring out the importance of the semiotic without thereby denying the importance of the symbolic. This has entailed a profound consideration of the mother's 'place' as *chora* as well as the place of the father as the embodiment of the symbolic Name-of-the-father. In sum: without the symbolic intervening as order, identity, consciousness, etc., there would be no art as we understand it in western society, because there would be no language as communication. On the other hand, without the semiotic, the symbolic would lack any form of materiality with the result that there would still be no art or language as communication.[17] Indeed, much of the inspiration of Kristeva's work in the seventies derives from the view that the semiotic in fields such as psychoanalysis, linguistics, and art had been seriously neglected. To her, this neglect seemed to correspond to a fundamental misconception of the real and potential effects of so-called avant-garde art works: for example, those of Lautréamont and Mallarmé in the latter part of the nineteenth century, and those of Joyce, Artaud, Kafka, and Abstract Expressionist painters in the twentieth.

What is sometimes difficult to grasp in Kristeva's work, and perhaps even more difficult for an Anglo audience to accept, is the fact that, for the theorist of the semiotic, there is no clear separation between art, society, and language on the one hand, and the individual subject as the outcome of the interaction between the semiotic and the symbolic on the other. This means, for one thing, that Kristeva does not separate out the (western) societal category of 'family' from the dynamic psychoanalytic triad of mother–child–father. As Kristeva sees it,[18] the category 'family' and the societal beings, mothers, fathers and children, are exclusively of the symbolic order. Moreover, society itself is a product of the symbolic. Because the discipline of sociology has tended to be concerned only with the symbolic (without necessarily acknowledging this), it has not been able to move beyond the sphere of representation and the symbolic as its precondition. Many strictly sociological interpretations of works of art, therefore, tend to focus on the (symbolic) message, for which the work is seen as a vehicle, rather than on the (semiotic) nature of the aesthetic achievement.

Consequently, the difference between sociology's approach and that of Kristeva is of some importance. Hence, when Kristeva speaks about a person's (be he or she artist or analysand) relation to a mother who is entirely accessible and evident in a speech without limits, or of a father who is only too visible in the precision and order of every paragraph, it is in the psychoanalytic sense of the dynamic interaction between the semiotic and the symbolic that this should be understood. By assessing psychoanalysis in purely sociological terms, however, is to mis-read the situation. For example, because it is often presumed that fathers and mothers must always be empirically present (i.e. reduced to a question of gender), saying (as I said earlier) that the ryhthms and flows of 'Blue Poles' are equivalent to 'Pollock's battle against the symbolic father', becomes, for the sociological approach, a source of scepticism. From a psychoanalytic perspective, by contrast, 'Blue Poles' embodies the clash, constitutive of Pollock's subjectivity, between the drive flows and energy of the semiotic *chora* and the form-giving symbolic.

To the extent that lines take precedence over points in 'Blue Poles', to the extent that the colour and the texture of the paint as such is perceptible and nothing is represented, incest is connoted. By this we mean that the symbolic as any form of limit, separation, or distancing is, if not entirely absent, at least radically diminished. Thus do I feel that the painting incorporates – envelops – me as viewer in an experience marked – as in other Abstract Expressionist works – by a plurality of points of interest instead of a single point of origin, typical of representational paintings based on perspective. This is why, too, the 'I' is brought into question: for it is complicitous with the symbolic father from whom a name, and thus an identity are derived. A painting like 'Blue Poles', then, is one where the semiotic is in dominance. Of course, the semiotic is also present in representational painting.

Indeed, in Kristeva's analysis of some of Giotto's works,[19] colour

131

as such – source of the semiotic – is seen to be of fundamental importance – especially indeterminate blue:

> Thus all colors, but blue in particular, would have a noncentered or decentering effect, lessening both object identification and phenomenal fixation. They thereby return the subject to the archaic moment of its dialectic, that is, before the fixed, specular 'I', but while in process of becoming this 'I' by breaking away from instinctual, biological (and also maternal) dependence.[20]

Kristeva shows that Giotto's paintings,[21] as well as being made up of figures as agents of the biblical narrative, equally consist of vast expanses of colour, particularly blue which, of all colours, is 'on this side of or beyond the object's fixed form; . . . it is the zone where phenomenal identity vanishes'.[22] While the history of western painting tends to view Giotto's works as the first groping steps towards perfecting the technique of perspective, and thus as the precursor of the domination of the symbolic (father) in painting, Kristeva argues that these works can also be viewed as giving roughly equal weight to the semiotic dimension (colour, form, etc); they do not simply privilege the symbolic (narrative figuration, representation). And after Giotto, Bellini's paintings of the Madonna and Child reveal motherhood primarily as 'a luminous spatialization, the ultimate language of a jouissance at the far limits of repression, whence bodies, identities, and signs are begotten'.[23] This implies that the artist, perhaps more than any other person, recognizes that a mother is also an unrepresentable body (chora), a locus of jouissance because she is both other and inseparable from the subject's own self. For, strictly speaking, the mother is prior to the subject's entry into the symbolic signalled in particular by the mastery of language, and thus prior to the capacity to posit another like oneself – a capacity indicated, for instance, by the mastery of the pronouns 'I/you'.

Art as rejection (negativity)

In summary, the semiotic is both a kind of material base for the symbolic and *sui generis*. It cannot be grasped in conceptual thought and forms the basis, as Kristeva would have it, of 'all avant-garde experience since the late nineteenth century'.[24] To focus uniquely on the general notion of the semiotic, however, is not sufficient for understanding the way avant-garde art can be a revolutionary force – this being Kristeva's prime concern in *La Révolution du langage poétique*. 'Semiotic', then, needs to be more refined, more subtly articulated, and more nuanced if it is to illuminate the process(es) of avant-garde art. We need, therefore, to explain in some detail the concepts of 'negativity', 'rejection' and 'drives'.

As with Kristeva's essays on the nature of language in the late sixties and early seventies, her trajectory in *La Révolution du langage poétique* and in the collection of essays called *Polylogue*,[25] consists in exploring and analysing a domain generally assumed to be beyond thought and knowledge. We know already that the semiotic is pre-symbolic and prior to the emergence of the division between signifier and signified. More pertinently, though, the semiotic '*precede[s]* the distinction between "subject" and "object"'.[26] The difficulty now is to accept that the radically other of thought and the symbolic is not simply an *other* posited by thought itself. In other words, the semiotic domain is not to be confused with the negative belonging to thought itself, a perfectly representable and knowable negative. Philosophically, the semiotic may be linked to the negative, but it is not the Kantian negation produced by a knowing, judging subject. To grasp the true import of Kristeva's theory here, we have to come to grips with a negative that transcends Kantian negation: Hegelian negativity. Negativity, Kristeva reminds us, is the fourth term in the Hegelian ternary dialectic.[27] It is, in effect, the very movement or 'ground' of the dialectic. 'Real ground', says Hegel 'contains a differentiated content'.[28] These roughly equivalent Hegelian terms of 'ground', 'movement', and especially 'negativity', have been neglected by the Marxist tradition, and Marx himself, possibly because of the Feuerbachian humanist appropriation of Hegel. But whatever the reason, the result has been that Marxism, like conservative modes of thought, has been unable to develop a genuinely materialist account of art and society. In other words, Marxism, too, has remained at the level of Kantian negation, the level of the symbolic, and has failed thereby to understand the potentially revolutionary force of the avant-garde's exploitation of the semiotic.

Philosophy, and within philosophy, phenomenology, had, at least until the late sixties, been considered to have provided the most sophisticated theory of the subject.[29] Although offering an extremely elaborate and complex view of subjectivity, even phenomenology, like Marxism, fails to move outside the limits of the symbolic. For Kristeva, phenomenology's reliance, in the work of Husserl in particular, on the 'transcendental ego' means that a posited, ultimately static element is functioning as the precondition of meaning. Notions like '*hyle*' (the matter of meaning), 'impulse', 'negation', and similar terms, are always within the range of the activity of the intellect – that is, of a transcendental ego that is always presupposed even if it cannot be demonstrated. The great merit of phenomenology is to have investigated hitherto neglected areas like the nature of experience. However, in Kristeva's view its limit is revealed when it becomes evident that the transcendental ego cannot be transcended. In brief, the phenomenological subject is ultimately the unitary subject of 'thetic' consciousness where the division of subject and object is eternalized. More specifically, Kristeva says

(1) that the *hyle*, which is always functional (in the Husserlian sense) since it is signifiable, apprehended, or named, appears directly to thetic consciousness, (2) that it is the projection of consciousness' positionality, and (3) that the same is true for everything that may appear heterogeneous to the noematic network of phenomenology – from 'perception' to the phenomenological 'drives' making up the ante-predicative sphere.[30]

The limit of phenomenological research is that it always, and inevitably, refers back to an ultimate unity, a posited subject of experience, a Cartesian subject in fact[31] which is already an 'I', already the result of the distinction between subject and object. The 'thetic', then, is precisely the positionality deriving from the distinction between subject and object. And Kristeva further says that

All enunciation, whether of a word or of a sentence, is thetic. It requires an identification; in other words, the subject must separate from and through his image, from and through his objects.[32]

This thetic phase is the precondition of the subject of the *énonciation*, which, as Kristeva acknowledges, approximates phenomenology's transcendental ego:

Let us first acknowledge, with Husserl, this thetic character of the signifying act, which establishes the transcendent object and the transcendental ego of communication (and consequently of sociability), before going beyond the Husserlian problematic ....[33]

Before we go 'beyond the Husserlian problematic' and explain Kristeva's theory of 'rejection', the importance of the thetic should be underlined. For the thetic is also the precondition of the difference between signifier and signified, denotation and connotation, language and referent; in effect it is the basis of all theses and antitheses, of all oppositions. As Kristeva notes on numerous occasions,[34] there is no language without the thetic; it is a necessary boundary originating in the mirror stage and is the basis of all structural relations. Mention of the mirror stage links the thetic clearly with the symbolic paternal function – the condition of signification and representation. When, in a poetic work, the semiotic violates the order of the symbolic, the thetic itself is challenged. For, says Kristeva, poetic language would 'wipe out sense through nonsense and laughter'.[35] That is, it would induce a jouissance that is prior to the mirror stage, and thus prior to the thetic. Or again: 'modern poetic language ... attacks not only denotation (the positioning of the object) but meaning (the positioning of enunciating subject) as well.'[36]

Phenomenology does make some headway towards understanding the position of the subject in the signifying process, but its subject is still the relatively rationalistic subject of an always already posited symbolic order. Kristeva, however, is interested in the process whereby this subject is constituted, an interest precisely spelled out in her development, within a framework of Hegelian negativity, of Freud's theory of drives. The linking of drives to negativity is summarized in Kristeva's concept of rejection.[37]

Negation is a logical operation carried out by a judging consciousness. Negativity is the precondition of the judging consciousness and its logic. Indeed, negation and dichotomy, Kristeva indicates, have to be distinguished, from negativity and heteronomy.[38] Maybe because there is still a slightly logical connotation to the term negativity, and thus an absence of a sense of expenditure and drive energy, the term 'rejection' becomes the more appropriate term for describing the pre-verbal, heterogeneous semiotic function.[39] Rejection could be described as what is repressed – kept at bay – in the operation of the symbolic. It consists of a process of drive charges characteristic of what Kristeva calls after certain psycholinguists, the 'concrete operations'[40] of the pre-symbolic phase of the individual's development. Gestures, refusal (as opposed to negation: saying 'no'), laughter, holophrastic utterances, echolalias, etc., are examples of these concrete operations which are never entirely repressed or expelled from the symbolic. The point, therefore, is that through these operations, the energy charges of the drives become *part of* – not language – but the signifying process. The drive activity of the body is what is *rejected* by, but is present in, the symbolic. Drives, as a result, cannot be understood within Kristeva's framework simply as bio-physiological processes.[41] Even less should they become a kind of origin of human behaviour, or the basis of vitalism and posited as a life force. In fact, for psychoanalysis, the drives are on the side of death and the pleasure of destructiveness, of sadism.[42] The drives, then, are 'already semiotic' energy charges which

> extract the body from its homogeneous expanse and turn it into a space bound to exterior space; they are the forces which trace the *chora* of the process.[43]

Although corporeal and biological, drives appear in an 'already social' space,[44] and are thus already part of the signifying process. For Kristeva, it is inadequate to assign the drives to a non-social domain – even though they also constitute the basis of a transgression of the social.

Rejection, then, is part – albeit the most dominant – of the drives. More specifically, psychoanalysis links it in a fundamental way to the anal-aggressive drive. In a succinct formulation, Kristeva says indeed that rejection is 'precisely the semiotic mode of this permanent aggressivity'.[45] Emerging just prior to the mirror phase, the anal-aggressive drive is equivalent to the separation of the subject from the mother through the expulsion of the maternal object. Here, the importance of Freud's oft-cited 'Fort-Da' story in *Beyond the Pleasure Principle*,[46] becomes clearer. For the child's expulsion and retrieval of the cotton reel would not simply *symbolize* the disappearance and re-appearance of the mother, but would constitute, in its repetition, the presence of anality, and evidence of the subject's expulsion of/separation from the mother. Put another way, the child's separation from the mother that the interdiction against incest articulates (the 'no' of the (symbolic) law) is founded on rejection. Hence Kristeva's statement that, 'Negativity is the rejection that the subject represses in saying "No" . . . .'[47] Although rejection is the precondition of the symbolic, and thus of language and symbolization, it is heterogeneous to it. If rejection is not regulated and the discharge of affect is not at least partially repressed by the Oedipal phase, the very formation of symbolicity can be seriously inhibited, giving rise to psychosis. Language acquisition thus implies the suppression of the intensely pleasurable anal drive, the drive separating the subject from real objects. Hence the expulsion of/separation from the (maternal) object is also constitutive of the object-in-reality. The latter is only signifiable as being *in absentia* in the sign: that is, the object is *posited* as real in the symbolic. Were the suppression of rejection in the symbolic to be absolute, were all affect to be expelled from language, the result would be an impossibly rigid and regulated symbolic realm. Rejection as semiotic processes constantly shakes up the symbolic, renders it unstable and open to potentially new forms:

> rejection therefore constitutes the return of expulsion . . . within the domain of the constituted subject: rejection *re*constitutes real objects, 'creates' new ones, reinvents the real, and re-symbolizes it.[48]

Two signifying modalities permitting 'the survival of rejection to the extent that they harmonize the shattering brought about by rejection', are what Kristeva calls 'oralization' and 'homosexual phratry'. The first amounts to a 'reunion with the mother's body' evoked by the material, non-denotative, 'vocalic' body, a body of the 'throat, voice, and breasts: music, rhythm, prosody, paragrams, and the matrix of the prophetic parabola; the Oedipus complex of a far-off incest . . .'.[49]

Homosexual phratry (evocative of Freud's primal horde), on the other hand, while always inseparable from 'oralization', breaks up the unity of a single rationality, punctures the homogeneity of a system – pluralizes the law, in effect, or at least refuses to accept the existing law. It introduces the *other* into the symbolic. Mallarmé's poetry is an example of the rhythms, etc., of oralization, while the 'logical distortions' in Lautréamont exemplify homosexual phratry. One could also think here of the nonsense poetry of Edward Lear and a Spike Milligan Goon script.

Rejection makes negativity a positive force or an expenditure (cf. Bataille). Negativity is thus not pure nothingness, the other side of a symmetrical, logical opposition. It is a semioticized expenditure. As the term 'expenditure' implies, rejection is not a constant or even static force, but is rather the movement of excitation and discharge. Such an alternation between excitation and discharge opens the way to a difference in energy charges forming the basis of an engram, or mark, the basis of thetic heterogeneity: '. . . rejection generates thetic *heterogeneity* under very precise biological and social conditions . . .'.[50] The conditions of the sign's emergence are thus also set up. Certain avant-garde texts have, as Kristeva sees it, tapped into this differential movement of expenditure, thereby disturbing the conventional and familiar forms of the pheno-text: its syntax, grammar, meaning, and logic.

The family as a productive unit and all institutions of society founded on representation fight to keep rejection at bay, if they do not completely repress it. The degree to which rejection, and thus the semiotic, is repressed goes precisely to the heart of Kristeva's analysis of the role of the artistic avant-garde in late-nineteenth-century France. Put most simply, in a society where rejection is entirely stifled, symbolic structures remain the same and there is a risk that rejection will emerge in an entirely destructive, violent, and negative form, as occurred under modern fascism. If Marxism (towards which Kristeva's attention is directed on a number of occasions in *La Révolution du langage poétique*[51]) is to realize its desire to change society, to make it the object of a practice, and to live out the dynamic insight of class *struggle*, then it cannot merely resort to being a humanism; that is, it cannot allow itself to become a form quite familiar to the static ego of representation and the state. Indeed, to be viable as a non-bourgeois political force, Marxism cannot afford to reject the import of Hegelian negativity (which, we recall, is not negation) and accept the Feuerbachian compromise of 'man' (i.e., ego, consciousness, homogeneity, etc.). The hostile attitude many Marxists exhibit, and have exhibited, towards the artistic avant-garde, is a sign that Marxism has not avoided this humanist trap.

For Kristeva, genuine dialectical materialism 'stresses *process* over identification, *rejection* over desire, heterogeneity over signifier, *struggle* over structure'.[52] By focusing on rejection and thus the semiotic, Kristeva sees herself as providing a truly 'dialectical materialist theory of signifiance';[53] here, her break with Marxism is thus not yet irrevocable.

To say that the semiotic, and thus rejection, is heterogeneous, is to say that the effects of rejection – in art, for example – cannot be predicted or grasped by existing symbolic forms. As Kristeva puts it, the heterogeneous element is that which 'the symbolizing social structure ... cannot grasp'.[54] As heterogeneous rupture, poetic language at the end of the nineteenth century is a greater challenge to capitalist society than Marxist politics – provided that the poetic artistic work is understood to be more than the individual artist's creation (in which case it would remain a 'signifying experience') and actually becomes a challenge to, if not the transgression of, the existing historical form of the symbolic. As transgression in this sense, poetic language becomes a 'signifying practice'.[55] The difference between 'experience' and 'practice' here is homologous with the difference between 'subjective' and 'objective'. Practice is therefore equivalent to a loss of subjectivity in a 'nonsymbolized outside': 'Practice is determined by the pulverization of the unity of consciousness by a nonsymbolized outside, on the basis of objective contradictions and, as such, it is the place where the signifying *process* is carried out.'[56] More succinctly, Kristeva has called transgression 'the key moment in practice', and transgression is the transgression of the unity 'proper to the transcendental ego'.[57] Practice, therefore, is the key to understanding the possible political and social implications of poetic language.

Because practice is a reconnecting of subject and object in an autonomous movement, and is not simply reducible to self-conscious action (in which case it would follow the predictable path mapped out by the symbolic), it is also a key moment in putting the subject in process.[58] Consequently, self-conscious acts as such do not necessarily achieve anything new; practice, on the other hand, can usher in something new. And for Kristeva, laughter is the prototypical instance of a truly innovative practice:

> The practice of the text is a kind of laughter whose only explosions are those of language. The pleasure obtained from the lifting of inhibitions is immediately invested in the production of the new. Every practice which produces something new (a new device) is a practice of laughter: it obeys laughter's logic and provides the subject with laughter's advantages. When practice is not laughter, there is nothing new; where there is nothing new, practice cannot be provoking: it is at best a repeated, empty act.[59]

The text, then, is not a political force at the level of the symbolic, the level of a univocal (ideological) message which would be communicated to an addressee. On the contrary, avant-garde texts fulfil what Kristeva calls their 'ethical' (and thus ultimately political) function, when the signifying mechanisms are themselves put into question in a practice. Hence the ethical function of the text has nothing to do with ideological purity, but with a semiotic practice which 'pluralizes, pulverizes, "musicates"' all ossified forms. And Kristeva continues this line of thought by saying that,

> This conception of the ethical function of art separates us, in a radical way, from one that would commit art to serving as the representation of a so-called progressive ideology or an avant-garde socio-historical philosophy.[60]

The semiotic disposition

So as to illustrate and clarify the way that the semiotic geno-text organizes itself in the pheno-text, Kristeva carries out, in *La Révolution du langage poétique*,[61] a detailed analysis of works by both Mallarmé and Lautréamont. Four different levels provide the focus of this analysis: the morphophonematic, the syntactic, the pronomial, and the contextual. These levels constitute part of what she calls the 'semiotic disposition' of the text, which is normally outside the province of scientific (especially linguistic) research.

Before noting the general features of Kristeva's analyses, we return for a moment to 'Blue Poles', and Jackson Pollock painting.

The vermilion dances in 'Blue Poles'; but only because it is a broken line traversed by other lines, that is, by other colours – particularly the cobalt of the 'poles'. The yellow 'explodes' and also flows. White drips down and, like the aluminium, works in fine webs of line. The point, overall, is that the 'pulverized' image becomes a pure rhythm of intensities: there is only colour and line (and thus the paint itself), but 'rhythmed', semioticized, so that the spectator can 'experience' the pure expenditure of energy involved – the expenditure of the anal drive, as Kristeva would have it. Expenditure produces stasis, or 'un arrêt éphémère' ('an ephemeral stop').[62] Expenditure thus presupposes stasis – the breaks in the lines in 'Blue Poles', the 'explosiveness' of yellow, etc. – which, in Pollock's work, or the work of any artist, is semioticized and becomes 'art' as it emerges within the social sphere. In this way the destructiveness of the drive (it attacks the symbolic) is made to serve creative ends. Through rhythm Pollock provides an analytic insight into the basis (the materiality) of painting, and possibly into the basis of art itself. The challenge to the symbolic posed by the 'pulverization' of the image is now seen to induce (or even force) a confrontation between the materiality and the drive energy constitutive of the primary phase of the symbolic order. In other words, Pollock's art reveals that the real is to be equated more with the material foundation of painting than with the representations in the symbolic which so seduce the ego. Such would be the way, therefore, that 'Blue Poles' comes to illustrate, but rather is the semiotic dimension of the signifying process.

Similarly, in Hans Namuth's photographs, Pollock's own image begins to disintegrate in the blur of movement (the partial obliteration of the figure in a clash between light and dark), which becomes equivalent to Pollock's expenditure of energy into his paintings. Seen in this way, these paintings become the mark of an energy expenditure which *is* Pollock painting; they do not express Pollock in any way. Indeed, as the mark of a network of energies which constitute this artist as a symbolic being, 'Blue Poles', and works of a similar genre, constitute Pollock as much as they are supposedly created by him. At least this is the conclusion we draw in light of Kristeva's concept of the material, semiotic dimension of the signifying process. Consequently, because Pollock is insepar- able from the *production* of his works, and that, as a result, a 'Blue Poles' would 'pulverize' the meaning and unity constitutive of the punctual, unitary subject, Kristeva begins to speak about a signifying *practice*. This concept of practice is explained in the discussion of Mallarmé's and Lautréamont's poetry. Let us now focus on this discussion.

Mallarmé

From what has been said already, it follows that Kristeva will not be concerned to isolate the true symbolic meaning of Mallarmé's poetry. Nor will she translate Mallarmé into everyday communi- cative language, or even describe accurately the formal linguistic features of Mallarmé's writing – whether or not the latter seems to make 'sense'. Still less will Kristeva analyse syntactic structures for their own sake. To adopt these or similar approaches is to remain tied exclusively to the pheno-text, and oblivious of the workings of the semiotic geno-text. For Kristeva, even Chomsky's generative theory with its distinction between 'competence' and 'performance' that could signal a breaking away from a severely formalistic linguistics, is still imprisoned in a static, phenomenological view of language and the subject:

> generative theory concentrates its attention on what we have called a *symbolic* functioning, sustained by a cartesian subject foreclosed to the signifier. In consequence, this theory is not interested in the *process* of the subject which may be glimpsed in the semiotic processes of condensation and transposition.[63]

Like most strictly linguistic approaches to language, generative theory thus does not broach what Kristeva calls the 'translinguistic',[64] 'trans-symbolic' rhythm of the geno-text, which 'is a battle against syntactic linearity in and through its inevitable necessity'.[65]

In light of this translinguistic/trans-symbolic sphere, Kristeva analyses 'semiotic devices', such as rhythm, repetition, condensation, and metonymy, etc., which reveal the drive basis of the symbolic order. This analytic process, however, only assumes its full significance within specific social and historical conditions. In fact, the thesis expounded in *La Révolution du langage poétique* is that an artistic practice is inseparable from a specific social formation, whether or not this is generally recognized at a social level. Thus the end of the nineteenth century in France brought with it a new 'signifying economy': the poeticization of prose which can be called the 'text'.[66] The text is neither poetry nor prose, but 'theorizes poetry' by retaining the possibility of denotation and the thetic. As opposed to the previous transformation from poetry to prose in the thirteenth century [67] which had made prose the bearer of a unique truth, the text emerges at the end of the nineteenth century to signify a 'plural' and 'uncertain' truth.[68] Mallarmé's work thus comes to exemplify, in Kristeva's hands, the constitution of the text as such. How precisely is this so?

Generally speaking, Mallarmé's poetry (for example 'Prose' analysed by Kristeva[69]) discloses the drive basis of phonation through 'musicalizing' the natural (national) language. Because French – unlike English, German, or Russian – has a monotone syllabic accentuation, making the musical resources of the language apparent becomes a problem. Mallarmé, says Kristeva, along with the French avant-garde in general, brought out the key to the potential uniqueness of the French language: *timbre*. In this regard, sonorous differences are achieved through the phonemic[70] drive base perceptible in displacements, condensations, transpositions, and repetitions. These latter often distort, if they do not destroy, syntax and grammar – as occurs in Mallarmé's 'Un coup de dés', a poem which, in addition, accentuates the challenge to syntax and grammar through the unique disposition of the words on the page. As mentioned earlier,[71] Ernest Fraenkel has produced designs evocative of ocean waves which are based on the 'typography' of 'Un coup de dés'.

To emphasize the importance of timbre in Mallarmé's poems is, at the same time, to point out that there is no single, unified meaning underlying the letters on the page. Rather, a pulverized unity becomes perceptible at the semiotic level of sound differences. Thus just as we have said that Pollock uses colour and line as the rhythmic trace of an *expenditure* of energy, so we could say that Mallarmé comes to present sounds as the same sort of rhythmic trace. These sounds consist of what Kristeva calls 'oral' and 'anal' phonemes indicative of intensive drive activity which are particularly evident in the infant's first morphemes – for example, in the French, '*mama*' and '*papa*'. Here Kristeva argues that the phoneme /m/ is evocative of sucking, and is thus 'oral', while /p/ is explosive, and thus 'anal'. Whether or not such an argument is sustainable in this particular case, the overriding idea is that the acquisition of language involves a period in which drive activity dominates the production of sounds. Evoking this period of language acquisition in artistic works can be a means of breaking loose from a very constricting historical form of the symbolic: its institutions and modes of representation. Mallarmé's 'timbre' poetry, therefore becomes a way of breaking out of ossified symbolic forms such as, perhaps, realist narrative. In highlighting the rhythm of phonic differences, or the timbre of the language, Mallarmé at the same time highlights the 'semiotic *chora* which underlies the language system'.[72] Furthermore, Kristeva sees Mallarmé achieving in literature what Webern's *Klangfarbenmelodie* – sound-colour melody, a timbre melody – achieved in modern music. And this is interesting, because Schoenberg, the leader of the 'Second Viennese School' of which Webern was a member, said that 'People must realize that there comes a time when a musician is no longer at ease using the same old interval-progression.'[73] In other words, the familiar and entrenched musical form based on the diatonic scale had become, for Schoenberg and his school, a limit that *Klangfarbenmelodie* would transcend by pluralizing tonal values, thereby producing rhythms of sound differences in a timbre melody. And, just as language is shown by Kristeva to be irreducible to a symbolic system of communication, so music is shown by Schoenberg and his students, Berg and Webern, to be irreducible to the diatonic scale.

While the 'semiotic devices' pointed to thus far have been phonetic, graphic, and to a lesser extent, intonational, they can also be semantic. Indeed, the drive-based operation of 'condensation' which Freud – along with the term 'displacement' – made famous in his *Interpretation of Dreams*,[74] is crucial for pluralizing meaning. Thus an image, word, or *sémème* (effect of meaning deriving from a specific group of words) may be invested with a 'plurality of significations and drive operations' not apparent in the pheno-text due to the effect of repression. In this vein, Kristeva observes that in the sixth verse of Mallarmé's poem, 'Prose', 'The signifying differential /*floeR*/ "fleur" [flower]' when compared with its appearance in other Mallarméan poems 'is the condensation of semantic features[[75]] like *"maternité"*, *"oralité"*, *"sein"* [breast], but also of *"sublimation"*, *"virginité"*, *"beauté"*, *"esthétique"*, *"calme"*, *"sérénité"*, and *"ironie"*, or *"mort symbolic"* [symbolic death], *"folie productrice d'art"* [madness producing art] . . .'.[76] Kristeva cites the poems, 'Les Fleurs' ('Flowers') and 'L'Azur' ('Azure') as examples of how 'fleur' figures in other poetic contexts thereby pluralizing the semantic base of Mallarmé's poetry.

Read beyond all *formal* limits (grammar, etc.), Mallarmé's poetry is a 'surplus of symbolicity' where even denotation becomes semiotic: 'the denotative textual object is also the semiotic functioning of the text'.[77] Most of all, though, Kristeva emphasizes[78] that Mallarméan poetic rhythm gives expression to the death drive which underlies, and at the same time threatens, every signifying practice. The death drive (total expenditure of energy) emerges at the point where communicative language is about to be extinguished.[79] As rhythm in Mallarmé's work, it shatters syntactic linearity (see 'Un coup de dés') and carries within it an intimation of the destruction of the symbolic. Rhythm *and* a surplus of symbolicity both animate Mallarmé's work: death *and* life are there in creative tension. The semiotic and the symbolic are thus evocative of death and life.

Lautréamont

With Lautréamont's prose poetry, Kristeva focuses on the multiplication of discursive instances characteristic of fiction. The subject of Lautréamont's writing, Kristeva notes, is a divided multiple subject which comes to occupy 'all discursive instances'.[80] Now in the 'normative usage' of language, 'subjectivity allows the localization of a moment in a pronoun which, without being isolated in itself, sustains definite relations with others'.[81] The key pronouns in this situation are of course those of the first, second, and third person (I/you/he). The possibility of these three fundamental discursive instances derives from a successful entry into the symbolic: 'I' (subject/son) separate from 'you' (mother) because 'he' (father) intervenes. This is the famous Freudian triangular structure so crucial, as will be seen in more detail later, both to Kristeva's theory of the text located within a social and economic formation, and to her psychoanalytic theory of the constitution of society. At this point, let us note that all pronouns are a fictional (purely symbolic) presentation of the subject because the 'true' subject is the corporeal subject in process, constituted, as we have seen, in and through displaced and condensed drive activity: the locus in effect, of the semiotic and the symbolic.

Every fictional discourse presupposes the capacity of the writer to occupy all discursive positions in the text, whether or not these simply be the characters of the fiction. Not every fictional piece, however, makes this process of the production of fictive discourse visible. The realist novel, for example, hides its procedures behind verisimilitude. Lautréamont's strategy is just the opposite. In dividing and multiplying itself through an exaggerated process of 'shifterization',[82] Lautréamont's subjectivity becomes kaleidoscopic, with, says Kristeva,

> the subject of the *énonciation* occupying all possible subjective positions, which amounts to producing all possible discursive situations between *I/you/he*. One can say that fiction produces an *incessant permutation of shifters*. . . .[T]he 'I' which normally transcends this act, due to shifterization and permutation, ceases to be a fixed and localizable point and becomes multipliable according to the discursive situations.[83]

Lautréamont's *Les Chants de Maldoror* thus subverts the notion of a single narrative voice, not by destroying narration as such, but by multiplying this position of unity. To say that there are several 'I's is not to imply the repetition of 'one', of unity, but to produce precisely *more than one* position of unity. It is, in short, to challenge the constrictiveness of the conventions of realist and normalist narrative so dominant in the second half of the nineteenth century.

Lautréamont's *Poésies* has a slightly different semiotic status to *Les Chants*. While the latter demonstrates that the subject of writing is not reducible to the writing 'I', so *Poésies*, in Kristeva's hands, demonstrates that the addressee (reader) of a text is also a discursive convention which can be subverted. How is this so?

Every discursive act has its basis in a generalized presupposition. This includes a whole corpus of preceding texts as well as the text's addressee. Both explicitly and implicitly a text addresses the universe constituted by these other texts. Thus in *Poésies*, references are made to a whole range of writers, philosophers, religious and mythical figures of all kinds.[84] Of course, from the position of the symbolic, what is presupposed appears to be prior to the text, just as the writer/author seems to be independent of writing and not constituted by it. As Kristeva says, J. L. Austin's work shows that the presupposed is an 'illocutory' act quite different from a denotative discursive act where language is used to describe something (outside language) for someone (outside language). As immediately obvious illocutory acts, Austin cites what he calls 'performatives': promising, opening a meeting or naming a ship, marriage vows, etc. In effect, 'performatives' are examples of the 'performance of an act *in* saying something as opposed to performance of an act *of* saying something . . .'.[85] As we noted in Chapter 3, recognition of the illocutionary aspect of language can lead to the question of whether any act of language is exclusively descriptive, or 'locutory', as Austin puts it. Or rather, it leads to the question of whether the locutory aspect is but a necessary linguistic *convention* – despite its appearance as being a vehicle for portraying reality.

Kristeva argues that if the locutory aspect of language harbouring what is presupposed is indeed a convention of the symbolic like syntax and grammar, it will be susceptible to subversion. And in fact texts like *Poésies* show that the presupposed may be effaced by rejection, just as it (rejection) shatters subjective unity and morphomatic or syntactic normativity.[86] By making the presupposed vulnerable, the modern text shows it to be essential to the normative (locutory) usage of language. To bring the presupposed into question, to 'transform', for example, the locution presupposing an interlocutor into an illocutionary act, is again to reveal the text as a *'signifying practice'* rather than a *'discursive act'*.[87] And *Poésies* effects such a transformation – in part, by denying propositions of the presupposed discourse in 'oppositional transformations having a negative effect', or by subtly modifying the presupposed discourse in 'oppositional transformations having an indefinite effect'. As an example of the first kind of transformation, Kristeva gives, amongst others, the following:

> Pascal: *'J'écrirai mes pensées sans ordre . . . .'* [Lit: *'I will write my thoughts without order . . . .'*].
> Ducasse [Lautréamont]: *'J'écrirai mes pensées avec ordre . . . .'* [Lit: *'I will write my thoughts with order . . . .*][88]

Logically, Lautréamont directly opposes Pascal here. In an example of an indefinite opposition, however, the logical relation is far from clear-cut – as the next example shows:

> Pascal: *'. . . et leur font des impressions fausses.'* [Lit: *'. . . and make them false impressions.'*]
> Ducasse: *'. . . leur font des impressions que je ne garantis pas fâcheuses'.* [Lit: . . . *make them impressions that I cannot guarantee to be unpleasant'.*][89]

It would be necessary to go into more detail than is possible here to explain, clearly and conclusively, how Kristeva charts the movement in *Poésies* away from the locutory level of logic and ideology towards the illocutory level. Suffice to point out, though, that the above examples of statements by Pascal and Lautréamont illustrate the way that such transformations begin to become ambiguous. In particular, Kristeva says, the "je ne garantis pas" renders ambiguous, not only this transformation, but all Lautréamont's statements. Ambiguity, Kristeva suggests, is increased by the rhythmic constraints of the text which blur meaning.[90] Such blurring of the pheno-text's meaning is precisely what brings about an illocutory effect. For the more meaning is unclear, the less so is the *fact* of the rhythm of the statements, the *fact* of the text (both 'pheno-' and 'geno-') itself. Now, the text's mode of coherence is no longer to be found in the logic of the locutory, or pheno-level, but rather in poetic negativity – the level beyond, as it were, the symbolic's Kantian negation.[91] Oppositional transformations having an indefinite effect at a locutory level, now become exemplary of the ambiguity bringing the rhythm of the geno-text into view.

In its simplest form, the thesis upon which the above argument is based is that both Mallarmé's and Lautréamont's writings ask to be appreciated not only as vehicles of a message – whether poetic or scientific – but also as being poetic in the broadest sense of a 'signifying practice'. It is now incumbent upon us to discover the socio-historical import of this signifying practice.

Poetic language in history and society

In the last section of *La Révolution du langage poétique*, 'L'Etat et le mystère', Kristeva argues that in order to make real headway towards the social and economic transformation of society, the very basis of the social has to be confronted. Not to do this is to risk having the same socio-economic conditions reconstituted under a new name: for example, state socialism becoming another version of bourgeois social relations. The point, once again, is that a Kantian negation – which can give rise to a relatively legitimized opposition – must give way to Hegelian negativity which brings the symbolic order as such into question. A full appreciation of the force of this argument requires that we discuss Kristeva's Freudian view of the basis of society.

As has been said on a number of occasions in this chapter, the social and the symbolic are almost synonymous in Kristeva's eyes, especially as language is above all a social instrument. But what is the symbolic in the psychoanalytic perspective here being outlined? The short answer is that it is, above all, order or regulation of some kind, especially as exemplified by the notion of the law. And so Kristeva says that for society as such to exist, 'subjects are called upon to participate in a law whose determinations and articulations they neither know nor control'.[92] Perhaps this is why myths about the origin of society tend to describe the origin of this law.

In the Freudian version of the mythical origin of the law, the sons kill the primordial father in order to possess his wives. The sons thus commit a murder and after the event suffer guilt and remorse. As a result, *in the name of the father*, the sons renounce their claim to the father's women. In the name of the *dead* father, then, the sons pay homage, symbolically, to the one they have killed and thus put an end to the state of unbridled jouissance in which there would be no obstacle between mother and son. Kristeva sees this murder and its renunciation as concomitant with the interdiction against incest, which, for Lévi-Strauss, is constitutive of the symbolic law and society as such. Lévi-Strauss thereby confirms the Freudian thesis – at least to the extent of agreeing that the possibility of society depends on some kind of regulation of human relations. For their parts, the sons desire direct access to the mother which the interdiction against incest – and thus the symbolic – opposes.

'Murder', therefore, is a name for this unthinkable point 'before' the law. But, Kristeva argues, it also alludes to something very real: the operation of the drives as rejection and jouissance. Rejection and jouissance do not disappear with the institution of the symbolic, but are repressed. Indeed, as we have seen, the drives are the foundation of the symbolic just as, in Freud's myth, murder becomes the foundation of the law. In every culture and in every society – *qua* society and culture – a specific interaction may be observed between the symbolic and drive energy. In short, every society could be described as a particular articulation of (relatively) repressed drive energy. Within certain religions and cultures, sacrifice has historically been the way in which rejection as such has been made explicit. Sacrifice is the re-enactment of the founding death ushering in the symbolic: it could be 'the killing of a man, a slave, a prisoner, an animal'.[93] Sacrifice – to summarize Kristeva's earlier remarks – is in fact constitutive of the thetic moment dividing the symbolic from the pre-symbolic. It is violent and at the same time controls violence in becoming the *symbol* of social order. From Kristeva's perspective sacrifice is not, as René Girard argues,[94] an 'unleashing of animal violence', but a 'violent and regulatory'[95] thetic moment.

While religion takes over sacrifice, thus 'theologizing' the thetic and even eliminating violent jouissance altogether, art is, in Kristeva's words, the 'semiotization of the symbolic'.[96] Art has great potential to facilitate social transformation. For it is not simply destructive – as is the case with the uncontrolled violence of fascism and, sometimes, of anarchism – nor does it depend on *organized* force, or violence – as does the revolutionary party (with the risk of institutionalizing violence within the framework of the symbolic it is trying to dislodge) – but is a practice of expenditure capable of confronting often ossified versions of the symbolic: the subject, the family, the state.

In broad outline, 'L'Etat et le mystère' treats Mallarmé's and

149

Lautréamont's texts in terms of how these become signifying practices confronting a particularly static version of the symbolic embodied in the bourgeois representative state and society in late-nineteenth-century France. Their art brings into view the nature of the text within an economic and social formation: the issue of class consciousness and the limits of power, anarchism as a political strategy, the institution of marriage, nationalism, the basis of sovereignty and, especially, the nature of the relation between the mother and society – the mother as the 'mystery' of reproduction in society. It now remains for us to outline the way the avant-garde text confronts the state and opens up another way of relating to reproduction in a capitalist society. First of all, however, we need to know what the form of the modern state was in nineteenth-century France.

For Kristeva, the distinguishing feature of the modern state is that it is the embodiment of representation. In short, the One stands for the Many, to use Hobbes' terms[97] – or, as Kristeva says, the state claims to be the collectivity of all collectivities, the set of all sets, as was pointed out in Chapter 4. Kristeva's point is that such a notion is a fiction: the state is not 'the masses become subject', but a representation, a projected unity deriving from the symbolic. The state is the myth that the institutions comprising it (parliament, bureaucracy, family, science, etc.) are the embodiment of reality. The State as representation also has its basis in the order pertaining to the Name-of-the-Father – otherwise called the paternal function – which keeps rejection at bay. The state in this sense is founded on a law which is 'phallic': it refers to the Name-of-the-Father as the basis of signification – the phallus being the signifier of all signification, and the precondition of representation. Whether or not the phallus can be convicted of the sins of which it has been accused by Jacques Derrida and certain feminists, representation can certainly be the basis for privileging the static, punctual, symbolic subject which stifled the 'subject in process' in nineteenth-century France through the agency of a dominant state apparatus. Under such conditions, the state is revealed as fetishism writ large: it becomes a *substitute* for the ensemble of social relations – for the ensemble of social *differences*, more precisely. Here the state fetishistically privileges the symbolic, by substituting the latter (and thus itself) for reality. Furthermore, the social contract on which the state is founded, generally tends to exclude the drives from social life and in so doing denies the thetic moment

150

(separation of symbolic from pre-symbolic through a murder, etc.). Fetishism here becomes another name for the denial of the crime at the origin of society.

Unsurprisingly, Kristeva finds that those societies with a very highly developed state apparatus are also those based on a system of the production of goods. In such western capitalist societies, the family is no longer the fundamental unit of production, but becomes a marginalized point of the reproduction of the species. The reproduction of the species, however, points to the importance of the woman, particularly as mother, in society. This *place* of the woman, ushering in sexual difference, is beyond the ken of a fully-fledged, state-dominated excessively paternalistic society. This is because sexual difference, like the founding crime, shows up a lack in the symbolic. The symbolic, says Kristeva, is fundamentally phallic; but in order to comprehend sexual difference, it needs to become 'genital':

> In other words, the paternal law hides genital jouissance and ensures procreation for the survival of society, provided, of course, that the importance of the mother remains unconscious or condemned to mystery.[98]

Genitality, however, cannot be entirely represented by the paternal law because it exceeds the latter's singular, unitary, phallic nature. 'Mystery', too, integrates the woman into the symbolic; it socializes difference, wipes out the evident lack in the symbolic and homogenizes sociality. Religions here make a cult of woman as mystery setting her apart from society *in* society. Mystery, which appears in the symbolic, is not therefore a means of giving permanent identity and thus equality to women, but a way of ensuring 'bonds between men'.[99] What is denied in particular, says Kristeva, is a maternal jouissance which, while being the symbolic's foundation, can never be contained within it. The mother in a state-dominated bourgeois society, however, is contained within a determinate unitary category. This is the 'phallic' mother at the threshold of the opposition between nature and culture. Elsewhere, Kristeva writes of the 'phallic' mother that:

> if . . . there were no one on this threshold, if the mother were not, that is, if she were not phallic, then every speaker would be led to conceive of its Being in relation to some void, a nothingness

asymmetrically opposed to this Being, a permanent threat against, first, its mastery, and ultimately, its stability.[100]

Hence, the phallic mother is a denial of the pre-symbolic, semiotic dimension of society and culture. Recognition of maternal jouissance in, for example, the 'music' of Mallarmé's text, or in the radical decentring of the symbolic subject in both Mallarmé and Lautréamont, forms what Kristeva calls the 'genitality' of poetic language which undermines fetishism in sexuality and language: it exceeds the limits of the imaginary subject's scope and shatters the unity of an excessive social homogeneity.

France in the second half of the nineteenth century is a particularly acute example of an excess of the symbolic and representation manifest in a narrow paternalism, *étatism*, and colonialism. In short, there is a generalized fetishism which includes a fetishization of the pheno-text (cf. realism and naturalism). And it occurs at the very heart of political and social upheavals: the 1848 revolutions, the *coup d'état* of Louis Napoleon in 1852, the Franco-Prussian war of 1870, and the Paris Commune of 1871. None of this political turmoil achieved – even for the left with its theory of class consciousness – a weakening of the existing system of the symbolic because all sides – proletariat, peasants, bourgeoisie – believed in the existing symbolic order. On the other hand, Kristeva does not deny that the above events had an effect on the existing social order. The Commune, for instance, was a definite, if unsuccessful, challenge to authority.

In such circumstances, the avant-garde artist will be politically successful to the extent that he or she subverts the existing mode of the symbolic order, rather than engaging in an open ideological confrontation. The avant-garde poetic text in this way becomes a permanent confrontation with the law. Or as Kristeva says, 'Music in letters is the counterpart of the parliamentary *oratio* ....'[101] Similarly, the text comes to give a voice to what had been so vigorously excluded from the social scene: genital jouissance. Mallarmé's text, in particular, 'is the first – ambiguous and prudent – attempt to transpose, in a text at all levels, genital jouissance in its relation to procreation'.[102] Lautréamont's *Chants*, for their part, are not only the story of Maldoror's war 'against the Name-of-the-Father', but also represent in the narrative the irruption of the drive in the symbolic'.[103]

When Kristeva says that 'no language can sing unless it

confronts the Phallic Mother',[104] she means that no progress can be made in the presentation of genitality (difference) in the text unless the negativity-rejection of 'music in letters' pluralizes the imaginary, mystical unity of a mother at the origins of the symbolic who, *qua* unity, becomes masculinized.[105] And so because the musicalization of language is bound up with the individual's relation to others, sexuality is fundamental to textuality. The text is therefore a 'family affair'; hence Kristeva's very close scrutiny of everything Mallarmé and Lautréamont write about the paternal function as well as *how* they write about it. In the avant-garde text sociality is subverted because the text (both geno- and pheno-) subverts representation, the unitary subject, the idea of the phallic mother, and thus the bourgeois family structure. The revolutionary force of poetic language links into the social revolution as a *practice* which prepares the way for another form of the symbolic order.

I shall not go into any more detail in our attempt to distil the essential part of Kristeva's complex, subtle, and often elaborate analysis of Mallarmé's and Lautréamont's writings. Rather, I conclude this chapter by reiterating the importance of the infinite. For if Lautréamont in particular breaks down symmetrical oppositions – such as father–mother – and introduces into the narrative the drive which, in a sense, embraces them, this negativity also evokes the infinite discussed in Chapter 4. The infinite, in fact, is another name for negativity, even as rejection. For we recall that the infinite is not the infinite sum of finite numbers (in which case it would be logically finite), but a 'transfinite' number, forming the basis of all finite numbers and exceeding them. This means that the infinite is not entirely of the symbolic order, but is also of the order of the real. It, too, challenges unity and thereby becomes another mode of access to the semiotic.

Notes

1 See 'L'Etat et le mystère', Section C of *La Révolution du langage poétique*, pp. 359–600.
2 For Kristeva's discussion of the limits of the phenomenological theory of the subject, see in particular, *Revolution in Poetic Language*, pp. 19–37, and *passim*.
3 For Kristeva, jouissance is inseparable from drive charges, rhythms, flows, and the constraints which generate these flows through a 'damming up' or what Freud calls repression.

4 See Julia Kristeva, *Revolution in Poetic Language*, Part I, pp. 19–106.

5 1952, 211 x 487.5 cms, Australian National Gallery, Canberra.

6 Barbara Rose (ed.), *Pollock Painting*, photographs by Hans Namuth (New York, Agrinde Publications, 1980), no pagination.

7 Hans Namuth in ibid.

8 Lee Krasner in ibid.

9 Julia Kristeva, 'La Voie lactée de Jackson Pollock, 1912–1959' ('Jackson Pollock's Milky Way, 1912–1959'), in *Art Press*, no. 55 (January, 1982), p. 6.

10 Kristeva, 'L'Engendrement de la formule', p. 284.

11 ibid.

12 See ibid., p. 303, 'A *generative*, infinite, plural *textuality* replaces *the* signifier.' Kristeva's emphasis.

13 ibid., pp. 351–2.

14 Kristeva, *Revolution in Poetic Language*, p. 25.

15 ibid.

16 See also Kristeva's discussion of this in *Powers of Horror*, pp. 13–15.

17 See Kristeva, *Polylogue*, p. 14.

18 See Kristeva, *La Révolution du langage poétique*, pp. 453–9.

19 Julia Kristeva, 'Giotto's Joy', in *Desire in Language*, pp. 210–36, esp. pp. 210–22.

20 ibid., p. 225.

21 See for example, Giotto, 'Interior of the Arena Chapel, Padua', ibid., p. 213.

22 Kristeva, 'Giotto's joy', p. 225.

23 Julia Kristeva, 'Mother according to Bellini', in *Desire in Language*, p. 269.

24 Kristeva, *Revolution in Poetic Language*, p. 185.

25 Eight out of these twenty-one essays have been translated in Kristeva, *Desire in Language*.

26 Kristeva, *Revolution in Poetic Language*, p. 34.

27 Kristeva, *Polylogue*, p. 14.

28 G. W. F. Hegel, *Science of Logic, Volume II*, trans. W. H. Johnston and L. G. Struthers (London, George Allen & Unwin, 4th impression, 1966), p. 91.

29 See Chapter 1, p. 15.

30 Kristeva, *Revolution in Poetic Language*, p. 32. 'Noematic' may be defined as 'reflective perception'. It is intimately linked to the notion of the objective world in the experience of a knowing subject, as opposed to the objective world as it *is* in reality. Phenomenology thus recognizes a gap between experience and reality.

31 Kristeva, *Revolution in Poetic Language*, p. 32.

32 ibid., p. 43.

33 Kristeva, *Desire in Language*, p. 131.

34 See for example, ibid. and p. 132; *Polylogue*, pp. 107–8, and see *Revolution in Poetic Language*, pp. 43–50.

35 Kristeva, *Desire in Language*, p. 142.
36 Kristeva, *Revolution in Poetic Language*, p. 58.
37 See ibid, Part II, 'Negativity: rejection', pp. 107–64.
38 Kristeva, *Polylogue*, p. 64.
39 ibid.
40 See ibid., p. 66.
41 See Kristeva, 'The System and the Speaking Subject', p. 28.
42 See Kristeva, *Revolution in Poetic Language*, pp. 151–2 and 171.
43 Kristeva, *Polylogue*, p. 69.
44 ibid., p. 67.
45 Kristeva, *Revolution in Poetic Language*, p. 150.
46 Sigmund Freud, *Beyond the Pleasure Principle*, *SE*, vol. XVIII, pp. 14–15.
47 Kristeva, 'Le Sujet en procès', in *Polylogue*, p. 65.
48 Kristeva, *Revolution in Poetic Language*, p. 155.
49 ibid., p. 153.
50 ibid., p. 171.
51 See in particular, Kristeva, in *La Révolution du langage poétique*, pp. 375–90.
52 Kristeva, *Revolution in Poetic Language*, p. 179. Kristeva's emphasis.
53 ibid., p. 181.
54 ibid., p. 180.
55 ibid., p. 195.
56 ibid., p. 203.
57 Kristeva, 'The system and the speaking subject', p. 25.
58 See Kristeva, *Polylogue*, p. 134.
59 Kristeva, *Revolution in Poetic Language*, p. 225.
60 ibid., p. 233.
61 See Part B, 'Le Dispositif sémiotique du Texte', pp. 205–358.
62 Kristeva, *Polylogue*, p. 107.
63 Kristeva, *La Révolution du langage poétique*, p. 266.
64 ibid., p. 258.
65 ibid., p. 270.
66 See ibid., p. 289.
67 Outlined in Kristeva, *Le Texte du roman*, see above, Chapter 4.
68 Kristeva, *La Révolution du langage poétique*, p. 289.
69 See ibid., pp. 220–1 and 239–63.
70 'Phonemic' derives, of course, from 'phoneme', which may be defined as the significant (i.e. meaningful) sound of a language.
71 See Chapter 4, and Ernest Fraenkel, *Les Dessins trans-conscients de Stéphane Mallarmé: à propos de la typographie d'un coup de dés* (Paris, Nizet, 1960).
72 Kristeva, *La Révolution du langage poétique*, p. 225.
73 Arnold Schoenberg, *Style and Idea: Selected Writings of Arnold Schoenberg*, trans. Leo Black (London, Faber & Faber, 1975), p. 102.
74 See S. Freud, *The Interpretation of Dreams*, *SE*, vol. IV, pp. 279–309.
75 That is, '*sèmes*' in the narrow sense of the term.

76 Kristeva, *La Révolution du langage poétique*, p. 249.
77 ibid., p. 290.
78 See, for example, ibid., pp. 258, 611, 615–17.
79 See Kristeva, *Polylogue*, p. 341.
80 Kristeva, *La Révolution du langage poétique*, p. 317.
81 ibid., p. 315.
82 Where the meanings of the pronouns vary with the context – or, as Benveniste would say, with the act of discourse. See Chapter 3, and Roman Jakobson, 'Shifters, verbal categories and the Russian verb', in *Selected Writings*, vol. II (The Hague, Mouton, 1971).
83 Kristeva, *La Révolution du language poétique*, pp. 317–18.
84 See ibid., p. 341.
85 J. L. Austin, *How to do Things with Words*, ed. J. O. Urmson and Marina Sbisa (Oxford, Clarendon Press, 2nd edn, rep. 1980), pp. 99–100.
86 See Kristeva, *La Révolution du langage poétique*, p. 340.
87 ibid.
88 ibid., p. 346. Kristeva's emphasis.
89 ibid., p. 350. Kristeva's emphasis.
90 ibid., p. 352.
91 Here, Kristeva also recalls the notion of a 'non-synthetic' union discussed in 'Poésie et négativité'. See above Chapter 4.
92 Kristeva, *La Révolution du langage poétique*, p. 478.
93 Kristeva, *Revolution in Poetic Language*, p. 70. For a useful general outline of the points being made here, see ibid., pp. 72–85.
94 Cf. René Girard, *Violence and the Sacred*, trans. Patrick Gregory (Baltimore, Johns Hopkins, 1977).
95 On Sovereignty, see Georges Dumézil, *Mitra-Varuna: Essai sur deux représentations indo-européennes de la souveraineté* (Paris, Gallimard, 6th edn, 1948).
96 Kristeva, *Revolution in Poetic Language*, p. 79.
97 See Thomas Hobbes, *Leviathan*, Michael Oakshott (ed.) (New York, Collier, 8th printing, 1971), pp. 127–8.
98 Kristeva, *La Révolution du langage poétique*, p. 457.
99 ibid., p. 456.
100 Kristeva, *Desire in Language*, p. 238.
101 Kristeva, *La Révolution du langage poétique*, p. 402.
102 ibid., p. 495.
103 ibid., p. 467.
104 Kristeva, *Desire in Language*, p. 191.
105 ibid., p. 242.

6

Horror, love, melancholy

Célines's . . . horrified laughter: the comedy of abjection . . . An apocalyptic laughter.

And yet, in these times of dreary crisis, what is the point of emphasising the horror of being?

Powers of Horror

Today Narcissus is an exile, deprived of his psychic space, an extraterrestrial with a prehistory bearing, wanting for love.

Tales of Love

It is true that someone unemployed is less suicidal than an abandoned lover but, in times of crisis, melancholy imposes itself, speaks, does its archaeology, produces its representations and its knowledge.

Soleil noir

We have seen that within Kristeva's psychoanalytic framework the semiotic dimension of poetic language corresponds to an experience with the mother. For the artist this mother is also a chora of drive energy, or 'semiotic mobility' that is present in, and potentially disruptive of, language and representation. A technocratic, state-dominated social milieu can severely contain the semiotic both in the sense of a severe and overly strict father, and in the sense of placing everything within a representation.

Horror

In her essay on abjection, *Powers of Horror* (*Pouvoirs de l'horreur*) published in 1980, Kristeva renews her interest in the psychoanalytic status of the mother.[1] *Powers of Horror* is the first of a series of works providing an intense elaboration of three familiar emotional states, or structurations of subjectivity analysed as indicative of the times in which we live: horror, love, and melancholy. The analyst, confronted with the sufferings and joy, fantasies and drive states, etc., of analysands, tries to link analytic listening to the social milieu. Abjection as the psychoanalytical elaboration of universal horror thus connects up with the 'times of dreary crisis', as our epigraph says. But precisely 'what is the point of emphasizing the horror of being?' The short answer is that the control exerted by horror – the abject – can only be the greater if it remains hidden, unknown – unanalysed. In addition, while the abject remains hidden so does the 'other side of religious, moral, and ideological codes on which rest the sleep of individuals and the respites of societies. Such codes are abjection's purification and repression.'[2] Through a refusal to confront the abject, therefore, a fundamental aspect of individual and social life remains in oblivion, and our understanding and capacity to cope are thereby greatly diminished.

All of this is to jump the gun just a little. For in order to understand the full impact of abjection, we need to follow the trajectory of the psychoanalytic elaboration of it: from its place in a theory of the subject, through its appearance as defilement in societies like the Indian, thence to its elaboration in the Judaeo-Christian text, and finally, to its emergence in the 'apocalyptic laughter' of Louis-Ferdinand Céline's writing and, perhaps, in all truly literary works.

The abject as formative of the 'I'

We recall, first of all, that in psychoanalytic theory of Lacanian inspiration, the acquisition of language during the mirror phase (6 to 18 months) marks the intervention of the symbolic (Name-of-the-Father) into the child's universe, and his/her separation from the idyllic state of harmony and continuity which, psychically, *is* the mother. A resultant experience of loss is constitutive of language and desire. This loss, we have noted,[3] is illustrated by

Freud's 'Fort-Da' anecdote. In effect, the acquisition of language allows the subject to symbolize his/her pre-symbolic existence – a time when the 'I' (subject) was united with the 'mother' (object). The extent to which this prior state *is* symbolizable is a measure of *actual* separation. We are now evoking an Edenic state for which, like Rousseau's golden age, we are all more or less still searching. To experience this loss, to be subjects of this loss and thus subjects of language, is to be quintessentially human. In my unarticulated fantasy, then, I desire the idyllic state which existed before my separation from my object. Before separation, too, all my desires were satisfied; in fact, desire as such did not exist, and I wished for nothing. Now, every as-yet-unsatisfied desire awakens the original sense of loss; satisfaction of them, the original harmony. Let it be underlined: I *desire* this state. For Lacan, moreover, one is fundamentally a subject as the subject of desire.

Kristeva, on the other hand, suggests that the Lacanian position needs to be nuanced: its strokes are just a little too bold. Indeed, are there not things (let's not call them objects) outside of me which do not give me the least satisfaction, and which I find repulsive. Whence, then, comes this repulsion, or, in its strongest form, this horror? If the objects in the world are a fundamental displacement of my desire for my mother, what is the status of these other things?

In broad outline Kristeva's answer is that before the full intervention of the symbolic begins, a prior state is necessary, one which will be the repressed desire and the symbolic. Before the 'beginning' of the symbolic, there must have already been moves, by way of the drives, towards expelling/rejecting the mother. We are reminded here of the anal phase discussed in the previous chapter in relation to the thetic. The point is that the symbolic is not, of its own accord, strong enough to ensure separation; it depends on the mother becoming abjected. '*The abject would thus be the "object" of primal repression.*'[4] In other words, the abject is what allows the drives to have complete and uninhibited reign. With the various little rituals tied to cleanliness, toilet training, eating habits, etc., the 'mother' is gradually rejected through becoming, at the pre-symbolic level, the prototype of what the drives expel. As Kristeva says, it 'is a violent, clumsy breaking away, with the constant risk of falling back under the sway of a power as securing as it is stifling'.[5] After the successful imposition of the symbolic, abjection tends, at least in western cultures, to remain as a kind of background support for the symbolic and its attendant ego; it is the ego's quite *un*desirable face. Such is the way that the abject may be understood as the dark side of narcissism; it is precisely what Narcissus would not want to have seen as he gazed into his pool. The abject is the mud of Narcissus' pool, 'the moment of narcissistic perturbation'.[6]

From an analytic point of view, however, the abject is above all the ambiguous, the in-between, what defies boundaries, a composite resistant to unity. Hence, if the subject's identity derives from the unity of its objects, the abject is the threat of unassimilable non-unity: that is, ambiguity. Abjection, therefore, is fundamentally 'what disturbs identity, system, order'.[7] Thus, the corpse which is both human and non-human, waste and filth which are neither entirely inside nor outside the socio-subjective order, are examples of the abject. And so too are the 'traitor, the liar, the criminal with a good conscience, the shameless rapist, the killer who claims he is a savior'.[8] Abjection thus corresponds to fundamental hypocrisy in morality and politics. The immoralist (Kristeva says 'amoralist') who openly flouts the existing moral order in light of a different set of principles is not abject, but the amoral oscillator is: he who, slyly and unpredictably, at one time conforms to existing moral principles, and at another secretly flouts them. Even worse. In light of Kristeva's insight, we see that the epitome of abjection is the one who is outwardly beyond reproach (like a judge), and yet secretly getting away with murder. In a word, the one who is abject lacks authenticity, that is, lacks any detectable moral consistency. Such consistency could be 'beyond (conventional) good and evil', as Nietzsche showed. For her part, though, Kristeva suggests that corruption is the most common 'socialized appearance of the abject'.[9] Such, then, is the way that the concept of abjection would constitute a stimulus for reflection in moral and social philosophy, not to mention politics.

Phobia

Phobia further complicates both the articulation of the structure of subjectivity, and the concept of abjection. With a phobia, fear goes together *with* an object. For example, in Freud's famous case study,[10] Little Hans has a fear of horses. But what is it exactly that the phobic person is frightened of? In a highly nuanced discussion, Kristeva answers this question by saying that the phobic is frightened of the unnameable: the lack, or absence at the origin of language which psychoanalysis links to castration. Within the structure of castration, it is the mother's lack of a penis which cannot be symbolized: that is, her difference cannot be symbolized. With Little Hans, therefore, the object, horse, serves as a sign of a fear of the void. How does this fear (ultimately, of castration) become displaced onto an object, thus resulting in a fear of *something* that is not a void? And what is the connection with the abject?

According to Kristeva, the phobic often exhibits great verbal skill. This is certainly the case with Little Hans. It is as though, at the time of intense ego formation, he were trying to name everything and bring it into the symbolic. The void, or lack, resists this naming. A sign, inseparable from its object (because of the frailty of the subject's signifying system), comes to be put in the place of the unnameable void. The horse, then, *is* Little Hans' unnameable indicated by the symptom of fear. Fear is the mark of the failure of language to provide a symbolization (object) to contain drive activity. Fear is thus also the mark of the failure of the paternal function to separate the subject from the mother.[11] The unnameable – precisely because of its link with castration and separation – provides the subject's signifying system with its severest test. Analysis, for its part, tries to assist in the development of symbolization and to help the subject turn the phobic object into a metaphor for the unnameable. This metaphor serves to control the drive activity (fear) which blurs the distinction between word and thing.

We can now see that the fear of a non-object (unnameable), is the fear of separation. This 'object' is in fact an 'abject referent'.[12] The phobic 'object' is thus another form of abjection which interferes with the smooth working of the symbolic. Writers, says Kristeva, are particularly embroiled in a contest with a fear of the void: 'The writer is a phobic who succeeds in metaphorizing in order to keep from being frightened to death; instead he comes to life again in signs.'[13]

Phobia and loathing, therefore, are two fundamental forms of abjection resulting from an instability in the symbolic/paternal function and thus an imperfect separation from the mother. Far from being a clearly articulated object of desire which would signal, ironically, a satisfactory entry of the subject into the symbolic, the mother is 'ab-jected' and becomes a kind of non-object of drive affect, the inaugurator of a struggle (cf. the writer) to bring language as metaphor to the place of separation/castration in order to keep abjection at bay. In other words, Kristeva argues that in *signifying* horror, a reconciliation with the maternal body becomes possible.

The abject as defilement, and Biblical abomination

Defilement

On reading Kristeva, it seems that western capitalist society is founded on a rigorous imposition of the symbolic law: the law of the father. This law (in the family as well as in religion), is the privileged place as far as the articulation and constitution of society and the subject are concerned, and in this sense, it gives western society its very definite patriarchal character. And while every society *qua* society is patriarchal to a degree,[14] other societies like the Indian give almost equal weight to the 'authority' of the mother. In such societies, the symbolic interdiction against incest needs to be supported by abjection (of the mother) articulated through a network of religious rituals, sacred rites, and purifying acts.

Not just murder, then, but also incest constitutes, the co-ordinates of the separation between subject and object which is, simultaneously, the precondition of the emergence of subjectivity *and* the formation of society. A combination of anthropology and psychoanalysis now appears to squeeze out the kind of sociological framework based on a dichotomy between the individual (subject) and society.[15] For, from Kristeva's perspective at least, the constitution of the subject is now inseparable from the constitution of society rendering obsolete the debate about the individual *or* society, subjectivity *or* objectivity, structure *or* individual autonomy, etc. Rather, the constitution of the subject–object dyad, and thus the social code, would be founded on the division between murder (leading to the imposition of the symbolic), and incest (leading to a turning away from the mother). This division, argues Kristeva, is the 'two-sided sacred'.[16] The 'sacred' is another name for the divided foundation simultaneously giving rise to social and individual life. No sacred, then, without murder and incest, 'totem' *and* 'taboo', to use Freud's terms.[17]

Filth and defilement which exist – in light of Mary Douglas' work[18] – on the border of identities and threaten the unity of the ego, epitomize the separation from the mother; they epitomize the mother's *not* being an object of desire. Hence, blood – especially menstrual blood – nail clippings, hair, bodily wastes, etc., which render the boundary of the body indistinct and ambiguous, are subject to ritual acts whose purpose is to ward off defilement, and thus abjection. Similarly, the corpse and all items subject to decay – that is, objects with an ambiguous objective status – become subject to ritual activities in a variety of forms. As the mother is a threat to boundaries – standing as she does for their effacement – rituals, in reinforcing identities, at the same time reinforce separation: that is, the existence of subject and object.

But not all things belonging to the body's borders are polluting, Kristeva observes. In fact, menstrual blood and excrement are the privileged elements here. Why these in particular? Precisely because, Kristeva claims, 'those *two* defilements stem from the *maternal* and/or feminine, of which the maternal is the real support'.[19] Excrement is also on the side of the 'maternal' to the extent that it is the pre-symbolic basis of one's own/clean body (*corps propre*). Here we are dealing with what is simultaneously clean, proper, and one's own. Excrement, then, plays a role in the 'marking out' of the body as such, but pre-linguistically under the 'semiotic authority' of the mother. 'Through frustrations and prohibitions', says Kristeva, 'this authority shapes the body into a *territory* having areas, orifices, points and lines, surfaces and hollows, where the archaic power of mastery and neglect, of the differentiation of proper–clean and improper–dirty, possible and impossible, is impressed and exerted.'[20] Excrement as fundamentally 'dirty' (*impropre*), therefore, will *not* be part of me, but an alien outside. Excrement, indeed, helps constitute the difference between an inside and an outside linked to the separation from the mother. Defilement as such marks the boundary between the 'semiotic authority [mother] and symbolic law [father]'.[21] And, in the formation of objects, defilement is on the border signalled in purifying rites by *acts* not by symbols. It is as though the acts of purification functioned on the same pre-symbolic, or 'translinguistic' level as the defilement itself. The act can be seen perhaps to encapsulate the cathartic energy of the semiotic. In effect, the abject is not controlled by the (symbolic) law, but by the energy drives that, in the end, are its condition of possibility. Consequently, Kristeva defines such acts as a 'writing of the real'.[22]

Overall, it is 'not surprising to see pollution rituals proliferating in societies where patrilineal power is poorly secured ...'.[23] Without going into the details of the societies and cultures invoked to illustrate her point,[24] let us simply say that one of the more interesting possibilities opened up by Kristeva's work here, concerns the way social cohesion does not have to be based entirely on the strong imposition of the symbolic order as instanced by the representative state. What a comparative study of western and non-western societies might show, in short, is that acts in themselves can constitute a universe of relative social cohesion.

The work of the French anthropologist, Pierre Clastres,[25] echoes just such an approach. He argues that not only is social cohesion successfully maintained in societies without a representative state apparatus, but that the history of peoples without a state, and thus 'without history', is 'the history of their battle against the state'.[26]

And for his part, Claude Lévi-Strauss has argued that art work like facial painting and tattooing 'stamp onto the mind all the traditions and philosophy of the social group'.[27] In particular, facial painting would be an example of a 'writing of the real' because, far from representing the face, or even presupposing a 'face' as surface, 'the design *is* the face, or rather it creates it. It is the design which confers on the face its social existence ...'.[28]

Biblical abomination

Kristeva's analysis of Biblical abomination and defilement broadly centres on the extent to which the maternal and the feminine are presented in the Old Testament as 'unclean'. Judaism breaks away from religions of sacrifice to establish a religion of dietary and corporeal prohibitions that, on closer examination, turn out to exemplify the logic of separation and the notion of the maternal as abject. Thus milk is prohibited because, argues Kristeva, it is 'a food that does not separate but binds' mother to child.[29] On this basis, milk connotes incest. Other prohibitions relating to the corpse and to the leprous body point up the fragility of boundaries constitutive of identities. In particular, as a 'decaying body, lifeless, completely turned into dejection, blurred between the inanimate and the inorganic, a transitional swarming, inseparable lining of a human nature whose life is undistinguishable from the symbolic – the corpse represents fundamental pollution'.[30] Kristeva's point is that Biblical abomination, with all the prohibitions and ritual purifying acts that this entails, opens the way for the imposition of 'the logic that sets up the symbolic order'.[31]

Abomination presupposes a polluting 'outside' that threatens identity. After Christ and the New Testament, however, pollution, or sin, emanates from *within* the speaking being, and sin comes to be intimately linked to the spoken word and language in general, so that to *confess* one's sins ushers in 'a wholly different speaking subject'.[32] Abjection, therefore, becomes internalized with Christ's arrival, but to the extent that it is spoken, taken up, and articulated in and through the symbolic order, it can be kept at bay. It is as though Christ simultaneously heralded the steady repression of the maternal element and the evolution of that mode of social and political rationality called 'western'.

At the same time, Christianity missed a great opportunity for allowing the subject to come to terms with abjection through his own speech following the elaboration of *felix culpa* by Duns Scotus during the early fourteenth century. *Felix culpa* is the possibility of *speaking* sin (i.e. evil, abjection) and thus of coming to terms with it, of controlling it rather than being controlled by it, if not of eliminating it as Hegel thought. But, argues Kristeva, the history of the Church shows that *felix culpa* provoked the 'fiercest censorship' and 'punishment'.[33] For this reason, the artist, and in particular the writer, have tended to provide the means of the *felix culpa*.[34] It is in this light that Kristeva analyses Céline's writing.

Apocalyptic laughter

For Kristeva, Céline's writing 'speaks' horror. It brings it into view in carnivalesque fashion, and reveals the other repressed face of human existence – the one with a direct line back to the mother who gives life, but also death, who thus wrecks 'the infinite'. In this sense, Céline writes beyond the symbolic: the evil which he shows and embodies is not moral, that is to say, philosophical evil; it is rather barely symbolizable apocalyptic evil. Céline, says Kristeva, is *inside* horror desperately striving to give it a name – to *speak* it. Nearly all of his narratives 'converge on a scene of massacres or death'[35] presented in the style of *hyperrealism*. For example:

> He sticks his finger into the wound . . . He plunges both hands into the meat . . . he digs into all the holes . . . He tears away the soft edges . . . He pokes around . . . He gets stuck . . . His wrist is

caught in the bones . . . Crack! . . . He tugs . . . He struggles like
in a trap . . . Some kind of pouch bursts . . . The juice pours out
. . . it gushes all over the place . . . all full of brains and blood
. . . splashing . . . . [36]

For Céline, emotion was at the beginning. However, unlike
Rousseau who said the same thing,[37] this was not a romantic
horizon uniting '*les belles âmes*', but the pointer to a struggle to
reveal precisely what Romanticism repressed: horror. Thus while
Rousseau worked to exclude horror from his fiction – even as
Kantian negation – Céline's writing is 'beyond good and evil': it is
abject, that is, for Kristeva, apocalyptic. In effect, Céline's work is
a spectacular break with Romanticism.

It is not only *what* Céline writes which interests Kristeva,
though, but more importantly *how* he writes – his style, in a word.
As can be seen from the passage quoted above, the three
suspension points, onomatopoeia ('Crack!'), and the overall
staccato effect begin to mark out the Célinian style. These
elements, when coupled with the use of slang (evoking the spoken
word) and radical deformations of syntax, give this writing its
melodic, poetic, and hence maternal aura. Slang, Kristeva shows,
'produces a semantic fuzziness, if not interruption, within the
utterances that it punctuates and rhythmicizes . . .'.[38] By challenging syntax (i.e. the structure of well-formed sentences, the basis of
communicative language), Céline's style effectively challenges the
symbolic, putting the reader in touch with the drive dimension of
language. Rhythm and intonation, highlighted by the three
suspension points, give the Célinian utterance an explosive quality.
Indeed, slang and three dots, and the ellipses implied by them,
shatter the well-rounded, gentle beauty of a nineteenth-century
prose style and introduce the rugged, violent beauty of horrified,
apocalyptic laughter. To highlight this laughter, Kristeva speaks of
the 'trans-syntactic inscription of emotion',[39] that is, of the semiotic
level of the signifying process.

But initially Céline's reader will recognize that the subject
matter *is* apocalyptic: marked by violence, catastrophe, and death.
In fact, Kristeva notes, it evokes that tradition of apocalyptic
writing found in the 'Revelation of Saint John the Divine' in the
New Testament.[40] The names of Dante, Rabelais, and Balzac are
given as Saint John's successors. Unlike the writers of this
tradition, though, Céline does not represent the apocalypse; he

does not, moreover, distance himself from what he writes so that he may judge, comment, condemn, or lament. Rather, Céline, as Kristeva reads him, speaks from *within* horror: he

> has no threats to utter, no morality to defend. In the name of what would he do it? So his laughter bursts out, facing abjection, and always originating at the same source, of which Freud had caught a glimpse: the gushing forth of the unconscious, the repressed, suppressed pleasure, be it sex or death.[41]

This means that despite Céline's virulently antisemitic pamphlets[42] – pamphlets written in the same melodic style as other works – an ideological, or moralistic reading of his work is partly beside the point because it *shows* us abjection. We do not like (how inadequate this word is!) what we see; but this, too, is beside the point. For abjection is precisely what we do not, consciously, want to see. There is, on the other hand, a certain emotionally charged fascination with abjection. Horror *and* fascination are here entwined. How can the speaking being cope with such a contradiction? Kristeva's answer is: not by more repression, but through a kind of laughter (the expenditure of affect): an *apocalyptic* laughter, given that we are faced with abjection.

Love

Love is impossible without a separation from the mother. This, in large part, is what Kristeva argues and seeks to illustrate in her book, *Tales of Love*. Images of western love (Eros, Ahav, Agape), its dynamics as played out by Narcissus, Don Juan, Romeo and Juliet, and the Virgin Mother, and its being taken in charge by psychoanalysis and literature, all form the backdrop to Kristeva's 'Stories' of love.[43]

Despite the intimidating diversity of such a trajectory, the constitution and dissolution of the psychic space called love finds a thematic constant in the psychoanalytic elaboration of it. Love is fundamental to psychoanalysis in the transference, opening the way to the treatment. The latter, as Kristeva sees it, is fundamentally a defusing, and thus assuaging, of a difficult separation from the mother. Our separation from our mother enables us, as Kristeva will later say,[44] to become narcissists, that is, to develop an identity, an ego. As we shall see in more detail later, love for another is, for the psychoanalyst, premised on the capacity for a certain self-love – not in the pathological sense of being in love with one's own body which so obsessed nineteenth-century psychiatry, but in the sense of being at ease with a particular image or model of oneself: an ego ideal. Whence comes this ego ideal, however? *Tales of Love* assumes its discursive and analytic momentum in attempting to answer this question.

From the very beginning of its unfolding, separation is psychically painful. A sense of loss, or emptiness (void) comes to exist where once there was a satisfying and oblivious union with the mother. Kristeva refers here to Freud's concept of an amalgam of the two parents which becomes the basis of an 'archaic' or 'primary' identification: the 'father of individual prehistory'.[45] The father of individual prehistory occurs prior to the formation of an object accompanying the emergence of the subject in language; it is thus prior to any ideal, but is none the less the *basis* of all idealization – especially in love. Or is it that every form of idealization, whether moral, political, intellectual, or artistic, is inscribed in the structure of love? This is the issue that Plato opens up in the *Symposium* and *Phaedrus*, as Kristeva analyses them.

What Plato's dramatized image of Eros encapsulates is not, strictly speaking, 'Platonic' love. On the contrary, 'Eros is essentially manic'.[46] And it is so because even in its idealizing and divine aspect, 'sublime' Eros has to work both to prevent 'manic' Eros from breaking through and wreaking orgiastic destruction and death, and to prevent a successful repression of manic Eros from toppling over into depression and melancholia – and even death through suicide.

Plato's amatory discourse thus begins (because we are immediately dealing with eroticism and thus an object of desire) at a point after the separation and the institution of the law: 'erotic, manic, or idealistic man does not touch the mother. The taboo has been imposed once and for all: language and the law are already there'.[47] The presence of an eroticized object is thus indicative of *symbolic* forms invested with affect: too much affect and the symbolic itself is shattered. Or, as Plato's famous illustration in the *Phaedrus* puts it, the soul, or psyche, is a team of two winged horses – one the equivalent of manic Eros, the other the equivalent of sublime Eros – guided by a charioteer. Sublime Eros is here engaged in an intense struggle to idealize the love relationship against the manic force urging that immediate pleasure be taken from the love object. Love in Plato – the Platonic soul – is therefore primarily about this struggle which takes on an unexpected aspect when, in the *Symposium*, attention moves to the nature of the loved object itself. What is it, Socrates asks, that is really lacking in a human being and is thus sought after most of all? In his dialogue with the very wise Mantinean woman, Diotima, Socrates receives an answer to his question. He is told that what the lover lacks above all is beauty, or rather 'the power to give birth to beauty', to create physically, but most of all, symbolically; for man loves immortality above all else. Thus, the greater the ideal (symbolic), the greater the prospect of immortality. In this sense, the philosopher loves beautiful creations (and thus beautiful women to the extent that they create lives) which turn out to be ideals of immortality brought to ward off death. Such is the enlightenment Socrates gains from Diotima, a woman, a potentially divine woman, a perfect creation of the symbolic, and, as a result, a phallic woman. The psyche, or soul, as Plato delineates it, then, turns out to be homosexual, that is symbolic, ideal, phallic. Plato's notion of love, therefore, is designated by Kristeva, following Lacan, as '*âmosexuel*' (âme = soul).[48] The *âmosexuel* loves beauty and thus immortality, but also risks placing the bar of idealization too high. Anxiety and melancholia – death, in a word – break through. Thus do we have Thomas Mann's *Death in Venice*, extolling ideal beauty (albeit in a man – but that also means symbolically), and at the same time confronting the reader with 'that esthetic melancholy at the heart of a shameful and disillusioned homosexual passion'.[49]

That the philosopher's amatory discourse on the erotic soul, has to do with the oscillation between erotic love and the love of the ideal means, for the psychoanalyst, that a primary identification with an other – 'the father of individual prehistory', the 'Imaginary Father' – has already taken place. This primary identification – as much imposed as it is made, due to the tenuous state of separation – becomes the basis of the first movement away from the mother towards the place of the father. In fact, an earlier version of Part I of *Tales of Love* ('Freud and love: treatment and its discontents'), was called 'L'abjet d'amour'[50] – 'The abject of love' – a title evoking the movement away from the (abject) mother towards the (ideal) father. Upon this movement depends the possibility of love, and thus ego-formation, through an identification with an ego ideal. The ego, therefore, is inseparable from a *capacity* to love which, in turn, is inseparable from a sense of loss – an 'emptiness'

– at the origin of ego-formation and narcissism.

Although narcissism covers over the emptiness wrought through separation, it *is* a separation – and thus a certain instability of the symbolic and the ego – with which we are dealing. As Kristeva puts it, narcissism is a screen for emptiness.[51] A certain degree of narcissism is thus a precondition for love. However, the narcissistic person is not necessarily capable of love; for love requires a Third Party (Other) whose role is to make possible the identification with another who is like oneself. Consequently, the other (object) of love is impossible unless the Other (Ideal) is also involved.

The potential failure of the Ideal and love, and the attendant psychological problems flowing from this are precisely Kristeva's major concern in *Tales of Love*. In short, for the contemporary western society of a *fin-de-siècle* twentieth century, the idealizing pole of love is under threat, in particular, because there is no longer any socially authentic ideal of love – or even an authentic lover's discourse unless it be one of 'extreme solitude'.[52] For Kristeva, Eros in today's society has begun to emerge as predominantly manic, with the result that the psychoanalyst is, more and more frequently, hearing in the fragmented speech of the psychotic or 'borderline' patient about a gap waiting to be filled by an idealization approximating Christianity's love as Agape. Psychoanalysis is thus being called upon to provide the opportunity – formerly offered by religion – for the subject to experience the transformative effects of opening oneself up to the other through the Other; that is, of opening oneself up to love.

But is not love a rather improbable, not to say vague, notion for the psychoanalyst to work with? In fact, would it not be better if the analyst refused to be swayed by such an illusion and rather set about delineating, rigorously and scientifically, the true basis of love's illusion? Kristeva's response to such questions is to argue that, on the contrary, it is not the concept, or indeed reality of love which is found wanting, but the rationalistic, scientific framework presuming to judge it, a framework unquestionably without love. For Kristeva will show that love – especially in the images and myths constituting a kind of proto-history of western subjectivity – is the embodiment of both the symbolic *and* the semiotic, language *and* affect, knowledge *and* joy (Spinoza), etc. The proto-history of subjectivity focusing on love, would also reveal another side of ourselves through widening our imaginative and symbolic powers. Put another way: the history of love has analytic effects. This

should be more clearly understood when we explain the relationship between love and psychoanalysis in more detail. Now,
however, we shall travel more of the path marked out by the
history of subjectivity in *Tales of Love*.

The Song of Songs

Plato, we saw, gave Eros to the western amatory discourse. And
while a kind of union exists between Eros and philosophy in Plato,
psychodrama (conflict in the soul) and the ideal give love a
symbolic bias: the Platonic discourse is on the side of an always-
already-formed ego, and not on the side of an ego in the throes of
formation.

The Song of Songs[53] in the Old Testament is, Kristeva argues, of
a very different order. Far from exemplifying a Platonic discursive
order from which almost all lyricism and rhythm have been
evacuated in both principle and practice, the Biblical text contains
lyrical meaning in each of the parts of an unstructured whole.
These parts are thus *equal* to the whole, and thus evoke the infinite
in Cantor's sense. The parts, then, are a condensation of affect, a
metaphor of 'lyrical meaning' which undermines the notion of a
logical whole. When this insight is coupled with the explicit
references to death contained in the more highly organized smaller
unities of the Song of Songs, the realm of the death drive begins to
mark out a new psychic space quite distinct from that of the
Greeks. Lyricism and idealism, death *and* immortality, thus come
together in the Biblical 'incantation'. Finally, in the Song of Songs
it is a woman – 'the amorous wife' – who is speaking/incanting.
And, as it is in loving that one becomes a subject in this Biblical
text, Kristeva suggests that here is born 'the first Subject in the
modern sense of the term'.[54]

Narcissus

With Ovid's Narcissus – so dear to psychoanalysis – we come to
the very basis of the western psyche, the precondition of its love.
Through *Tales of Love* we recall Narcissus before his reflection in
the pool as he suffers the sense of loss entailed in the process of ego
formation. Narcissus wants desperately to unite with the perceived
other which is in truth the image of himself. He wants otherness:
he is in love with his image; but he also refuses it: he will not

171

accept a real other to replace the image. Narcissus, says Kristeva, is thus 'a borderline case',[55] and a common one at that. The story of Narcissus opens up a new dynamic in western subjectivity where the youth beside the pool, at the very point of desiring an object outside himself, thereby confirming his subjectivity, does not quite succeed: desire fails and Narcissus dies. Despite nineteenth-century psychiatry's concern to point out that Narcissus died *because* of his narcissism (perversion), Kristeva sees the death as equivalent to the failure of narcissism to develop with sufficient strength. Narcissus has nothing (no object) to fill the psychic space; in fact Narcissus' object *is* psychic space (the image) as such.[56]

Focusing on Plotinus' *Enneads* in order to illustrate Narcissus' place in the early Christian era (AD *c.* 250), Kristeva notes that with the intense concern with the One, real alterity is eliminated: 'The soul then loses its specificity, it is no longer completely itself, it is outside itself, in *extasis*.'[57]

Freud's notion of narcissism, Kristeva continues, suggests neither a pathological nor a sublime state. Even Christianity did not condemn narcissism outright. Rather, it said love yourself – but through an ideal, through Christ. Freud explains, in similar fashion, that love of self is not pathological provided it takes place through an ideal of oneself: an ego ideal. Because the ego drives are also infected with death drives, without an other, without an object outside of itself, the amorous ego may well hide a suicidal ego. And the latter is a possibility if the mother inhibits separation, and thus the formation of an ideal, because she sees the child as an ideal already. Love then becomes difficult because the ideal never becomes an object. In fact a pre-object is the only form of objectification.[58] To remain, as do Narcissus and the ideal child, at the passive, pre-objectal stage, is thus to thwart the formation of an adequate social being. Only the artist who is not enthralled by the pre-object, but plays with it in rhythm and lyricism, colour and forms, etc., can give it a truly social dimension. As Kristeva puts it, art 'manages to have us love it . . . .'.[59]

Agape

With the arrival of the Pauline doctrine God is interpreted as *agape*, or 'man should love God'. Unlike Eros which rises to the object, agape descends to its object. Are we then back once again in the realm of passive Narcissus? The answer is 'no' because Paul also entreats humanity to *recognize* that God loves everyone. He calls for an active enlightenment leading to a full encounter with the symbolic: with God as the Ideal. To be sure, an active identification with the Ideal requires the sacrifice of one's own body, expressed symbolically as the 'I' being everything 'through the Name of the Father'. And Kristeva quotes from the Bible by way of illustration as follows:

> I live now not with my own life but with the life of Christ who lives in me. The life I now live in this body I live in faith: faith in the Son of God who loved me and who sacrificed himself for my sake. (Gal. 2:20)[60]

Clearly, we are a long way from antiquity; for the ideal is there already in me – if only I would recognize it: 'I' is everything in the ideal, even if the body is nothing. Through the symbolic (active principle), I surpass all passivity – masochism included. And in opening myself up to the symbolic (Other), I will love the other as myself. Narcissus has indeed been transcended.

Has passion similarly been transcended, however? Passion is always present, says Kristeva[61] (for we are dealing with the death of the body as in the crucifixion), but the believer in Christ goes beyond it: that is, it is taken in hand symbolically. In psycho-analytic terms, a complete separation from the mother is as much a painful and passionate affair as it is the way to tranquillity in the Father's love.

Both Bernard of Clairvaux and Thomas Aquinas further illustrate the dynamics of love in Kristeva's account[62] – the former putting passion into the very constitution of the ego ('the ego is affect'), the latter giving a new impetus to narcissism by arguing that the love of self (*Amor sui*) is the first move in loving others.

While it is true that in the work of Saint Bernard, *affectus* has a passive connotation, love, which is one of the four affects (the others being joy, fear, and sadness), is fundamentally a passionate striving for the Other (God), not a rational contemplation. Love is a 'saintly violence' that strives to overcome the resistance of the flesh. Love thus *depends* on this resistance in order to be what it is. Even more: according to Kristeva, it is not certain that carnal love is absolutely evil, but more the case that the flesh is both necessary and inevitable: the flesh gives body to spirit, just as the spirit sanctifies the body. In any event, despite readings of Saint Bernard which would like to eliminate all ambiguity on this point, and turn the theologian's thought on love into a radical dualism, or indeed, into a monism of the spirit, Kristeva argues that ambivalence cannot be erased – as is illustrated by the following quotation:

> We also love our spirit in carnal fashion when we break it through prayer, with tears, sighs, and moans. We love our flesh with a spiritual love when, after we have subjected it to the spirit, we exercise it spiritually for the good and watch with judgment over its conservation.[63]

Kristeva proposes, then, that love in Saint Bernard is fundamentally ambiguous and ambivalent: it is *as much* spirit as flesh, *as much* affect as contemplation of the ideal. Here, at the point before rationalist philosophy had turned the ego into a purely philosophical entity, the psychoanalyst sees an ego which is constituted in love: *Ego affectus est* – not in thought: *Ego cogito*. Love, indeed, opens out onto the terrain of that which today is called the unconscious. Above all for this reason, Kristeva argues that the writings of Bernard of Clairvaux take on an extremely modern aspect.

In Aquinas, love of self is not at all a source of guilt. Indeed, Kristeva shows that 'the love of others originates in the love of self' because the love of one's own being is inseparable from being in general, which is good. Therefore, love of self is good. In fact, through love, the individual's being and goodness become connected to the being and goodness of God – the Ideal. For his part, Aquinas shows that love is the tendency for the individual to become *united* with God, and at the same time is the striving by an irrevocably divided subject to become united with itself.

Just as importantly, Kristeva is keen to emphasise that for Aquinas love is inseparable from knowing and reason: one cannot love the good without knowing what it is – nor can reason be excluded from love given that it is through the *ratio diligendi* (reason in loving) that the link is made between the self and God. Like Saint Bernard, then, Aquinas, too, writes at a time before the Cartesian project had separated the subject's being as knowledge and reason, from love. Now, the analyst begins to see the extent to which a so-called rational society is not only suspicious of love, but sets up a strong resistance to the notion of the unconscious.

Myths of love: Don Juan, Romeo and Juliet, the Virgin Mother

The mythical figures of Don Juan, Romeo and Juliet, and the Virgin Mother, like the previous discourses on love, mark out an extra dimension of love's psychic space.

With regard to the Don Juan myth, Kristeva poses the question as to whether there is indeed anything like love revealed there. How can love exist in such a milieu of inconstancy and deception – not to mention egotism – where Don Juan is concerned? Part of the answer is that while there may be deception, the ideal is not absent. Indeed, Don Juan is in love with an inaccessible ideal woman with whom no real woman can compare: his mother, in a word. Because Don Juan never meets his match in his flight from one woman to another, his love is a love of conquering, that is, of power. Even more: in his entrances and escapes, in his repeated lack of attachment, Don Juan shows himself to be in love with the *game* of power. The game of course is entirely symbolic, entirely a product of language. This is why Don Juan has no interiority or, to put it more pointedly, why Don Juan is not a humanist, for he is identical to – is nothing more than – his fictional being.

But, if Don Juan is nothing but a fiction, whence comes his pleasure? For Kristeva remarks that there is hardly any reference to Don Juan's sensuality. This is, she suspects, because the focus in the myth is on a game of seduction based on signs. As seducer pure and simple, Don Juan is engaged in perversion: he brings nothing to a proper conclusion but seems to be captivated by a kind of phallic jouissance 'made up of displacements and combinations'.[64] The upshot is that Don Juan himself is entirely seduced by the symbolic power of the phallus.[65] The only way to break that power, Kristeva seems to say, is through a joyful death: reuniting with the inaccessible mother. Thus does Don Juan give himself up to the stone arms of the Commandant.

Through Kristeva's analysis, we begin to see that Don Juan is a unique entity, a unique, ephemeral entity (not a character, for this connotes fixity). And he is so primarily because he does not live the original separation from the mother as a wound. There is no mark of the wound in his language, and yet this wound is language's precondition. Separation is lived as phallic jouissance. There is no melancholy. Repression is, in a sense, absolute. Don Juan thus usurps God's position. Another consequence of this is that much as he *knows* guilt, fear, and the horror of death intellectually, Don

Juan does not *experience* them because his separation from the mother is so absolute. Don Juan is in fact the realization of love without affect – the quintessential, post-separation fantasy. We understand now, even better than before, why it is that Don Juan goes to his death so nonchalantly, if not joyfully. For him, says Kristeva, 'the reversal of Christly passion is glory alone'.[66]

We have seen in Aquinas that love is in knowledge and reason. With Romeo and Juliet, Kristeva finds, amongst other things, that death infects love, and that love is always lined with hate. How precisely does Kristeva see these things unfolding in Shakespeare's masterpiece?

Immediately we note that Romeo and Juliet's love – as is well known – is a defiance of the law. Here, the law is doubly significant. Firstly, it ensures the separation that fuels love's passion, and, secondly, it evokes hate: the hatred that the Montagues and Capulets have for each other. Hence the importance Kristeva attaches to Juliet's line, 'My only love sprung from my only hate!' (I.v.139).[67] From the hatred existing between the two families comes the transgression embodied in Romeo and Juliet's love for one another. 'My *only* love', says Juliet, which means her only, and *ideal* love. Thus do transgression (of the law) and idealization go together, Shakespeare shows us. And Kristeva takes up the point by considering the nature of idealization as such in the play.

In this regard, the sun, 'metaphor or metaphors', becomes the ideal *par excellence*: the lovers experience a 'mutual dazzlement', a mutual blindness, at the very point of idealization. Such blindness at once links love with the night – with death. Without death, or at least the prospect of death, the separation giving rise to idealization in love, is threatened. It is almost as though without death, love dies, turns into hate. Death, therefore, becomes the protection against the normal, banal couple in marriage; or, if passion continues, it risks running through the 'entire gamut of sadomasochism that the two partners already heralded in the yet relatively quiet version of the Shakespearean text.'[68] Thus do Romeo and Juliet appear as an impossible couple. Idealization, however pure, cannot sustain a thwarted eros. This is why Juliet unconsciously desires Romeo's death: '"come, gentle night, . . . and, when he shall die,/Take him and cut him out in little stars,/And he will make the face of heaven so fine,/That all the world will be in love with night . . ."'(III.ii.19–24).[69]

Love nevertheless involves a drive towards fusion: a deathly fusion with the mother. Such a fusion is also the equivalent of the death of the symbolic and conscious subject. Marriage is thus a threat to identity, for it is a marriage with the mother: an effacement of separation, a union with an other. In Shakespeare's play, the ambivalent position of the mother is spelled out, Kristeva shows, in the following lines: "'The earth that's nature's mother is her tomb;/What is her burying grave, that is her womb'"(II.iii.9–10).[70] From Kristeva's point of view, hatred is to be seen as a protection against total fusion, against death, in effect. In this context, to go beyond the couple is to go beyond the mother. Marriage is therefore the reverse side of the myth of Romeo and Juliet, a myth to which we moderns may well have recourse in our yearning for love and our hatred of marriage.

In her essay, 'Stabat Mater',[71] Kristeva turns away from the love of the impossible couple and precisely towards that which sustains it: the idealization of the mother in primary narcissism. Christianity provides a perfect image of such an idealization in the Virgin Mother. Mary turns death aside, that is why she is a virgin in the logical explanation offered by John Duns Scotus for which Kristeva has obvious sympathy. Mary also has to thwart death, Kristeva argues, in order to enter into the symbolic order on a parity (that is, having equal symbolic status) with the Father. The possibility of a discourse on motherhood depends, therefore, on the myth of the Virgin, or its equivalent, in order that motherhood may have a discourse, that is, have a clear symbolic status. The extent to which such a discourse is both problematic and difficult can be gauged when it is realized that an attempt is being made to give a symbolic status to primary narcissism: the time of the first separation from the mother, the time of the unnameable pre-object.

The latter, evoking the archaic narcissistic wound (separation), is what a mother's love seeks to render less threatening to the child. Love, although always occurring after separation, may however be too strong and become an obstacle to the formation of an identity. In such circumstances, love overpowers the symbolic as we saw above and hate becomes the only means of 'self' preservation. The experience of men and women here, says Kristeva, tends, from a psychoanalytic point of view, to be quite different. Because an Oedipal conflict is less explicit, a daughter sometimes finds it difficult to separate from her own mother before becoming a mother herself. As a necessarily separate entity (separation beginning with the physical act of childbirth, which Kristeva describes in her own case), the child is also symbolic, and indeed becomes the phallus for Kristeva as for Lacan. It is in this sense that motherhood can be a normalizing and fulfilling experience. The Virgin, then, provided a discourse for this experience which, today, is 'without a discourse'.

Further into the analysis, the Virgin Mother thus embodies a kind of perfection of fulfilled femininity. Mary's separation from Christ is complete, and He makes a perfect entry into the symbolic. His not having been conceived in sin (= flesh) is the confirmation of this. Mary is moreover the 'perfect' mother in the analytic sense because Christ is not her only desire: God, as the Holy Ghost and the Ideal, is also. Mary thus does not marry the flesh, but the Ideal as such. She then occupies all three symbolic positions of mother, daughter, and wife. In other words, the absence of the flesh makes Mary simultaneously the mother, daughter, and wife of Christ.

Historically, Mary has competed with the troubadour's Lady as the 'focal point of men's desires and aspirations'.[72] Although initially carnal, courtly love also promoted the Lady to a pure ideal like the Virgin. It is of course *as* ideal that the Virgin and the Lady exclude all other women. They are 'alone of all their sex'.[73] This very uniqueness distinguished the so-called feminine ideal from the masculine ideal model to which one relates through identification. Indeed, the task of the feminine ideal is not to portray union, but separation. This is clear from what we have said regarding the Mother of Christ. The mother *qua* mother has an unconscious desire to take the child back into herself, to make the child once again one with her. Love cannot really flower in such a situation; for it presupposes, as we have seen, a degree of detachment and separation. Put another way – and recalling the 'father of individual pre-history' (Kristeva's 'Imaginary Father') – love has to come partly from the father. Mary is a perfect mother, therefore, to the extent that she gave up her Son out of love for God, the Father. But not without suffering, not without emotion.

Accordingly, Mary inspires a kind of 'baroqueness' (plenitude of signs) in art premised on 'metaphors of nonspeech, a "semiotics" that linguistic communication does not account for'.[74] Perhaps, Kristeva speculates, a mother's suffering and joy are at the heart of modern art ('for those who are attached to it'). In effect, the presence of 'emotion' (see Rothko) would be – as we suggested with Pollock's work – a 'sublimated celebration of incest'.[75]

To some extent, aspects of modern art had already been foreshadowed with the troubadours. For them, the woman is a purely imaginary addressee, a pretext for the song of love, which, says Kristeva, is essentially an incantation: it is thus fundamentally semiotic, with rhythm and melody dominating over the message to the Lady.[76] The troubadour's song is therefore joy as such: a 'direct inscription of jouissance', an excess of meaning, a '*plus-que-sense*', as the French text has it.[77]

Jeanne Guyon

The story of love continues with the notion that the last insight into the structure of love and narcissism before Descartes comes to dominate the western discourse on subjectivity, is to be found in the life and work of the seventeenth-century French quietist, Jeanne Guyon (1648–1717). Quietism and the life of Guyon bring together an aspect of love which may be less visible today, but is no less present: love experienced from the position of the imaginary father himself. Such a love, to be sure, is a kind of regression to the very basis of narcissism, to the very point of separation and the unnameable: it is an experience of the void. This is a love, then, without an object unless the void itself be that object. The result is that a subject struggles to 'be', on the basis of a complete loss of self in a union with God. Instead of trying to name the unnameable, Guyon attempts to be the unnameable in silence as a way of easing the pain of separation. On the edge of psychosis, her quietistic silence is thus at the other extreme from the artist's necessarily 'exploded and pulverized' *naming* of the unnameable. Unlike Cartesian rationalism which makes the dream 'a representation that is identical with the one that makes up the idea',[78] Jean Guyon's writing is a 'logorrhea' on the 'brink of aphasia'. To the extent that one can gauge, Kristeva seems to suggest that although it lacks the clarity and precision of rationalism, Guyon's written logorrhea, is a way of 'stretching the boundaries of the nameable'. In short, there is here a subject of a silent *énonciation*, albeit one that is archaic and unrepresentable. This notion of love as expanding the 'boundaries of the nameable' is particularly significant for Kristeva's theory of love. As we shall see, for the analyst, expanding symbolic and imaginary boundaries is fundamental to the treatment. Such analytic effects can extend to the reader of Guyon, provided one reads with love.[79]

In sum, Guyon's situation is modern because it marks out the structure of narcissism displayed in the confrontation 'with what is nonrepresentable', and the 'imaginary father' as the 'zero degree' of subjectivity – a father 'who loves us, not the one who judges us'.[80]

Love as metaphor

To consider metaphor from a psychoanalytic perspective, Kristeva argues, is *not* to see it as another way of naming, that is to say, as a kind of displaced mode of the symbolic. Rather, metaphor is on the side of the semiotic. For the analyst, it is equivalent to a condensation of affect, or psychical energy, in dream work. As Freud explains 'the intensity [of psychical energy] of a whole train of thought may eventually be concentrated in a single ideational element. Here we have the effect of "compression" or "condensation" which has become familiar in dream-work'.[81] The Freudian dream, therefore, is quite different from Descartes' dream as the actual repesentation of the idea. Descartes wants to eliminate affect, Freud to include it. Metaphor for Freud, and for Kristeva, would thus be the *'affectus'* brought to light by Bernard of Clairvaux in *ego affectus est.*

Love links up with this condensation of affect in the act of enunciation. Put simply, the evocation of the loved one in words is in itself a rather empty gesture. A description of the ideal alone is not enough if the lover's discourse is to be more than a linguistic phenomenon. On the other hand, love is seen by Kristeva as a kind of synthesis of the metaphor and the ideal, or as a combination of drive energy and an external referent. More than this, though, the affect of metaphor and the impact of the act of enunciation is strongest, precisely 'where the object slips away',[82] and the 'univocity of signs undergoes equivocality'.[83]

In Baudelaire, the theme of perfume most closely approximates the notion of metaphor as condensation – as love. For perfume, at least in Kristeva's reading, has 'fusional connotations that condense the intoxicated memory of an invaded maternal body'.[84] Perfume gives the Baudelairean text its great lyricism by dissolving the object, or rather by merging all objects into one, namely, the poet's contemplation. Baudelaire's contemplation now becomes the equivalent of condensation – of metaphor – as such. Perfume, Kristeva continues, is the most powerful metaphor for that archaic universe, preceding sight, where what takes place is the conveyance of the most opaque lovers' indefinite identities, together with the chilliest words: 'There are strong perfumes for which all matter/Is porous. They seem to penetrate glass' (*The Flask*).[85]

Metaphor as perfume in Baudelaire, as 'synaesthesia', is love as the dissolution of otherness, as the metamorphosis of self into . . . what? Into the metaphor as pure condensation, to be sure. This is what fusion with the mother is all about. More specifically, though, how does one cope with this loss of identity? In Baudelaire's case, through dandyism, in today's society, perhaps through 'punk', is Kristeva's reply.

Dandyism as 'punk' before the fact, then, would be a way for Baudelaire to cope with loss of identity and a wounding of narcissism. In this sense, dandyism is not simply an individual choice which could be analysed sociologically. It is also a kind of desperate assertion of independence – of social survival – against the mother. Dandyism is the symbolic appropriation of the maternal position. The question still remains as to why the dandy needs to draw attention to himself ('those flowing locks, pink gloves, coloured nails as well as hair'), why, indeed, he feels the need to be anti-social, rather than asocial. Kristeva's answer is that industrial technocratic societies do not give recognition to those who wander 'at the borders of the speakable and the visible',[86] entailed by the loss of identity in poetic writing. This realm, once controlled by myths of 'Earth, Sovereign and God', is thus that of language's musicality. Now both the dandy and the punk seem to be saying: 'I cannot bear being without some form of symbolic existence in a fully articulated form'.[87] Both need *some* kind of social presence.

If being in love involves being the other, of recognizing subjectivity as an 'open system' (we shall return to this), industrial society, in Kristeva's view, has no love for the semiotic poet. Even though the position of all artists is precarious in industrial society, that of the one who dissolves identities and meanings is more so. And to the extent that the amatory condition itself tends to inspire a writing of pure lyricism, such a society has no love either for the one in love, as this passage forcefully demonstrates:

If through a writing that is synonymous with the amatory condition – an experience at the limits of the identifiable – the writer can find no other place in the bosom of bourgeois society than that of a refugee at the side of nonproduction nobility or the Church, which protects fetishes under the symbolic umbrella, we can only interpret that as an indictment of that very society rather than the evidence of the writer's error or 'failure'.[88]

Love of power, power of love: subjectivity as an open system

Quite unlike Baudelaire, Stendhal does not go the way of 'fusion', but of 'distancing'. Writing will distance the author of *On Love* from the intimidating feminine authority which provokes anxiety. Writing turns Stendhal into a superman confronted by a superwoman.[89] Because Stendhal finds real women unapproachable, he writes his 'amorous journey'. In other words, Stendhal's written conceit is nothing but a veil over his real fear in the presence of the feminine body. Love here is thus a love of the power which would conquer the threatening woman. Nevertheless, it will always be the way the *woman* loves and acts, and is invariably in control, which is fundamental to the Stendhalian perspective, according to Kristeva. To love a woman is, for Stendhal, to be effectively engaged in a battle for self-preservation – a battle which often ends in the death of the lovers.[90]

If, because of the love of power, Stendhal's text in the end signals a certain closure to the other and to love, Georges Bataille's writing may be a last-ditch effort, before the crisis provoked by the disintegration of psychic space ensues, to give expression in the twentieth century to a truly amatory discourse. This would not be in the sense of a code to be followed, but as an 'opening up' to another through a broadening of imaginative powers. Bataille's *My Mother* thus shocks with its clash of opposites (darkness as light), and also with its impossible synthesis of a 'scientific' description of perverse relationships (obscenity), and the 'excessiveness' of love's anguish. Such a synthesis leads to an incoherent 'immoderate' narrative which 'tries to convey . . . the idealization and the state of shock germane to amatory feeling'.[91] Kristeva sees Bataille's writing as a medium which brings the reader to a new awareness precisely through a state of shock, even to the extent that the reader might discover another self.

Even more, however, Bataille's obscene narrative tries to describe the real itself: the mother's sex. But it cannot, for the real cannot be 'uttered', as Kristeva says. The attempt, none the less, leads the speaking being 'to fly off the handle' in an immense 'language ordeal' where the impossibility of obscenity ever reproducing the real means that it can only ever be spoken obliquely 'through an erotic, meditative narrative – an amorous one'. To this extent, the obscene opens up the possibility of idealization.

Overall, Kristeva's remarks on Bataille help us to recognize that this writing is also a coming to terms with primary narcissism. It is an attempt to confirm the separation from the pre-Oedipal mother – 'archaic holder of my identity' – source of life . . . and of death.

Crisis in the 1980s, on the other hand, means that there is no longer the coming to terms with primary narcissism revealed by Bataille's text. In fact, the individual, dispossessed of any amatory code through which the idealizing dimension of love might be expressed, is also deprived of the psychic space a clear separation from the mother entails. Intoxication of all kinds ('from drugs to sacred music') closing off the individual to the social world outside has, for many, taken the place of psychic space as such: the space of narcissus and of love. To the psychoanalyst, this intoxication is a symptom of suffering which he or she feels duty bound to ameliorate. Most of all, intoxication deprives the subject of the imaginary and symbolic wherewithal to be a truly living being, rather than a 'corpse under care'.

The psychoanalytic transfer (basis of the treatment) does not derive from a claim to have created a new amatory code for the twentieth century. Instead, the wager is that a fulfilling separation from the mother is possible and that, as a result, analysis should be seen to some extent as 'an apprenticeship in separation'.[92] Such an apprenticeship involves enlarging one's own imaginary and symbolic capacities.

Of course, if the subject were essentially closed off from the other like some kind of maternal monad, love and the enlargement and maintenance of psychic space would be impossible. By contrast to such a conception of the subject fundamentally in a world of its own, Kristeva proposes, in conjunction with developments in logic and biology (see von Forster), that the subject is an 'open system'.[93] To illustrate the notion of 'open system', Kristeva suggests that rather than thinking of the outside as a threat, or perhaps analogous to 'noise' in information theory, we should see it as a stimulus to change and adaptation. The 'outside' as a perturbation then becomes an 'event' in the life of the subject, broadening horizons and creating psychic space. Resistance to this event leads to an atrophying of psychic space and thus of love. On the other hand, when a perturbation is absorbed by the psychic system and does not remain a threatening trauma, the psyche becomes increasingly more complex. The more complex and more supple it becomes, the more adept it is at coping with difference – with the other as difference. Now, the other ceases to be a threat and becomes, in his or her very individuality, a participant in my identity. This process, Kristeva also calls love:

> We ... know the mechanisms of this transfer which makes the human psyche an *open system* capable of self-organisation on condition of maintaining a kind of link with an other: these are the *identification* of primary narcissism 'revealing' the subject, and an *idealisation of the word* of the other. I have called this the amorous state.[94]

Based on love, treatment in analysis therefore gives the psyche over to the other as difference and variation with the aim that this should happen more or less permanently.

To be able to accept that every work of art that is not simply a cliché is, in all likelihood, capable of inviting a multiplicity of ways of appreciating it, is also to recognize that art is an opening up of the psyche, similar to love. Art, potentially, has analytic effects: 'The amorous and artistic experiences, as two interdependent aspects of the identificatory process, are our only way of preserving our psychic space as a "living system", that is, open to the other, capable of adaptation and change.'[95] It is in this sense that one can understand why Kristeva refuses to offer an ultimate interpretation of the literary text but, on the contrary (as she says elsewhere) keeps 'asking questions'.[96] Or, as we saw with Bataille, the history of love will have analytic effects if we read it with love: that is, with the capacity to turn our reading into an 'event' of our own subjectivity that is also partly constitutive of this subjectivity. When love is not possible, we lose part of ourselves; we begin to die and perhaps then realize that love is life. Such would be our distillation of Kristeva's message.

Melancholy

Signs and affect

If love is a striving (largely fuelled by symbolic idealization) for a union with an object, melancholy, as Kristeva outlines it, corresponds to union with Lacan's Real: that is, for Kristeva, with the mother and death. This, then, is a union based on a withdrawal from the symbolic, from life. Melancholia, and its more temporary variant, depression, would constitute an example of an unsuccessful separation from the mother and a failure of primary narcissism to emerge. The melancholic/depressive is thus not simply displacing hatred for an other into his or her own ego, as Freud maintained;[97] rather, the melancholic's sadness would be

> the most archaic expression of a non-symbolisable, unnameable narcissistic wound that is so premature that no external agent (subject or object) can be referred to it. For this type of narcissistic depressive, sadness is in reality the only object. More exactly, it is an ersatz of an object to which he attaches himself, and which he tames and cherishes, for want of something else.[98]

Consequently, while Freud sees melancholia as a particular kind of object relation, Kristeva argues that the problem is located in the failure of the relation as such to materialize. There is no object for the melancholic, only a sadness as an ersatz object; or, as Kristeva goes on to say, there is only a 'Thing' (*chose*), a vague, indeterminate 'something', a 'light without representation', or, as in Nerval's metaphor, a 'black sun' (*soleil noir*).[99]

The melancholic does not search for meaning (constituted through a synthesis of signifier and drive affect); rather, despair, or pain (*douleur*), is the melancholic's only meaning. What we have, at least in part, then, is a failure to develop of imaginary and symbolic capacities (language, in a word) which would ensure a successful separation and a viable identity for the subject. Indeed, in its extreme form melancholia is a living death. It will be interesting to see how one can possibly become an artist under such circumstances. For to be drowned in affect (the Thing) and the slave of changing moods entails the collapse of the symbolic and the consequent impossibility of art: that is, precisely, a living death. Against this, art would be a rebirth (resurrection) for the artist in signs. The analytic effects of art would thereby come to the fore once again.

Unlike a true psychosis neither melancholia nor depression results in the complete collapse of the symbolic and the loss of the use of signs. Rather, for the melancholic/depressive, language is always 'foreign', never maternal. Words have become detached from their drive base and marked with a deathly stillness. Melancholia prevents an eroticization of the death drive (as manifested in hate), and this distinguishes it from neurosis; but above all, melancholia prevents an eroticization of the separation from the mother: that is, the mother is not a lost object, the subject dies in her place. Such would be the logic behind the melancholic's (deathly) immobility.

Consequently, in an almost mirror reversal of love as eroticization, the melancholic's words become cut off from their drive base and emotions become detached from symbolic constructions. Melancholia holds the drives and the symbolic quite apart. An extreme rationalist relying on a strict mind–body dualism might thus be a potential melancholic. Would this mean that Descartes was the 'perfect' melancholic? Kristeva does not say. What she does say, is that the failed synthesis of drive and symbol may be summarized in terms of a denial of the '*dénégation*'[100] fundamental to language. For it is language's *dénégation* that unites words with objects. Kristeva explains:

> Signs are arbitrary because language begins with a *dénégation* (*Verneinung*) of loss, at the same time as a depression occasioned by mourning. 'I have lost an indispensable object which happens to be, in the last instance, my mother', the speaking being seems to say. 'But no, I have found her again in signs, or rather because I accept to lose her, I have not lost her (here is the *dénégation*), I can get her back in language.'[101]

The melancholic's denial of *dénégation* (which is also a denial of representation) means that signs do not have the force either of bringing the mother back, or of expressing the pain of loss. Rather than expressing emotion and affect, the subject *becomes* these: melancholics, in short, act out what needs to be put into signs and symbols formed in response to the loss of the object (the mother). This detachment of signs from an object, corresponds to an attachment to the Thing: the object as *not* lost. A chasm now forms between the melancholic subject and its objects, and it is the psychoanalyst's task, as Kristeva sees it, to provide a symbolic 'graft'[102] for reconnecting the two domains and turning the Thing into an object. Can the artist do something similar?

Soleil noir will, in all likelihood, become renowned for its analysis of Holbein the Younger's painting of 'The Corpse of Christ in the Tomb' (*'Der Leichnam Christi im Grabe'*), and we shall consider this, as we shall also consider, albeit more briefly, Kristeva's analysis of de Nerval's poetry, the writing of Dostoyevsky, and that of Marguerite Duras – the modern, melancholic stylist. But first, art and melancholia should be generally explained.

To begin, we may suppose that the artist tends towards the melancholic pole of the psychic spectrum. Every imaginary artistic work, even those geared to provoke a strong emotional response, is executed with a certain detachment. The artist exemplifies an attachment to the Thing through there being a continuity between the artist's life – or *'comportement'*, as Kristeva says[103] – and his work; but this, not in the sense that a life is represented in the work, but because the work is *part* of the artist's life. Perhaps, then, Dostoyevsky's excessive gambling, equivalent to an evacuation of drive energy, would be the precondition for the detachment and (as he remarked himself) clarity of mind necessary for him to write his moving fiction. Finally, the artist would evoke the attachment to the mother through the semiotic dimension of the signifying process, where the transposition of affect becomes rhythm, alliteration, intonation, etc. The artist, unlike the melancholic, has control over the use of signs; the true artist is not naïve: style (coherence) predominates. The work of art is thus the possible mark, Kristeva suggests, of a 'vanquished' depression.[104]

While the psychotic is incapable of carrying out all linguistic operations successfully, the melancholic can master signs, but not affect. In short, the denial centres predominantly on the primary inscription of affect in the symbolic. Artists, though, are like neither the psychotic nor the melancholic in that they very often articulate the primary inscription of loss semiotically (see rhythm, etc., mentioned above, p. 124), and so give loss a mode of articulation. Holbein's 'The Corpse of Christ . . .' gives a unique vision of loss, Kristeva will argue.

Holbein

Hans Holbein the Younger was far from being a melancholic himself. For one thing, he produced the series of engravings called the 'Macabre Dance' – an eroticized representation of death. Moreover, the detachment and coldness often evident in his work has an historical determinant: the Reformation and the emergence of a 'melancholic moment' in Europe, especially in the north (Calvin, for example) where severity comes to embody truth. This moment, says Kristeva, 'mobilizes' Holbein's 'aesthetic activity'.[105]

In such a context, Kristeva suggests, some of Holbein the Younger's paintings, and especially 'The Corpse of Christ . . .', take us very close to a presentation of signs completely bereft of drive affect typical of melancholia. In other words, Holbein's dead Christ, unlike the paintings of Grünewald or Mantegna, goes very close to illustrating the denial of *dénégation* and the evacuation of drive affect characteristic of the melancholic's constructions. This effect is achieved in the painting in question through a 'minimalism' which, firstly, isolates the figure of Christ through depicting the body entirely alone in its crypt; and, secondly, gives no hint of an idealization of the body, no sign of transcendence, or of passion (semiotic features). Indeed, the spectator cannot easily identify with this painting. For as Kristeva says, it is not a sign of grief, it *is* grief. To identify with death entails life becoming a 'macabre dance'.[106] Of course the same spectator may be directly affected by the painting through being given a premonition of his or her own death. Indeed, there is no coded rhetoric in Holbein's painting to alleviate the anguish of the intimation of death. Holbein's minimalism (which implies the invisibility of signs) places the spectator in touch with death and its synonyms: the unnameable, the real, the void, etc. Holbein thus evokes the sadness of separation, enables us to relive it in signs (albeit, minimal), and to come as close as possible to experiencing death as a depression, as a disruption in and of the symbolic: the equivalent of the death of God. Christ as the equivalent of the death of God is also the equivalent of the destruction of all identity and the death of man as a fundamentally symbolic being.

On the other hand, Christianity has, through facilitating an imaginary identification with the death of Christ, provided a way for bringing death into the symbolic; or at least it has provided a way for enlarging the imaginary and symbolic means available for coping with death:

The Corpse of Christ in the Tomb by Hans Holbein the Younger (1521). Reproduced courtesy of the Public Art Collection, Basel Kunstmuseum

In light of this identification, admittedly too anthropological and psychological in the eyes of a strict theology, man is nevertheless bequeathed a powerful symbolic device enabling him to live his death and resurrection even in his physical body, thanks to the power of imaginary unification – and its real effects – with the absolute Subject (Christ).[107]

Christ is the Absolute, imaginary subject (ego) forming the border between the real (Mother) and the symbolic (Father). The subject, therefore, comes to occupy the place of art itself, the place transcending death through signs. The analyst thus points to the following scenario: to transcend death (which is also the death of the symbolic), it is necessary to identify with it for all we are worth, expanding our imaginary capacities, and thereby overcoming the unnameable basis of our depression. 'To enter heaven, travel hell', as Joyce put it.[108] We need to put hell into the symbolic, to describe it, name all its aspects, experience it in imagination, and so constitute ourselves as subjects with (new) identities. We will become somebody through transcending non-meaning: the void, the unrepresentable, nothingness, etc.

Kristeva's further point is that Holbein's minimalism depicting death, almost reaches the point of no return: a death without resurrection. This is historically reinforced in Holbein's painting by the arrival of Protestant iconoclasm leading to such an extreme simplicity of signs that they almost become extinct. In this sense, 'The Corpse of Christ . . .' takes us to the limit of our imaginary capacities. What we cannot give an image, what constitutes a gap in our imaginary capacities, is death – and Holbein paints it. He thus paints the 'scission' in the psyche between 'death' and 'divine love' – the equivalent of a simultaneous opening up and closure of the psyche itself. As Kristeva succinctly writes:

> Between classicism and mannerism [Holbein's] minimalism is the metaphor of scission: between life and death, meaning and non-meaning, it is an intimate and fine response of our melancholies.[109]

Forms of resurrection: 'El Desdichado'; Dostoyevsky and forgiveness

If Holbein is any guide the art of melancholy would be a resurrection in the symbolic, and a means of assuming an identity. And Kristeva confirms this in her studies of de Nerval's poem 'El

Desdichado', and the writings of Dostoyevsky. We shall briefly summarize the analysis of the poem in question, before moving on to consider at slightly greater length the way that forgiveness and writing are linked in Dostoyevsky.

'El Desdichado' is the cry of the grief-stricken, 'disinherited' one (*el desdichado*; cf. Walter Scott's *Ivanhoe*). For Kristeva, the subject of the poem is disinherited of an object and the possibility of articulating, or symbolizing the pain of ensuing grief. As a result, the poem is more 'about' the archaic Thing than about an object; or rather, the poem, as the mark of melancholy, is at the same time the overcoming of melancholy in the act of producing the poem. Because the poem is also a 'vocal gesture'[110] exhibiting semiotic features ('alliterations, rhythms, melodies'), the reader can grasp something from it without understanding all its allusions. The poem is a 'soleil noir' – an impossible naming of the source of grief: the Thing. The latter becomes a kind of object giving rise to signs and a (provisional) preservation of psychic space: a resurrection.

With Dostoyevsky, suffering dominates the content of his novels and is constitutive of writing as such. This is the 'non-eroticized suffering' of 'primary masochism' or 'melancholy', 'the primordial psychic inscription of a rupture'.[111] Or again, we are dealing with a non-erotic mood of suffering which is 'neither inside nor outside, between two, at the threshold of the separation self/other, even before this is possible . . .'.[112] Hence, Dostoyevsky suffers voluptuously in order to write. In fact, Kristeva reveals that Dostoyevsky's belief is that suffering, and not pleasure, drives man. Consciousness here is a form of suffering. Given such a framework, it is impossible for human beings to be pure hedonists. The overcoming of suffering in signs, in imagination – in writing – constitutes one as a symbolic being. More directly, suffering is overcome through forgiveness, but forgiveness is fundamentally a symbolic affair, and thus potentially an affair of writing. Dostoyevsky's wager is that by putting suffering into signs, but identifying with it without reserve, we human beings will experience a resurrection. Consequently, we see in *Crime and Punishment* that Raskolnikov, the murderer, experiences forgiveness through becoming aware of his love for the devoted Sonia:

They wanted to speak, but could not; tears stood in their eyes. They were both pale and thin; but in those sick and pale faces the dawn of a new future, of a *full resurrection* to a new life, was already shining. It was love that brought them back to life: the heart of one held inexhaustible sources of life for the heart of the other.

They decided to wait and be patient. They still had to wait for another seven years, and what great suffering and what infinite joy till then! And he had come back to life, and he knew it, and felt it with every fibre of his renewed being, and she – why, she lived only for him.[113]

Love would, therefore, reconstitute Raskolnikov's psychic space and make him open to the other after having been closed off from others and the world in his downward spin into nihilism. Kristeva, however, suggests that we should see much more than the imaginary rebirth of characters in these novels, and recognize that Dostoyevsky's writing has analytic effects – first of all, for the reader, but most importantly for Dostoyevsky himself. Writing produces forgiveness; for it opens up suffering to the self and thus to the other as well. Hence, the significance of the fact that Raskolnikov 'knew' he had come back to life. Not to 'know' in these circumstances is impossible, because forgiveness presupposes a heightened state of consciousness and, therefore, a heightened sense of suffering entailing more forgiveness and leading to eventual jubilation.

In another important respect, forgiveness is a substitute for the act – for the acting out of violence, in particular. In this regard, Kristeva observes,[114] Dostoyevsky identified closely with his characters and knew them intimately. He thus 'travels hell' with them, does not leave them for a moment, and makes their rebirth inseparable from his own. 'Is it not', says Kristeva, 'in *signifying* hate, the destruction of the other and perhaps, above all, his own dying, that the human being survives as a symbolic animal?'[115] Signifying suffering, therefore, constituting an aesthetic distance between it and one's own self, would thus *be* forgiveness as such. In short, the analytic effects of writing merge into writing as forgiveness in Dostoyevsky: 'between suffering and acting out, aesthetic activity is forgiveness'.[116] And it is to a mother (or a substitute for her) to whom the writer (but we are all writers in this sense) turns in order to be forgiven. For it is she who has been killed by signs in the quest for individuality. Forgiveness, then, is fundamentally equivalent to a reconciliation with the mother.

A nihilist culture, however, finds it difficult to understand forgiveness. It is like Raskolnikov in prison before he comes 'back to life':

> he went over his actions again in his mind, and he did not find them so stupid or so absurd as they had seemed to him at the fatal time in the past. . . .
> 'Why does my action strike them as so hideous?' he kept saying to himself. 'Is it because it was a crime? What does "crime" mean? My conscience is clear . . .'.[117]

Up to this point in the novel, Raskolnikov does not feel any need to be forgiven, for he cannot believe that killing the old woman was a crime. He assumes that a crime is simply what is defined as such, a definition without absolute validity. Fundamentally, there would be no real crime, and therefore neither guilt nor forgiveness. But in particular, there would be no suffering for Raskolnikov, either in prison or outside; only wounded pride. Suffering only comes with love, and a capacity to believe in – that is, struggle to symbolize – some ideal instance. Without the ideal, the result is indifference to the point of death (e.g. Raskolnikov's collapse). Without the ideal, in other words, there can be no resurrection and, no doubt, hardly any aesthetic endeavour either.

Under the influence of the Byzantine conception of the trinity,[118] Dostoyevsky's position, according to Kristeva, is that without the father (ideal) there can be no son (individual ego), or being as 'real' (holy spirit). Or, to put it, as Kristeva does, in a psychoanalytic frame, Dostoyevsky's writing manifests the fusion of the Real, the Symbolic, and the Imaginary. In this trilogy, the polyphonic, dialogical – poetic – aspect of Dostoyevsky's writing would accompany both the ideal instance and the imaginary place of the writer.

Duras and writing at the end of the twentieth century

For the reader of *Soleil noir*, to move from Dostoyevsky and forgiveness to the analysis of the stylistically 'white' writing of a Marguerite Duras, is to move from art as resurrection and renewal, to a writing art that would realize an erasure of all signs of transcendence similar to the one witnessed in Holbein's 'The Corpse of Christ . . .'. As Kristeva says, with Duras never has reality been more cataclysmic, but never has there been such a poverty of symbolic means for coping with it.[119] Thus, Duras' writing, as Kristeva presents it, contains no ideal, no music (thus, no mark of the real: the mother), only a cold, logical, totally lucid self: the world as nothing but this self – this imaginary ego. Such writing is symptomatic of a world where people have gone mad quite rationally in full command of their faculties. Indeed, we are witness to a growing worthlessness of meaning and sentiment accompanied by complete lucidity. Consequently, everything would be controlled and cold in this Durasian world, our own distress 'neutralized without tragedy or enthusiasm . . . in the frigid insignificance of a psychic drowsiness, the ultimate but also minimal sign of pain and rapture'.[120] In short, Duras would show us the way to turn back from; a way derived, perhaps, from the very disenchantment Dostoyevsky fought against, and against which love, as the basis of the analytic treatment, also fights.

If Duras' writing is a valid sign of our contemporary experience, we have to ask whether our so called postmodernity is the breakthrough many have been waiting for. In the flight from dogma and the impossible precariousness of faith, may we not be risking a form of individual, and therefore collective, suicide – at least in the west? For Kristeva, the answer seems to be 'yes', and we should be awakened to the need to have a 'new loving world surface from the eternal return of historical and mental cycles'.[121]

Is this perspective not too pessimistic? More pointedly, is it valid? It remains now to discuss these and other issues – such as feminism – in the final chapter which attempts to give an assessment of Kristeva's œuvre.

Notes

1 We recall that the Mother was the semiotic *chora* in *Revolution in Poetic Language*.

2 Kristeva, *Powers of Horror*, p. 209. Translation modified.

3 See Chapter 5, p. 136.

4 Kristeva, *Powers of Horror*, p. 12. Kristeva's emphasis.

5 ibid., p. 13.

6 ibid., p. 15.

7 ibid., p. 4.

8 ibid.

9 ibid., p. 16.

10 See Sigmund Freud, 'Analysis of a phobia in a five-year-old boy ("Little Hans")', *SE*, vol. X, pp. 3–140.

11 See Kristeva, *Powers of Horror*, pp. 35–6, where Kristeva speaks of the father not holding his own.

12 ibid., p. 38.

13 ibid.

14 Thus, in referring to Lévi-Strauss, Kristeva says in *La Révolution du langage poétique*, p. 456, that 'as soon as society reaches a political stage, that is to say, finally, in every more or less ordered human society, rights belong to the father, whatever the modes of filiation'. In this sense, the right of the father is a structural necessity.

15 See Anthony Giddens' discussion based on such a dichotomy in *Social Theory and Modern Sociology* (Oxford, Polity Press in association with Basil Blackwell, 1987), pp. 59–61.

16 See Kristeva, *Powers of Horror*, pp. 57–8.

17 See Sigmund Freud, *Totem and Taboo*, *SE*, vol. XIII, pp. 1–162.

18 See Mary Douglas, *Purity and Danger* (London, Routledge & Kegan Paul, 1979).

19 Kristeva, *Powers of Horror*, p. 71. Kristeva's emphasis.

20 ibid., p. 72.

21 ibid., p. 73.

22 ibid., p. 74.

23 ibid., p. 77.

24 Particular mention should be made here of Kristeva's analysis of Indian society where, in sum, the absence of a radical opposition between man and woman (symbolic) is translated into a caste hierarchy. Relying heavily on Louis Dumont's work, she writes, at ibid., page 81, that:

> It is as if the more the balance between the two sexual powers was maintained by endogamy, the greater was the need to have *other* differences come into play. The inseparability, one might even say that immanence to endogamy, of the hierarchic principle, like the cloth and lining of a single organization, perhaps explains why marriage (the rite of joining, of maintaining the identity and balance of the two) is the only rite of passage that 'is not accompanied by any impurity' [Louis Dumont, *Homo Hierarchicus* (Chicago, University of Chicago Press, 1970), p. 53].

25 See, in particular, Pierre Clastres, *Society Against the State*, trans. Robert Hurley (Oxford, Basil Blackwell, 1977), pp. 159–86.

26 ibid., pp. 185–6.

27 Claude Lévi-Strauss, 'The Art of Asia and America' in *Structural Anthropology*, trans. Claire Jacobson and Brooke Grundfest Schoepf (Harmondsworth, Penguin, 1972), p. 257.

28 ibid., p. 259.

29 Kristeva, *Powers of Horror*, p. 105.

30 ibid., p. 109.

31 ibid., p. 110.

32 ibid., p. 113.

33 ibid., p. 131.

34 It is here that Georges Bataille's work serves to draw attention to the link between art and abjection. See Georges Bataille, *Literature and Evil*, trans. Alistair Hamilton (New York, Marion Boyars, 1985), and 'L'Abjection et les formes misérables', in *Essais de sociologie, Oeuvres Complètes* (Paris, Gallimard, 1970).

35 Kristeva, *Powers of Horror*, p. 149.

36 ibid., p. 150, from L.-F. Céline, *Death on the Instalment Plan*, trans. Ralph Manheim (New York, New Directions, 1966), p. 560.

37 See Jean-Jacques Rousseau, *Essai sur l'origine des langues* (Paris, Nizet, 1979), p. 41.

38 Kristeva, *Powers of Horror*, p. 191.

39 ibid., p. 204.

40 ibid., p. 205.

41 ibid., pp. 205–6.

42 The titles of these anti-semitic pamphlets by Louis-Ferdinand Céline are as follows: *Bagatelles pour un massacre* (Paris, Denoel, 1937): *L'Ecole des cadavres* (Paris, Denoel, 1938); *Les Beaux draps* (Paris, Nouvelles Editions Françaises, 1941).

43 For her own brief summary of *Tales of Love*, see Julia Kristeva, *Histoires d'amour – Love Stories*, London, ICA Documents (1984), pp. 18–21.

44 Kristeva, *Soleil noir*, p. 38.

45 Kristeva, *Tales of Love*, p. 26. Translation modified.

46 ibid., p. 79.

47 ibid.

48 The pun is stronger in French: see *Histoires d'amour* (Paris, Denoel, 1983), pp. 78–80, and *Tales of Love*, pp. 78–80 and p. 389, note 9.

49 ibid., pp. 77–8.

50 *Tel Quel*, no. 91 (Spring, 1982), pp. 17–32.

51 See Kristeva, *Tales of Love*, pp. 21–4.

52 Roland Barthes, *A Lover's Discourse: Fragments*, trans. Richard Howard (New York, Hill & Wang, 1984), p. 1.

53 See 'A holy madness: she and he' in *Tales of Love*, pp. 83–100.

54 *Tales of Love*, p. 100.

55 ibid., p. 115.

56 ibid., p. 116.

57 ibid., p. 120.

58 ibid., p. 126.

59 ibid., p. 127.

60 ibid., p. 146.

61 ibid., p. 145.

62 See, in ibid., the following chapters: 'Ego affectus est. Bernard of Clairvaux: Affect, Desire, Love', pp. 151–69; and 'Ratio Diligendi, or the triumph of one's own. Thomas Aquinas: natural love and love of self', pp. 170–87.

63 Saint Bernard, *Sermons divers*, 101, *Oeuvres Complètes*, IV, p. 69, cited in

   Tales of Love, p. 167.
64 *Tales of Love*, p. 200.
65 ibid., p. 201.
66 ibid., *Tales of Love*, p. 204.
67 See ibid., pp. 220–3.
68 ibid., p. 217.
69 ibid., p. 221.
70 ibid., p. 223.
71 ibid., pp. 234–63. First published as 'Hérétique de l'amour', *Tel Quel*, no. 74 (Winter, 1977), pp. 30–49.
72 Kristeva, *Tales of Love*, p. 245.
73 See Marina Warner, *Alone of All Her Sex: The Myth and Cult of the Virgin Mary* (London, Picador, 1985).
74 Kristeva, *Tales of Love*, p. 249.
75 ibid., p. 253.
76 ibid., pp. 281–2.
77 See Kristeva, *Histoires d'amour*, p. 268.
78 Kristeva, *Tales of Love*, p. 312.
79 ibid., p. 313.
80 ibid.
81 Freud, *Interpretation of Dreams*, *SE*, vol. V, p. 595.
82 Kristeva, *Tales of Love*, p. 267
83 ibid., p. 275.
84 ibid., p. 329.
85 ibid., p. 334.
86 ibid., p. 339.
87 See also, Kristeva's interview entitled 'Les Looks sont entrés dans Paris', *L'Infini*, no. 5 (Winter, 1984), pp. 14–19.
88 Kristeva, *Tales of Love*, p. 339.
89 ibid., p. 355.
90 ibid., p. 360.
91 ibid., pp. 367–8.
92 Julia Kristeva, *Au commencement était l'amour: Psychanalyse et foi* (Paris, Hachette, 1985), p. 71.
93 For Kristeva's treatment of the notion of the subject as an open system, see *Tales of Love*, pp. 13–16, 379–82; 'Evénement et révélation', *L'Infini*, no. 5 (Winter, 1984), pp. 3–11, and 'Les Looks sont entrés dans Paris', ibid., pp. 14–19.
94 Kristeva, 'Evénement et révélation', p. 5. Kristeva's emphasis.
95 Julia Kristeva, 'Joyce, le retour d'Orphée', *L'Infini*, no. 8 (Autumn, 1984), p. 5.
96 See Kristeva, *Powers of Horror*, p. 92.
97 See Freud, 'Mourning and Melancholia', *SE*, vol. XIV, p. 246.
98 Julia Kristeva, *Soleil noir*, p. 22.
99 See ibid., pp. 22–3.
100 I retain the French term *dénégation* as it corresponds more closely to

Freud's *Verneinung*, translated as 'negation'. See Sigmund Freud, 'On Negation' in *SE*, vol. XIX, p. 143, note 1, and p. 235, note 2, where Freud says:

> Negation is a way of taking cognizance of what is repressed; indeed it is already a lifting of the repression, though not of course an acceptance of what is repressed. We can see how in this the intellectual function is separated from the affective process. With the help of negation only one consequence of the process of repression is undone – the fact, namely, of the ideational content of what is repressed not reaching consciousness. The outcome of this is a kind of intellectual acceptance of the repressed while at the same time what is essential to the repression persists. (ibid., pp. 235–6)

Thus the negation is not a 'pure' negation, but a 'dénégation': an acceptance on one level of what is negated on another.

101 Kristeva, *Soleil noir*, p. 55.
102 ibid., p. 64.
103 ibid., p. 141.
104 ibid., p. 76.
105 ibid., p. 140.
106 ibid., p. 125.
107 ibid., p. 145.
108 Cited by Jean-Louis Houdebine in 'Joyce: littérature et religion', *Tel Quel*, no. 89 (Autumn, 1981), p. 69.
109 Kristeva, *Soleil noir*, p. 148.
110 See ibid., p. 172.
111 ibid., p. 186.
112 ibid.
113 Fyodor Dostoyevsky, *Crime and Punishment*, trans. David Magarshack (Harmondsworth, Penguin, reprinted 1967), pp. 557–8. Emphasis added.
114 See Kristeva, interviewed by Catherine Francblin in *Art Press*, no. 114 (May, 1987), p. 50.
115 Kristeva, *Soleil noir*, p. 192. Kristeva's emphasis.
116 ibid., p. 200.
117 Dostoyevsky, *Crime and Punishment*, p. 552.
118 That is, *per filium*, the fusion of Father, Son, and Holy Spirit, as opposed to the *Filioque* of the Latin Church, where each element of the trinity has a separate identity, and the Holy Spirit emanates from both the Father *and* the Son.
119 See Kristeva, *Soleil noir*, p. 231.
120 ibid., p. 236.
121 ibid., p. 265.

Part Three

Conclusion

7

The importance of Kristeva

> ... Cruelfiction!
> ... Array! Surrection!

> *Finnegans Wake*

Julia Kristeva's first book translated into English on Chinese women[1] quickly turned into a feminist work of some significance. Indeed, as Kristeva's writings (to the extent that they are well known outside France) are more often than not seen as part of feminist discourse, we first consider this fact, before moving on to an assessment of the Kristevan *œuvre*.

Feminism: for and against

Besides an overt political commitment to social equality, Kristeva brought to feminism a partial reworking of Lacan's psychoanalytic framework. With Kristeva, the pre-symbolic, semiotic domain came to figure within the very sphere of the Lacanian Name-of-the-Father where once it was entirely unrecognized. 'Chora', 'semiotic', 'negativity', 'heterogeneity' – 'music' ('ultimate position of meaning'[2]) – all form part of a vocabulary aimed at speaking what is at once unnameable and at the same time points to the name as 'legion':[3] a vast plurality of names. The unnameable, heterogeneous element is called 'feminine' in Kristeva's writing of the mid seventies. Our earlier commentary has endeavoured to show this.

To avoid psychosis, the feminine element (in men and women) needs to be inscribed within the symbolic order. According to Kristeva, the feminine semiotic may be potentially disruptive of an overly rigid form of the symbolic but it cannot humanly exist independently of it. By way of this more refined framework, a feminist politics was able to see that all social movements (of which feminism was one) were the outcome of a division more fundamental than one based on ideology, a division produced within the frame of reproduction – namely, sexual difference as psychoanalysis outlines it. To put it simply: the social sphere signified by the Name-of-the-Father is itself complicit with a patriarchy that makes the independent existence of the feminine impossible. For Kristeva, as we have seen, it is doubtful whether any society could be matriarchal in anything but name only – given that language (the symbolic) is the precondition of social life. In any event, Kristeva's approach to feminism could never be couched within an either/or polemical framework of either the feminine semiotic *or* the masculine symbolic.

But such a stance is far too equivocal for some critics. While they agree that the position of women is only explicable through reference to the basis of the social bond as such, a truly effective feminist politics, this view says, must seek to valorize a language of the feminine. Not to have such a language, theorists such as Luce Irigaray argue[4] – one that rejects patriarchy lock, stock, and barrel – is to continue to condemn women to silence, to deprive them of meaningful speech. For Irigaray, women thus need their own language in order to escape their oppression in a patriarchal society. Irigaray, then, is quite clearly against Kristeva who believes that in opposing the phallic sign with a feminine language there is a danger, firstly, of essentializing 'woman'; secondly, of falling back into mysticism; and thirdly, of privileging feminine '*signifiance*' instead of the phallus, thereby remaining within the same metaphysical enclosure that created the problem in the first place.[5] In effect, the feminine, the woman, is no more outside language than the man is outside *signifiance*.

One of Irigaray's advocates, Elizabeth Grosz, finds Kristeva's argument 'puzzling in feminist terms, to say the least':

[Kristeva's] ideal model of a transgressive subjectivity articulating itself is a male who has identified with and taken upon himself the representation of a femininity women can't speak: man mimicking the woman who reproduces man! – man unable to accept his difference from, and his debt to the maternal space which bore him.[6]

As well as condemning women to being unable to speak on their own behalf (Kristeva's avant-garde artist would *represent* femininity), Kristeva's so-called 'avant-garde revolutionary male' is, finally, 'unable to accept women's differences, whether bodily, psychic or social'![7] A later work by Grosz even suggests that Kristeva's theory of both the so-called male avant-garde and sexual difference implies an anti-feminist stance.[8] A number of remarks need to be made in response to this critique.

To begin, the full force of the word 'mimicking' appearing in the above quotation should be digested. For it is an unstable term, regardless of whether or not this is intended. 'To mimic' could be thought, in its etymological connection, with 'to mime': using only gesture and movement in a performance without words. The actor here, like the woman as feminine, would be constrained to silence. Mime, though, is a *presentation* of the act; it is thus a re-presentation, and this explains its link with 'mimesis', or imitation. It is mimesis, of course, which centres the issue in representation. Alice Jardine elaborates:

> Representation is the condition that confirms the possibility of an imitation (mimesis) based on the dichotomy of presence and absence and, more generally, on the dichotomies of dialectical thinking (negativity). Representation, mimesis, and the dialectic are inseparable . . . .[9]

If the male artist mimed woman without speaking, he might have been (because silent) close to 'being' woman – in which case Grosz's argument might have had some effect. As it is, even mime is inseparable from representation: the most apodictic form of the symbolic. To mimic/represent 'woman' is thus a clear way of *not* being woman and signalling a separation from the mother. This is to say that, fundamentally, a work of art is at the heart of the matter, and not the unspeakable real emerging in psychosis. In effect, the work of art as a 'délire manqué'[10] keeps psychosis at bay. This is why, according to Kristeva, the artist's creation, almost invariably, has to do with the phallic mother – the mother as castrated and thus *in* the symbolic. The mother as the embodiment of the real, on the other hand, can never as such appear in art; she may only be alluded to in the materiality of the work – as in the colour blue of Giotto's Padua frescoes. Above all, perhaps, we should note that each individual is, in psychoanalytic terms, a specific configuration of the Real, the Imaginary, and the

Symbolic: a 'borromean' trinity, to coin a phrase, evoking both Lacan and Dostoyevsky. It follows from this that social being is not the sole custodian of human characteristics. Grosz's argument against Kristeva, however, implies the contrary.

Nevertheless, it is true that rather than confirming the symbolic, the 'music in letters' (semiotic) is more disruptive of the symbolic and evocative of the feminine (but not necessarily 'woman'). Pollock's painting, we have suggested,[11] is on the side of the mother in this sense. There is still some way to go, however, before the semiotic in art is a pure imitation of the mother, or, as Grosz says, the mark of an inability to accept one's difference from the 'maternal space'. Indeed, to say this is to risk the appearance of making an exclusively clinical judgement about the work of art, whereas Kristeva keeps the relative autonomy of the work of art in view. And, although Grosz may not agree, every subjectivity approximates a work of art to the extent that

> [a]ll speaking subjects have within themselves a certain bisexual-ity which is precisely the possibility to explore all the sources of signification, that which posits meaning as well as that which multiplies, pulverizes and finally revives it.[12]

Because the speaking subject cannot be reduced to the male or female gender it is possible for the work of art to explore aspects of both the feminine and the masculine disposition. This means, as the Conclusion to *La Révolution du langage poétique* shows,[13] that the avant-garde text, in presenting both the dissolution of the symbolic effected by the semiotic, and thence the reconstitution of the symbolic through the attainment of equilibrium, as work of art mimes, not the woman, nor even the feminine – but the 'constitution and deconstruction of the subject: a subject in process/on trial . . .'.[14]

For feminists such as Irigaray and Grosz, however, art of the late nineteenth and early twentieth centuries is directly tied to political considerations relating to the position of women in western society. The key issue then supposedly centres on the fact that it is a male artist producing works of art, thereby reinforcing the inferior status of women in a patriarchal society.

Gayatri Spivak, for her part, as well as criticizing Kristeva for making unfounded generalizations about Chinese women and Chinese society,[15] finds 'something even faintly comical about Joyce rising above sexual identities and bequeathing the proper mind-set to the women's movement'.[16] While Spivak is aware that feminism cannot simply be about putting a positive sign in front of 'woman' and a negative sign in front of 'man', as the first generation of feminists had tended to do, she is clearly suspicious of the actual practical, political effect of a male avant-garde in the fight against the power of patriarchy. According to Spivak, there is a need to move 'beyond the texts so far favored by the French feminists' while relating the 'morphology of this critique' to the '"specificity" of other discourses that spell out and establish the power of the patriarchy'; this will then provide 'an excellent strategy for undermining the *masculinist* vanguard'.[17] Therefore, even though Spivak recognizes the force of an 'anti-feminist' feminism[18] inspired by a structuralist and poststructuralist anti-humanism, she clearly asks that the political credentials of the male avant-garde be scrutinized lest they be found wanting from a feminist perspective. For Kristeva, on the other hand, the avant-garde did not, and perhaps does not, have an *immediate* political agenda. Its political effect would at best be indirect. And this is important within Kristeva's analysis of western capitalist society for two main reasons. The first is that to enter the political arena at an (immediate) ideological level often results in one becoming ineffective because caught within the structure of binary opposi-tions fundamental to western political discourse. In any event, this arena is not the essence of social and cultural life – everything is not political – but only one aspect of it. Believing that there is no 'outside' to politics may be an important force in a precisely western social life.

In the second place, avant-garde artistic works, as presented in Kristeva's writing, are a signifying practice presupposing the limitedness of all binary oppositions (including 'man'–'woman'); in fact, the form of the avant-garde artistic work would – *qua* avant-garde work – escape binary oppositions. In Kristeva's terms, this means that it *includes* sexual difference within it. The danger of calling for the avant-garde (or indeed any art work) to have an immediately political disposition, centres on the very real risk of re-establishing constricting binary oppositions. In a commentary on a short story by the East German writer, Karl-Heinz Jakobs, Anne MacLeod illustrates this danger which is particularly acute when a certain type of feminism reduces its aim to the simple attainment of political power. Let us pause for a moment on this commentary.[19]

Like Spivak on the male avant-garde, MacLeod sees herself

approaching Jakobs' story called 'Quedlinburg'[20] from a decon-structionist perspective. Effectively, this means that the commentary aims to highlight the pitfalls of being oppositional within a social context that is, in good part, structured by opposition. MacLeod's pointed epigraph from Derrida succinctly encapsulates the theme of the argument presented: 'if the form of opposition and the oppositional structure are themselves metaphysical, then the relation of metaphysics to its other can no longer be one of opposition'.[21]

The theme of Jakobs' story deals with a change from patriarchy to matriarchy in the political and social structure of the fictional town of Quedlinburg. This town, then, is the site of a complete 'inversion' having, amongst others, the following features: abolition of love, marriage, and private property – as these are deemed to be sources of women's oppression; identity as the governing principle of thought is replaced by difference; ugliness is given precedence over beauty, and generally, legislation is enacted giving women full equality with men. A written constitution proclaims a system of 'truths' which are the direct opposite of those of the system the women denounce and believe they have already overthrown. The question to be faced, however, is: Did the women really overthrow the patriarchal system as they seem to believe? In this regard, MacLeod suggests that from Jakobs' story it is clear that 'the operations of patriarchy are such that it simply cannot be opposed because all oppositions already belong to it'.[22]

The final twist to the story comes when it is revealed that the men of Quedlinburg have gone along with the 'inversion' of social forms as a way of subverting the new matriarchy. Not opposition, but a complete identification with the source of power is the men's strategy.[23] As MacLeod sees it, the 'problem which becomes clear in and through writing ... is that discourse is a thoroughly alternativist system: it operates by means of binary oppositions'.[24]

In such circumstances, Kristeva's non-oppositional avant-garde becomes entirely pertinent. For its base in negativity rather than in the simple oppositional form of negation would become potentially subversive of a rigidly patriarchal society – precisely because it does not constitute a *recognizable* oppositional form. But the question whether or not such importance should be attributed to an avant-garde is less significant than the insight that the specific constitution of society is inseparable from the formation of individuals as subjects in process. The subject in process leads to the articulation of specific *social* forms: the two aspects are inseparable. Reproduction (of the species) is therefore implicit in production, and the semiotic, like the mother, is the real basis of sociality. However, as soon as these things are recognized, they are located in the symbolic. For Anne MacLeod the point is to unhinge thought based on binary oppositions, not to displace it or become another version of it. For Kristeva, this is at least partially achieved through a musicalization of language leading to an infinitization of meaning. I would say that in this context the musicalization of language is neither entirely of the semiotic nor of the symbolic; rather, it would be *sembolic*, provided that this neologism conveys the notion that, in practice, it is no longer a question of a binary opposition, or of a new synthesis. We recall, indeed, that this musicalization of language was seen by Kristeva in the mid-1970s as a way of allowing a non-destructive (whether of self or others) form of jouissance into the social sphere. Close off this avenue and the only outlet, the only recognition of the other face of social life, becomes drugs, madness, and violence – a destructive return of the repressed.

In a more explicitly political vein, Kristeva has said[25] that 'first generation' feminism claiming economic, political and professional equality for women, as well as 'second generation feminism' inspired by thinkers such as Irigaray, needs to give way to a third form that does not exclude the other two, but is cognizant of their dangers. These dangers, illustrated by Anne MacLeod, may be summarized as: a failure by first generation feminism (for example de Beauvoir) to recognize the risk of being incorporated into the male power structure, and, with the second generation, a blindness as to the risk of sectarianism and of becoming agents of the violence (terrorism) that the movement expressly opposes. Kristeva's 'third way' would see the 'very dichotomy man/woman . . . as belonging to *metaphysics*'[26] and, in particular, would advocate 'aesthetic practices' which explore, and also construct, the singularity of every speaking being: that is, a being who is the outcome of a multiplicity of 'possible identifications'. Aesthetic practices here are equivalent to transcending difference as a battle between rival groups of all kinds (including that of the sexes), in order to turn it into the basis of new possibilities for subjectivity. Indeed, this point made by Kristeva for the first time in 1979, can be seen to foreshadow the notion of subjectivity as an 'open system' elaborated in the early 1980s. It is a view of subjectivity to which we shall return. But first, let us focus on the overall evolution of Kristeva's *œuvre*.

From modernism to postmodernism?

The evolution of Kristeva's *œuvre* from the practice of a *sémanalyse* in the 1960s to reflections on art and melancholy in the latter half of the 1980s, invites us to ask about the structure of this evolution. In this regard, we note that at all stages Kristeva has never wavered from a concern to extend 'the limits of the signifiable', and to understand writing as an individuating 'experience of limits'.[27] Poetic logic (0-2), the semiotic, and subjectivity as an open system (founded on love as a multiplicity of identifications) only seem to confirm the predominance of this Kristevan concern. Nevertheless, a change has occurred in the period in question. For whereas Kristeva's writing up until, and partly including, *Pouvoirs de l'horreur* (1980), focuses on the restrictiveness of a western society which privileges a representative state apparatus and scientific logic – especially as far as aesthetic practices are concerned – her writings since 1980 embody a modified focus. Ostensibly, this consists in a more intense concentration on the subject in analysis and the importance of identification (and thus the analyst) in love and melancholy.

Looked at within a broader perspective, we see that the fight against an overly restrictive form of the Name-of-the-Father in the bourgeois representative state, and the consequent emphasis on identification and identity to the exclusion of forms echoing the feminine, now makes way for a return of identification as both a necessary component of love and a bulwark against melancholia – if not psychosis. It is as though a too-severe dethronement of the Father – of identity – produces a need to tip the scales in the other direction. Even more. Could we not see Kristeva's work of the eighties as a transformation of her work of the seventies?

Here, it must quickly be acknowledged that Kristeva herself does not accept such a hypothesis.[28] Rather, she suggests that this change in emphasis has resulted from her deepening personal commitment to analytic practice. Also, we need to recall, as I have suggested elsewhere,[29] that Kristeva has never argued for the privileging of either the semiotic over the symbolic, or for the dominance of the symbolic over the semiotic. On the contrary, her work urges a striving for a certain equilibrium in the social and psychic experience of individuals – between language (symbolic) as meaning, and (potentially) poetic non-meaning (semiotic): that is, for what can both erase and multiply meaning. Perhaps, then, it is not within the *œuvre* itself that a transformation has taken place, but in the relation of this *œuvre* to two different social and political contexts: the 1960s and 1970s – when the arrogance of representation was being brought into question and 'difference' was subverting the exclusiveness of 'identity'[30] – and the 1980s, when 'postmodernism' as a celebration, perhaps of difference but certainly of variety, captures the 'colour' of the times. Depression and melancholia begin to become audible on the analyst's couch, along with a speaking that often oscillates between the lucidity and delirium of the borderline case. The mother becomes the (implicit or explicit) point of reference in the subject's sadness, in place of the father in the neurotic's painful reminiscences. Consequently, postmodern anti-Oedipus may have won the day. Of course, to win in a situation where psychic equilibrium is needed, is in fact to lose. To strive for some kind of equilibrium is not to try and impose a single meaning onto the subject's utterances, but to recognize the inevitable crisis that is constitutive of the subject. Meaning and non-meaning come to exist side by side.

When Jean-François Lyotard defined the 'postmodern' as consisting in a certain 'incredulity toward metanarratives'[31] – by which he meant that the reduction of reality to a single meaning was no longer credible – did he, by that very act, pretend to resolve the crisis in meaning by giving us an ultimate interpretation of the times we live in at the end of the twentieth century? Similarly, is Lyotard's *interpretation* of a delirious reality where 'anything goes' a much-needed call to order before the anti-Oedipal, 'schiz-analyse' of current nihilism leads to a more or less generalized terror? Or again: is Lyotard's discourse on the postmodern not a slightly belated recognition by a philosopher of the non-meaning (delirium) always contained within meaning? Is the necessity for a work of art today to become 'postmodern' before it becomes 'modern',[32] simply another way of saying that new meaning can only arise after the dissolution of entrenched existing meaning: delirium giving rise to meaning? Needless to say, it would take more space than is available here to begin to answer these questions satisfactorily. Nevertheless, it can be said that Kristeva's work is somewhat tangential to this postmodern experience. Her focus as psychoanalyst is to confront the distress of the analysand and to mobilize interpretation – not with the aim of finding the true meaning of the subject's distress, and 'not to make an interpretative summa in the name of system of truths'; rather, the task

> is, instead, to record the *crisis* of modern interpretative systems without smoothing it over, to affirm that the crisis is inherent in the symbolic function itself and to perceive as symptoms all constructions, including totalizing interpretation, which try to deny this crisis: to dissolve, to displace indefinitely, in Kafka's words, 'temporarily and for a lifetime'.[33]

From this statement it would seem that the psychoanalyst places the very possibility of a philosophy of postmodernism into doubt. In effect, the times we live in are postmodern because they do *not* have a name; history has been put in question; it is (simply) a time of 'laughter and forgetting' (Kundera). An older generation is dimly reminded of its past by the passion for 'retro' fashion – in the arts, as elsewhere – so that when presented with art works of, say, the 1930s, a new generation says: 'It's just like the modern art of today.' Here, 'retro' *is* modernity; for there is no memory, or knowledge, of what came before.[34] Or rather, as Kristeva says, we can give a name to postmodernism in a spirit of equilibrium if it is in accordance with Kafka's 'temporarily and for a lifetime'. On this basis, we may begin to live our lives in crisis, but also with a degree of fulfilment.

For Kristeva, as analyst, a political solution to all of the individual's ills is not possible because the political sphere is only one aspect of human existence emerging within the truth of the individual as a divided subject, and thus not identical with him- or herself. It follows, therefore, that human existence also cannot be reduced to the social contract's version of it. Indeed, we have seen how the latter would in fact be founded on a murder, or a 'sacrifice' containing a potentially disruptive jouissance. But politics becomes the sphere of a dangerous dogma when it refuses to acknowledge that the social contract is always under threat from jouissance and thus always in the throes of being negotiated, and re-negotiated. The social contract has not been made once and for all – despite Rousseau, and after him, Marx. For those who have put their faith exclusively in politics, Kristeva's work is thus likely to be unsatisfactory. In focusing, or in appearing to focus, exclusively on the individual, this *œuvre* will not please those who invoke social conditions (but without always analysing the implications) to explain human experience. Without denying the importance of the political sphere, it is as though the Kristeva of the 1980s uses the theory of individuality as a singularity (e.g. infinity), to keep politics from becoming a substitute for dogmatic religious practices. The slogan 'everything is political' ceases to be illuminating and becomes destructive of the individual when it is used unreflectively (as it has been in the past) to support an ideology. And this attitude becomes represssive when it denies the potential individuating force of 'writing-as-an-experience-of-limits'.

The power of the analyst?

If Kristeva shows considerable sensitivity and insight into the nature and dangers of politics, it may be true, nevertheless, that in the analytic session itself, an imbalance exists in the power relation between the analyst and the analysand. Stephen Frosh outlines a possible critique here in the following terms:

> The structure of the psychoanalytic situation is not simply one in which one person unavoidably has some power over another; everything that is done herein serves to increase that power. The analyst remains mysterious while the patient discloses the most intimate recesses of her/himself; the analyst is silent while the patient speaks; the patient is observed and the analyst invisible; and everything that the patient says is scrutinised for hidden meanings, so that even criticism of the analyst is interpreted as belonging elsewhere. The analyst can never be confronted, s/he epitomises that subtle power that slips away, unspoken but dominant. In theory, as everything that occurs between patient and analyst is analysed, the uses [*sic*] of power may itself be examined; but this is always in the terms defined by the arc of psychoanalysis itself.[35]

True to the empirical approach of the British tradition, Frosh focuses on what he claims to be the *real* relationship between 'patient' and analyst outside the 'arc' of psychoanalysis. But such an approach only displaces the problem. For what is the nature of the discourse that is outside the arc of psychoanalysis and is making a judgement on it? Kristeva has a cogent response to the substance of Frosh's criticism.

First of all, it is pertinent to make a distinction between the structure of the analytic situation – how it should work in principle

– and its empirical form in light of this principle. The psycho-analytic situation governing the interaction between the analyst and analysand is not guilty, in principle, of the inadequacies levelled by Frosh because psychoanalysis is not a hermeneutic seeking to find 'hidden' meaning, but has to do, as we said above, with non-meaning, or delirium. It is even the reality of non-meaning, evoking the semiotic, that distinguishes psychoanalysis from other forms of discourse. It is, therefore, too simplistic to imply that psychoanalysis is claiming that its truth is superior to all others.

Secondly, the notion that the analyst 'remains mysterious' while the 'patient discloses the most intimate recesses of her/himself' betrays certain unanalysed assumptions in its very formulation. For, despite appearances, this is in fact to suggest a symmetrical (even if unequal) relation between patient and analyst that no one could guarantee. But most of all, what would 'intimate recesses' mean within the field of speech and language that underpins the analytic session? It connotes the idea of an 'essential self' confessing, and is thus a long way from a Lacanian inspired psychoanalysis.

As to the analyst's silence, Kristeva proposes that this is precisely equivalent to the way that non-meaning enters the situation: 'silence as frustration of meaning reveals the ex-centricity of desire with regard to meaning. Madness/meaninglessness *exists* – that is what interpretive silence suggests.'[36]

Two additional factors presented by Kristeva, partly commented upon already, when not neglected by Frosh are treated by him inadequately. The first is the counter-transference[37] where the analyst is 'constantly tracking his own desire' and his own attitude towards the analysand's discourse. The counter-transference is what more or less formally distinguishes analytic discourse from that of 'the classical interpreter, who interprets by virtue of stable meanings'.[38] The counter-transference in fact is one of the factors preventing the procedures of the analytic session from being strictly formalized.[39]

The second factor, highlighting the inadequacy of Frosh's account – at least as far as Kristeva is concerned – is that analysis has to do with the unnameable: 'that which is necessarily enclosed in a very questionable, interpretable, enigmatic object. The analyst does not exclude the unnameable.'[40] The unnameable both escapes meaning and at the same time is the basis of a 'phantasm' of a 'return to the origin'. In other words, some symbolic form, however insecure and provisional, has to come to fill the space (literally: the void) beyond language. The analysand unconsciously recognizes this in the expression of the suffering endured in the delirium.

Frosh is well aware of Lacanian psychoanalytic theory, as well as the difference in Kristeva between the semiotic and the symbolic, and yet he writes about the structure of the analytic session not only as though an empiricist, ego-psychology were the norm, but also as though there was a norm of psychoanalysis. Frosh's critique of the psychoanalytic session alone betrays a number of the failings he claims to have revealed. For he writes in a style which suggests that he has found the true 'hidden' meaning of the analytic session, while at the same time condemning to silence the more subtle approaches represented by analysts such as Kristeva. Despite the inadequacies of Frosh's criticism, however, the point is less that Frosh is 'wrong' and the Kristevan version of psychoanalysis 'right', and more that through Frosh we have been better able to illustrate Kristeva's approach to analysis.

Even so, it may be wondered as to whether or not psychoanalysis has, in certain respects, become too imperialistic, given that there hardly appears to be any realm of life (formation of society, history, art, politics, anthropology, etc.) upon which the analyst would not presume to comment. Like Lacan, and before him, Freud, Kristeva's work represents a vast range of interests. And certainly, to the extent that all other fields of endeavour are forced into a constraining framework provided by psychoanalysis, the danger of imperialism cannot be ignored. What should none the less be remembered is that, like philosophy, psychoanalysis also presumes to be a mode of thinking and interpretation. Its aim should be, and can be, to reveal and undo the restrictive assumptions which serve as the precondition for many dogmatic (because ultimately reductionist) ideologies and epistemologies.

More specifically, Kristeva's work has done two important things which derive from its being inspired by a psychoanalytic framework. The first is that it has gone a long way to specify the limits of analysis in non-meaning. As a result, it is highly reflexive but recognizes the limits of all reflexivity. In this sense, Kristeva has given a new impetus to the notion of philosophy as wisdom: philosophy as the recognition of the limits of philosophy. Secondly, at no stage has Kristeva attempted to present her own work as being a substitute for, or identical to, the object of analysis: it does not claim to be as poetic as the poetry it analyses, or as delirious as the analysand's speech. Indeed, perhaps it is in pretending to be just this that a real threat of imperialism arises. Lacan's discourse, to the extent that it claims to *be* itself a work of art, seems to run this risk, as does Derrida's writing in philosophy. Psychoanalysis as meaning *and* delirium, as symbolic *and* semiotic, as plenitude *and* void – such would be the ultimate imperialism. This is not to deny – far from it – that within Kristeva's analytic frame of reference, fiction and poetry appear. But it is to say that fiction and poetry are not identical to the analytic framework itself. Consequently, we find many stories (some very moving)[41] within analytic discourse, together with examples of lyricism: "'I am alone, therefore I am the creator'" – poetry of the paranoid moment at the end of the treatment.[42] Or again:

> forgotten time crops up suddenly and condenses into a flash of lightning that, if it were thought out, would involve bringing together the two opposite terms but, on account of that flash, is discharged like thunder. The time of abjection is double: a time of oblivion and thunder, of veiled infinity and the moment when revelation bursts forth. . .

– lyricism of an explication of abjection.[43] Fiction and lyricism are thus visible in this psychoanalytically inspired writing, but an old dichotomy is intentionally retained, despite its metaphysical origin: commentary (metalanguage) and the object of commentary, a dichotomy partly recalling Barthes' distinction between *écrivance* and *écriture*.

From a related but slightly different angle, there *is* a metalanguage (despite Lacan); for, asks Kristeva, 'what becomes of this "unconscious structured like a language", if "there is no metalanguage"?'[44] Commentary thus exists as a metalanguage without which the repressed would exist in a pure and unmediated form. Unconsciously, perhaps, Lacan's dismissal of metalanguage – by which he meant that the subject is constituted in and through language – turns out to be a final grab for mastery – hence the double-edged title of Kristeva's essay: 'Il n'y a pas de maître à langage' (there is no master of language) echoing Lacan's 'il n'y a pas de métalangage' (there is no metalanguage). Kristeva thus interprets 'il n'y a pas de métalangage' to mean; there *is* a (so-called) master of language (il y a un maître à langage) – possibly leading to a 'mummification of the transference'.[45] The morphology of this argument serves to illuminate Kristeva's position regarding the need to distinguish between psychoanalysis and its object. The two spheres cannot be entirely conflated.

Art and analysis

In light of art's increasingly relentless mediatization – where art as a product selling for huge sums adds to the fame, or infamy, of the artist – Kristeva speaks about art as production as well as product. In a world where the main antidote to the commercialization and professionalization of art is found by art 'serving [a] progressive ideology',[46] thereby confirming the symmetry of art as a (fetishized) product, Kristeva speaks of art as 'the possibility of fashioning narcissism and of subtilizing the ideal'.[47] The ideal, as we have seen in Chapter 6, is *in* the creative process itself. Art is a uniquely amateur activity in this sense. Kristeva elaborates:

> In the ideal hypothesis, the artist succeeds in probabilizing, in relativizing, his own production, as though it were a living system that lives only on condition of being open to the other. A life, a work of art: are these not 'works in progress' only inasmuch as capable of self-depreciation and of resubmitting themselves to the flames which are, without distinction, the flames of language and love?[48]

Hence, the art work is only there as a mark of the process of production which is also constitutive of psychic space. Is the artist's psyche thus the only one constituted in this process? Not in principle. For to 'identify' with this difference, to make it one's own in a sense, and thereby have it profoundly shake a fixed, even fetishistic, identity, is also to become an artist. To have produced this insight into art must surely be one of Kristeva's finest achievements – especially for her readers outside France for whom the connection between art and love is still very uncertain. Art, as art, therefore, is 'open to the other', as the above passage says. How does a work of art open itself up to an other? As an initial and indirect response to this question, let us consider the 'Anna Livia Plurabelle' episode in *Finnegans Wake*.

Here, we recall again that rather than simply being an identification with the Father, or the symbolic dimension of the signifying process, identification for Kristeva has far wider import.[49] Love as agape, introduced as the 'primary identification', or as the imaginary father of individual pre-history, constitutes a kind of pre-existent 'outside' close to the mother. It is the basis of a dynamic potential in the process of identification. For whereas I can, more or less self-consciously, identify with an other as familiar and as alter-ego, agape is what seems to come to me from a nether region outside my control. So while on the one hand, agape is a source of comfort in the first stage of separation (from my mother), and while God's love might also relieve a fearful loneliness, this 'outside' can itself be a significant source of fear and discomfort. For it would be the equivalent of the unfamiliar *in* me; I become a stranger to myself. An unfamiliar element as an unsettling strangeness, then, might also become the basis of another self. Or rather, the self might become a kind of locus of a plurality of identifications which I make mine. Or, to paraphrase Kristeva: identification in the fullest sense, entails the assimilation, both in a symbolic and a real sense, of another entity separated and different from the subject. Difference thus becomes the basis of the subject as an 'open system' modifying itself in light of new identifications. To refuse difference here, to be closed off to the dynamic aspect of identity, is also to begin to die – certainly in a symbolic sense, and probably in a physical sense as well. Without God – which means, without agape as difference – the speaking being in postmodern times risks becoming a stunted version of humanity. Love as both agape and eros can compensate for God – and so can art, in Kristeva's view. It is in this spirit that we return to *Finnegans Wake*.

I think, first of all, of Gayatri Spivak's comment (cited earlier) that there 'is something faintly comical about Joyce rising above sexual identities and bequeathing the proper mind-set to the women's movement'. For at the beginning of her essay on French feminism, Spivak speaks of walking in her grandfather's estate on the Bihar–Bengal border: 'Two ancient washerwomen are washing clothes in the river, beating the clothes on the stones.'[50] As is well known, Joyce, for his part, wrote to Harriet Shaw Weaver in March 1924 to say that the Anna Livia Plurabelle episode in *Finnegans Wake* was 'a chattering dialogue across the river by two washerwomen who as night falls become a tree and a stone. The river is named Anna Liffey.'[51] It is interesting that Spivak's text represses this echo of Joyce, given that the relationship between writing and reality is so clearly at issue in the episodes recounted by Spivak and Joyce respectively. Apart from the striking coincidence of theme, the two episodes form a homology: Spivak raises the problem of the relationship between the Indian washerwomen's experience and language (can western discourse do justice to it?), whereas Joyce raises the problem of how reality becomes the basis of language. In other words: Spivak is vexed by the problem of how reality can be put into language, whereas the Anna Livia Plurabelle episode is concerned with how language can become real.

Of course, to proceed in the above manner is to move quite quickly to an interpretation of the two scenes (recounted by Spivak and Joyce), so that the *process* of interpretation is vastly truncated. And it is indeed necessary to do justice to this process in order to make the reading of *Finnegans Wake* a 'work in progress'[52] potentially capable of modifying our psychic structure. A rush to interpretation risks forcing Joyce's work (or any work of art) into a rigid framework of the 'same' where the 'other' could not become part of ourselves, that is, become part of our own identity.

The Anna Livia Plurabelle episode begins:

O
tell me all about
Anna Livia! I want to hear all
about Anna Livia. Well, you know Anna Livia? Yes, of course, we all know Anna Livia. Tell me all. Tell me now. You'll die when you hear.[53]

The focus is on the *telling* of the story which will never stop. The telling is always incomplete and therefore based equally on meaning and non-meaning or difference. The focus on 'telling' echoes throughout the episode: 'O, tell me all I want to hear . . .';[54] 'Tell me moher. Tell me moatst';[55] 'Listen now. Are you listening? Yes, yes! Idneed I am!';[56] 'Onon! Onon! tell me more. Tell me every tiny teign. I want to know every single ingul'[57] . . . and so on, with references to 'never' stopping and 'Continuarration!',[58] the notion that 'every telling has a taling',[59] right up to the concluding lines of the episode:

Tell me of John or Shaun? Who were Shem and Shaun the living sons or daughters of? Night now! Tell me, tell me, elm! Night night! Telmetale of stem or stone. Beside the rivering waters of, hitherandthithering waters of. Night![60]

Non-meaning – the poetry – captures my imagination, grips me from outside myself. I accept the challenge Joyce lays down. I

217

allow myself to be integrated into what I cannot entirely understand. I accept the challenge of non-meaning; I venture to the edge of the abyss, where God as agape would have been perhaps only a century ago. I am also saying that I will try to interpret Joyce – or at least read him – rather than evacuate him from my imaginary.

'Night', then, is doubly inscribed in this episode of Anna Livia Plurabelle. As night falls, a head begins to turn into stone: 'Night! Night! My ho head halls.'[61] Night signals the end of *a* telling, and tells of the beginning of another: the tale of Shem and Shaun. A tree, a stone, a river, and a new story is what we have, as though the real were both obstacle and origin of language. For 'night' not only signals a continuation of the telling as such, it also recalls the poetic 'yes' of Molly's monologue in *Ulysses* mentioned in our Introduction. The repetition of 'night' is therefore equivalent to the poeticizing of language: words caught between the real and the symbolic, between the telling and the river, tree, and stone. Hence, we read elsewhere in *Finnegans Wake*, that 'The war is in words and the wood is the world. Maply me, willowy we, hickory he and yew yourselves.'[62] This inseparability of world (tree) and word recalls the old Celtic mythical Ogham alphabet of twenty letters, each letter being the name of a tree. The associations then seem unlimited. For much later we read: 'Listeneth! 'Tis a tree story.'[63] And what is the river if not this wandering, meandering tale – a 'meandertale',[64] or even more: a 'meanderthalltale'.[65] The 'meandertale' evoking the river is the result – as the *Wake* also helps us to realize – of a process of 'soundsense' and 'sensesound' (as we noted in Chapter 3) made possible by a 'warping process': 'His producers are they not his consumers? Your exagmination round his factification for incamination of a *warping process*'.[66] A 'warping process' evokes a 'work in progress', the title Joyce gave to *Finnegans Wake* before it was published. This warping process produced, in part, by punning and agglutination, would bring about a deformation of the symbolic that at one and the same time pluralizes meaning and gives rise to the *echo* (see 'Hush! Caution! Echoland!' – HCE) of the real: language returning to its origin in the semiotic, poetic dimension of the signifying process. This is the 'langscape'[67] of writing, Joyce suggests ... or is it 'landuage'?[68]

Now we see that, once begun, it is hardly possible to stop reading Joyce's writing, a writing without end geared to put the reader in question. Considered in this light, Kristeva's concept of identification shows that it is only through being willing to face the challenge, to be put in question as reader – to be feminized, as it were – that analytic effects become possible and art can become the way to a 'resurrection' through signs; or as *Finnegans Wake* says: 'Array! Surrection!'[69]

Kristeva's work thus focuses precisely on what Gayatri Spivak's text evokes, but also represses – even though the challenge presented to Spivak by her washerwomen is no less daunting. Kristeva shows that to be challenged by art is to be confronted by the void of non-meaning and the prospect of our own hell, our own suffering caused by a loss of identity inducing our melancholies and the truly tragic aspect of being. Kristeva shows, too – in her writing on love and art – that this suffering is also the way to a 'resurrection' as a renewal of the self in language. Once, to 'travel hell' was possible: for God was love (agape); now, God is dead and we are alone and afraid of the challenge of the void. Kristeva does not say how people can now be induced to accept this challenge. And for some she will be seen to be silent where she should be most illuminating.

On the other hand, there is no doubt that Kristeva sets out the problem a world without God as love poses for individuals in western society; and this is surely an advance. All the more so if we accept with Marx that a problem only arises when the 'material conditions for its solution already exist'.

Notes

1 Julia Kristeva, *About Chinese Women*, trans. Anita Burrows (New York, London, Marion Boyars, paperback edn, 1986).

2 Kristeva, 'Il n'y a pas de maître à langage', p. 139.

3 See Julia Kristeva, 'Nom de mort ou de vie', in Jacques Sédat (ed.), *Retour à Lacan* (Paris, Fayard, 1981), p. 179.

4 See Luce Irigaray, *This Sex Which is Not One* (Ithaca, Cornell University Press, 1985); '"Women's exile", interview with Luce Irigaray', trans. Couze Veun, *Ideology and Consciousness*, no. 1 (May 1977), pp. 62–76, esp. p. 64; Luce Irigaray, 'Femmes divines', *Critique*, no. 454 (1985), pp. 294–308. In English as *Divine Women*, trans. Stephen Muecke (Sydney, Local Consumption, 1986). See the following:

Defined as mother-substance, often obscure, even occult, of the verb of men, we need our *subject*, our *noun*, our *verb*, our *predicates*, our elementary sentence, our base rhythm, our morphological identity, our generic incarnation, our genealogy.

(ibid., p. 11)

5 See Kristeva, 'Il n'y a pas de maître à langage', pp. 134–5.

6 Elizabeth Gross, 'Philosophy, subjectivity and the body: Kristeva and Irigaray', in Carole Pateman and Elizabeth Gross (eds), *Feminist Challenges: Social and Political Theory* (Sydney, London, Boston, Allen & Unwin, 1986), p. 131.

7 ibid., p. 132.

8 Thus Gross writes, in 1989, that

> advocacy of the (male) avant-garde as spokesman for a repressed femininity coupled with [Kristeva's] call for a feminism that is not confined to sexual differences but analyses and confronts the question of sexual differentiation, the existence of masculine/symbolic and feminine/semiotic elements within each subject, imply the annihilation of women's struggles for sexual specificity and auto-nomy. (Elizabeth Grosz (*sic*), *Sexual Subversions* (Sydney, Allen & Unwin, 1989), p. 97)

Kristeva does not for a moment think that sexual difference is not important in the formation of subjectivity, however she does draw a clear distinction between this, and the more socially obvious gender difference.

9 Alice A. Jardine, *Gynesis: Configurations of Woman and Modernity* (Ithaca and London, Cornell University Press, 1985), p. 119.

10 Kristeva, *La Révolution du langage poétique*, p. 616.

11 See Chapter 5, p. 131.

12 Julia Kristeva, 'Oscillation between power and denial', in Elaine Marks and Isabelle de Courtivron (eds), *New French Feminisms* (Brighton, Sussex, Harvester Press, reprinted 1985), p. 165.

13 See Kristeva, *La Révolution du langage poétique*, pp. 611–20.

14 ibid., p. 616.

15 See Gayatri Chakravorty Spivak, 'French feminism in an international frame', *Yale French Studies*, no. 62 (1981), pp. 159–64.

16 ibid., p. 169.

17 ibid., pp. 178–9. My emphasis.

18 See ibid., p. 172.

19 See Anne MacLeod, 'Gender difference relativity in GDR-writing, or how to oppose without really trying', *Oxford Literary Review*, vol. 7, nos 1 and 2 (1985), pp. 41–61.

20 Reproduced in Stefan Heym (ed.), *Auskunftz: Neue Prosa aus der DDR* (Königstein/Ts., Athenäum, 1978).

21 Jacques Derrida, *Spurs: Nietzsche's Styles*, trans. Barbara Harlow (Chicago and London, University of Chicago Press, 1978), p. 117, cited in MacLeod, 'Gender difference . . .', p. 41.

22 MacLeod, 'Gender difference . . .', p. 48.
23 ibid., p. 49.
24 ibid., p. 51.
25 First published as 'Le Temps des femmes' in 33/44: Cahiers de recherche de sciences des textes et documents, no. 5, (Winter, 1979), pp. 5–19. Reprinted as 'Women's time' in Moi (ed.), *The Kristeva Reader*, pp. 188–213.
26 ibid., p. 209. Kristeva's emphasis.
27 See Julia Kristeva, 'Postmodernism?' in Harry Garvin (ed.), *Romanticism, Modernism, Postmodernism* (Lewisburg, Bucknell University Press, 1980) p. 137.
28 Personal interview at Université de Paris 7, 24 May 1988.
29 John Lechte, 'Art, love and melancholy in the work of Julia Kristeva', in Andrew Benjamin and John Fletcher (eds), *Abjection, Melancholia, and Love: The Work of Julia Kristeva* (London, Routledge, 1989), pp. 24–41.
30 See Gilles Deleuze, *Différence et répétition* (Paris, Presses Universitaires de France, 3rd edn, 1976).
31 Jean-François Lyotard, *The Postmodern Condition*, trans. Geoffrey Bennington and Brian Massumi (Manchester, Manchester University Press, 1984), p. xxiv.
32 ibid., p. 79.
33 Julia Kristeva, 'Psychoanalysis and the polis', trans. Margaret Waller in Moi (ed.), *The Kristeva Reader*, p. 319. Kristeva's emphasis.
34 Thus in a discussion about national identity, one of my first-year sociology students tells me that Max Dupain's 'Sunbaker' (black and white, 1937, and available from the Art Gallery of New South Wales in postcard form from a new print) 'looks just like a modern photograph'.
35 Stephen Frosh, *The Politics of Psychoanalysis* (London, Macmillan Education, 1987), p. 259.
36 Kristeva, 'Psychoanalysis and the polis', p. 310.
37 See Frosh, *The Politics of Psychoanalysis*, pp. 260–3, where the notion of counter-transference, although discussed at some length, is not seen to render problematic earlier statements about the 'power' of the analyst.
38 Kristeva, 'Psychoanalysis and the polis', p. 310.
39 Elsewhere, Kristeva points out that the end of treatment entails the 'dethronement' of the analyst's function. See Julia Kristeva, *Au commencement était l'amour*, pp. 67–9.
40 Kristeva, 'Psychoanalysis and the polis', p. 310.
41 See Julia Kristeva, *Au commencement était l'amour*, pp. 24–30, and story of Paul who surprised his mother with a lover, and who was forced to watch his father tortured to death.
42 ibid., p. 67.
43 Kristeva, *Powers of Horror*, pp. 8–9.
44 Kristeva, 'Il n'y a pas de maître à langage', p. 126.
45 ibid., p. 139.

46 See Kristeva, *Revolution in Poetic Language*, p. 233.

47 Julia Kristeva, *Histoires d'amour – Love Stories*, ICA Documents, p. 21.

48 ibid.

49 See Kristeva, *Tales of Love*, and also, 'Joyce "the Gracehopper", ou le retour d'Orphée'.

50 Gayatri Spivak, 'French feminism in an international frame', p. 155.

51 James Joyce letter to Harriet Shaw Weaver, 7 March 1924, in Richard Ellmann (ed.), *Selected Letters of James Joyce* (London, Faber, 1975), p. 301.

52 Kristeva has also used this phrase as a synonym for an 'open system'. (Cf. *Tales of Love*, p. 380.)

53 Joyce, *Finnegans Wake*, p. 196.

54 ibid., p. 198.

55 ibid.

56 ibid., p. 201.

57 ibid.

58 ibid., p. 205.

59 ibid., p. 213.

60 ibid., p. 216.

61 ibid., p. 215.

62 ibid., p. 98.

63 ibid., p. 564.

64 ibid., p. 18.

65 ibid., p. 19.

66 ibid., p. 497 (my emphasis). Regarding this 'warping' process as a *logos spermatikos*, see Jean-Louis Houdebine, 'Joyce: littérature et religion', *Tel Quel*, no. 89 (Autumn, 1981), pp. 41–73.

67 Joyce, *Finnegans Wake*, p. 595.

68 ibid., p. 327.

69 ibid., p. 593.

Select bibliography

The following is a bibliography of Kristeva's books published in French. The English translation, where available, is cited after the French text.

Séméiotiké, Recherches pour une sémanalyse (Paris, Seuil, 1969).

Le Texte du roman. Approche sémiologique d'une structure discursive transformationnelle (The Hague, Mouton, 1970).

Des chinoises (Paris, Editions Des Femmes, 1974). In English as *About Chinese Women*, trans. Anita Barrows (New York and London, Marion Boyars, paperback edition, 1986).

La Révolution du langage poétique. L'avant-garde à la fin du XIXe siècle. Lautréamont et Mallarmé (Paris, Seuil, 1974). First part in English as *Revolution in Poetic Language*, trans. Margaret Waller (New York, Columbia University Press, 1984).

La Traversée des signes (collective work) (Paris, Seuil, 1975).

Polylogue (Paris, Seuil, 1977). Eight of the twenty essays are in English in *Desire in Language. A Semiotic Approach to Literature and Art*, trans. Thomas S. Gora, Alice Jardine, and Leon S. Roudiez (Oxford, Basil Blackwell, reprinted, 1984).

Folle vérité (collective work) (Paris, Seuil, 1979).

Pouvoirs de l'horreur. Essai sur l'abjection (Paris, Seuil, 1980). In English as *Powers of Horror. An Essay on Abjection*, trans. Leon S. Roudiez (New York, Columbia University Press, 1982).

Le Langage cet inconnu (Paris, Seuil, 1981; SGPP, 1989).

Au commencement était l'amour. Psychanalyse et foi (Paris, Hachette, 1985). In English as *In the Beginning was Love: Psychoanalysis and Faith*, trans. Arthur Goldhammer (New York, Columbia University Press, 1987).

Histoires d'amour (Paris, Denoel, 1983; Folio essais/Gallimard, 1985). In English as *Tales of Love* trans. Leon S. Roudiez (New York, Columbia University Press, 1987).

Soleil noir, dépression et mélancolie (Paris, Gallimard, 1987). In English as *Black Sun: Depression and Melancholia*, trans. Leon S. Roudiez (New York,

223

Columbia University Press, 1989).
Étrangers à nous-mêmes (Paris, Favard, 1988).

A range of Kristeva's essays, from the above list and elsewhere, is available in English in:

Toril Moi (ed.), *The Kristeva Reader* (Oxford, Basil Blackwell, 1986).

Index

225